Hacking Mac OS® X Tiger™

Hacking Mac OS® X Tiger™

Serious Hacks, Mods and Customizations

Scott Knaster

Wiley Publishing, Inc.

Hacking Mac OS® X Tiger:™ Serious Hacks, Mods and Customizations

Published by
Wiley Publishing, Inc.
10475 Crosspoint Boulevard
Indianapolis, IN 46256
www.wiley.com

Copyright © 2005 by Wiley Publishing, Inc., Indianapolis, Indiana

Published simultaneously in Canada

ISBN-13: 978-0-7645-8345-2
ISBN-10: 0-7645-8345-X

Manufactured in the United States of America

10 9 8 7 6 5 4 3 2 1

1B/SZ/QW/QV/IN

For general information on our other products and services or to obtain technical support, please contact our Customer Care Department within the U.S. at (800) 762-2974, outside the U.S. at (317) 572-3993 or fax (317) 572-4002.

Wiley also publishes its books in a variety of electronic formats. Some content that appears in print may not be available in electronic books.

Library of Congress Cataloging-in-Publication Data:

Knaster, Scott.
    Hacking MAC OS X Tiger : Serious hacks, mods and customizations / Scott Knaster.
        p.cm.
    Includes index.
    ISBN-13: 978-0-7645-8345-2 (paper/website)
    ISBN-10: 0-7645-8345-X (paper/website)
  1. Mac OS.   2. Operating systems (Computers)   3. Macintosh
(Computer)--Programming. I. Title.
    QA76.76.063K594 2005
    005.4'465--dc22

                                      2005010350

About the Author

Scott Knaster has been writing about Macintosh programming since the days when Macs didn't run Unix. His books were required reading for Mac programmers for more than a decade and have been translated into several languages, including Japanese and Pascal. Scott has every issue of MAD magazine, which explains a lot about his philosophy of life.

Credits

Executive Editor
Chris Webb

Development Editor
Brian MacDonald

Technical Editor
Mark Dalrymple

Production Editor
Angela Smith

Copy Editor
Mary Lagu

Editorial Manager
Mary Beth Wakefield

Vice President & Executive Group Publisher
Richard Swadley

Vice President and Publisher
Joseph B. Wikert

Project Coordinator
Erin Smith

Graphics and Production Specialists
Lauren Goddard
Clint Lahnen
Lynsey Osborn
Melanee Prendergast
Heather Ryan
Amanda Spagnuolo

Quality Control Technician
John Greenough
Jessica Kramer
Joe Niesen
Carl William Pierce

Book Designer
Kathie S. Rickard

Proofreading and Indexing
TECHBOOKS Production Services

*To my Smart Friends, who helped
make this book possible.*

Acknowledgments

More than any book I've written, this one was the result of work by a lot of people.

A collection of folks I call the Hack Pack contributed their time and code to make the great programs in Part III. You can read a little about them and see their faces in Part III, but I acknowledge their brilliance and generosity here: Buzz Andersen, Josh Carter, Mark Dalrymple, Shane Looker, Jonathan "Wolf" Rentzch, and John A. Vink.

I asked a zillion questions while writing this book, and they were all answered quickly and thoroughly by smart and friendly people, especially Scott Boyd, Tim Dierks, Tim Dierks 2, Chris Espinosa, Miro Jurisic, Nevin Liber, Warren Magnus, Chris Page, Greg Robbins, Alex Rosenberg, Mike Rutman, Jon Pugh, Eric Shapiro, Andy Stadler, and Amanda Walker.

Ron Avitzur graciously allowed me to reprint his remarkable Graphing Calculator story, which is one of the greatest meatspace hacks of all time.

Thanks to Jorg Brown, Marshall Clow, Sanford Selznick, Keith Stattenfield, and Maf Vosburgh for their contributions, which for various reasons did not make it into this book.

Mark Dalrymple was a wonderful technical editor, applying his vast knowledge of Cocoa, Mach, puns, and badgers to the goal of producing a better and more accurate book.

Brian MacDonald is credited as Development Editor, but while working on this book I came to regard Brian as a collaborator. He is the best kind of editor, one who really "gets" what a book is about and helps make it better, rather than just ensuring it's done on time (although he did that too).

Eileen Calabro was the book's original Development Editor and helped get the project off to a good start.

Chris Webb once again provided me with an opportunity to tackle a wonderful topic, giving me a reason to play around with fun stuff and then write about it.

Carole McClendon continues to use her genius to smooth over every rough spot that pops up and move things forward.

Last and most, thanks to my family—Barbara, Jess, and Devi—for giving me everything I need.

Contents at a Glance

Contents

Part II: Mods

Part III: Hacks

Introduction

Can't we just leave well enough alone?

Well, no, we can't.

Apple spends a lot of time carefully crafting its computers and software, and when you get a Mac, you're generally very happy with what you have. But eventually, after you develop some comfort and facility with your new Mac, you want to find ways to accomplish tasks more quickly and efficiently. And then, after you become something of an expert, you start to realize the incredible depth of the features hidden inside the computer and operating system.

That's when curiosity takes over. You might visit an Apple retail store or a user group meeting and see someone using a cool shortcut or showing off a nifty feature you didn't know about. That's when you know you've crossed over and become a new kind of Mac user, one seeking knowledge about how to make your computing life not only more convenient but also more fun.

This book is for people like you (and me) who want to explore, investigate, improve, and play. If you're using a Mac, it's likely you *chose* to use it— it wasn't forced upon you by your company's information technology department. And if you chose to use it, chances are you're ready to discover more cool stuff to do. That's what this book is about.

About Hacking

No doubt you noticed the word *hacking* in the title of this book. I'm happy to report the rehabilitation of this word in recent years. Some time ago, hacking universally meant people who were up to no good. There's still a segment of the population that defines hacking that way. But a lot of other folks, including many technical types, have helped return hacking to a positive state, in which it means creativity, ingenuity, and imagination. In this book, hacking is the ability to find solutions and apply inventiveness and resourcefulness to everyday use of Mac OS X. That's not evil—that's good. And you don't have to be an expert to get into it—hacks come at all levels of experience.

About Mac OS X 10.4 Tiger

"Just about every computer on the market today runs Unix, except the Mac (and nobody cares about it)." — Bill Joy, co-founder of Sun Microsystems, 6/21/1985

Little did Bill Joy, or anyone else, suspect that not 15 years after this statement, the Mac would run Unix in the guise of Mac OS X. Mac users have always loved to customize and fool around with their systems, but after Mac OS X came out and the full power of Unix was available on every Mac, the power to hack around increased massively.

Although it's accurate to say that Mac OS X is a complete implementation of Unix, it's also much, much more than that. Apple includes dozens of powerful technologies and components in Mac OS X, such as Quartz graphics, the Aqua user interface, AppleScript, the Darwin core, and many, many more. Every one of those technologies adds more opportunities for personalizing and hacking.

And now we have Mac OS X 10.4 Tiger, the latest major version of Apple's operating system. Tiger adds wonderful new jewels to the collection, such as Dashboard, Spotlight, and Automator, that provide rich new areas for improving Macs in ways we're just beginning to understand.

The Unix foundation and Apple personality of Mac OS X provides a fertile target for learning and tweaking. With the addition of new features in Tiger, the Mac becomes an even better platform for us to work and play with.

Mac OS X has even caused Bill Joy to change his opinion: "Mac OS X is a rock-solid system that's beautifully designed. I much prefer it to Linux."—Bill Joy, December 2003

Who Is This Book For?

This book is for curious people of all kinds, especially those who have a Mac running Tiger. Some of the tips and hacks require Tiger, such as the Dashboard and Automator chapters, whereas others work in Tiger but don't require it. If you're not already running Tiger, you can use the descriptions of Tiger hacks and features as a way to find out more before you decide whether to upgrade. To get the most out of the hacks in Part III, you need some programming experience or a desire to learn.

What's in This Book?

This book is divided into three parts. The parts get a bit more technical as you go forward. The idea is to present a sort of sliding scale of geekiness, so that every Mac user can find something interesting and understandable, and those who want to learn more can gain technical chops as they proceed through the book.

Part I, "Tips," is filled with material that's accessible to all Mac users. Some of the tips in Part I are right there for you to discover in the user interface of the Finder and applications, while others walk you through basic skills in Terminal and other basic tools.

Part II, "Mods," takes the next step by discussing how to dig inside applications, see what makes them work, and change their appearance and behavior. The material in this Part takes a bit more skill and technical ability than that in Part I. With perseverance, however, you should be able to move on from Part I even if you haven't done this sort of thing before.

Part III, "Hacks," is real programming. In this section, master Mac programmers have contributed applications, tools, Dashboard widgets, a Spotlight importer, and other cool software, complete with descriptions and source code. If you're a programmer or you want to be one, the information in this section is invaluable for seeing how Mac programming is done. If you have no interest in learning to write code, you can still take advantage of the hacks just by using them, and you might be interested in seeing what source code looks like even if you don't want to create any yourself.

Conventions

All the tips, tricks, and hacks in this book work with Mac OS X 10.4 Tiger, and many of them are compatible with 10.3.x.

References to menus and menu items look like this: File → Save.

As you probably know, Macs come with one-button mice, but many people buy and use mice with more buttons, and they work fine on Macs. With a one-button mouse, you display contextual menus by holding down Control and clicking. If you have a multi-button mouse, you can right-click to show the contextual menu, so whenever I write about Control-click, those of you with multi-button mice should feel free to right-click instead, without fear.

When you type commands into Terminal, you should press Return or Enter at the end of the line to perform the command. I'm letting you know that now so that you don't get bored with me writing it over and over again in every set of steps that involves Terminal commands.

Pathnames are written in the POSIX format favored by Unix. This just means that I use slashes to indicate directory (folder) levels. So, /Developer/Applications/Xcode means that Xcode is inside a folder named Applications, which in turn is in a folder named Developer. Sometimes I follow the Unix convention of using the tilde character to refer to the current user's Home directory, so, for example, ~/Documents/ is the Documents folder in the current user's Home folder.

Editing Property Lists

In Mac OS X, applications and many other programs include files called property lists, which always end with the .plist extension. These files contain information about the programs they're associated with. Many of the tweaks and hacks in this book involve editing property lists.

You can edit any property list in Mac OS X using the Property List Editor application. This application is part of Xcode Tools, a developer kit that comes with Tiger and is also available for free download at connect.apple.com.

Some property lists are in text (XML) format. In addition to using Property List Editor, you can edit these in any program that handles text files, such as TextEdit. You can use a Terminal command named plutil to convert property lists to text format. For the full story on property lists, formats, and editors, see the section in Chapter 12 entitled "Looking at Preferences Files."

Disclaimer and Warning

Please back stuff up. You should have a backup strategy that backs up all your data regularly, but when you're trying out the things in this book, you should be even more cautious. Before you edit a property list or change an application bundle, make a copy of the file you're going to change. Doing so is quick and easy, and you can do it right there in the Finder. The first time you reduce an important application to a quivering mass of undifferentiated bits, you'll be very happy to have that backup copy.

Things can go wrong. Something might have changed in the system between the time this book was written and the time you try it out. A trick that works today might not work after the next software update. Despite the best efforts of the author, the terrific technical editor, and the wonderful Wiley folks, there might be (gasp) errors in this book. Your dog might eat your property list. Please proceed at your own risk.

Using the Code in Part III

There's no reason to type in the code from the hacks in Part III, unless you're interested in learning how to type. All the code is available on this book's companion Web site at www.wiley.com/compbooks/extremetech. If you want to report errors or otherwise get in touch with the author, please send e-mail to hackingtiger@papercar.com.

Final Word

Whether you're just entering the Macintosh universe with a new Mac mini, you've been deep inside Unix systems for decades, or you're a long-time Mac genius, I hope you find fun and enlightenment in this book. So keep your backups fresh and let's get started.

Hacking Mac
OS® X Tiger™

Tips

Welcome to Part I! This Part starts off with some gentle hacking in the user interface, building a foundation of fun and useful stuff you can do with Mac OS X. You'll find out about some of the strange and wonderful things you can do in the parts of the Mac you use everyday. These tips include making the Finder behave better, useful secrets of the Dock, and hidden tricks in System Preferences. There's a nifty section filled with Dashboard tricks, and a chapter with a bunch of cool things to do in applications, including iTunes.

After that, the technical level moves up a notch as I dig into interesting facts about startup and login time. I'll describe some of the best third-party utilities for customizing and maintaining your Mac.

As you probably know, your Macintosh runs Unix underneath that nice user interface. I'll show you how to acquire and run Unix software that isn't necessarily designed for Macs. Finally, there are a couple of chapters that show you some of the secrets of Terminal, the Mac OS X way to the Unix command line, and a few of the more useful and bizarre commands you can use therein. By the time you're finished with this Part, you'll be ready for the deeper stuff you'll find in Part II.

Finder

The Finder is the heart of the Mac OS X user interface. The Finder is so central to the Macintosh experience that beginning users don't even know it's there: It's just the desktop. Because the Finder is so important and used so often, Apple's crafty designers like to create well-worn paths and little tweaks that make it more fun and easier to wrangle. You're probably familiar with some of these, such as the power to choose from among column, list, and icon views and to customize the Finder toolbar.

In this chapter, you'll explore some of the cooler, odder, and wackier shortcuts and tricks in the Finder. In the hackiest tradition, you'll find some to be so valuable that you'll use them every day. Others are really fun, but are pretty much for demonstration purposes only. I trust you to figure out which ones are which.

List View Open Secrets

The Finder's list view hides the hierarchy of folders by using little controls called *disclosure triangles*. (That's not a very catchy name, is it? Clearly, Apple's marketing department could do a little work here.) Click a disclosure triangle next to a folder to see the contents of that folder, and click it again to close the folder.

You can use various keyboard shortcuts to control disclosure triangles in more powerful ways. When a folder is selected, you can press the right arrow key to show its contents or the left arrow to hide them. It works just as if you had clicked on the triangle.

If you hold down Option while clicking a disclosure triangle, the Finder recursively opens all the folders inside the one you selected. This is a quick way to see all the stuff in a folder and inside any subfolders it contains. You can perform the same trick by holding down Option while you press right arrow to open a disclosure triangle. This also works when you have multiple folders selected, which makes it even more powerful.

Instead of double-clicking, you can open any file or folder in the Finder by selecting it and pressing Command-down arrow, which acts exactly like the Open command in the File menu. If you also hold down Option (that's Command-Option-down arrow) instead, the original Finder window closes as the new ones open, one for each folder you have selected.

Note Command-down arrow is very versatile—it opens both folders and files. If you select a bunch of folders, documents, and applications and then press Command-down arrow, the Finder will happily open all of them. This can lead to disaster (or at least distraction) if this is not exactly what you want to do. For example, if your memory of these wacky shortcuts is a little off, you might decide to select a bunch of folders and files, hoping to see their contents (Option-right arrow), but instead (using Command-down arrow) opening all of them and their applications.

Attack of the Giant Icons

In case you haven't discovered it yet, the Finder's View Options dialog sports a slider for controlling the size of icons. You can make your icons appear at sizes ranging from tiny (16 by 16 pixels) to extra large (128 by 128). But with an extra tweak behind the scenes, you can have some real fun and create impossibly enormous icons.

To make this work, you must modify the Finder's property list. As described in the Introduction, you can use Apple's Property List Editor, although you can feel free to use a text editing tool if you prefer, because property lists are just text files. Here are the steps:

1. In the Finder, go to your Home directory.

2. Navigate to Library/Preferences: and select com.apple.finder.plist.

3. Choose File ➔ Duplicate to make a safe copy of Finder preferences. You'll need this in the unlikely event that you accidentally mangle the original.

Warning As I describe in the Introduction, it's a good idea to make a backup copy of preferences and other system files before you change them. Although I won't repeat this warning every time you edit a file, please keep it in mind.

4. Double-click com.apple.finder.plist to open it in Property List Editor. If you don't have Property List Editor and some other application opens, see the section "Editing property lists" in the Introduction.

5. In the Finder's property list, open Root.

6. Open StandardViewOptions.

7. Under StandardViewOptions, open the icnv (icon view) branch.

8. In the IconSize item, double-click the value to select it. It will be set to some number between 16 and 128, depending on the current global setting for the icon size.

9. Type **640** as the new value and press Return.

10. Save the file and close it.

11. Restart the Finder. You can do this by choosing Force Quit from the Apple menu, logging out and back in again, or by using the method in this chapter's "Quit the Finder" section.

When the Finder restarts, go to any folder and choose icon view. You should see something similar to the awesome monsters depicted in Figure 1-1.

To return the icon sizes to normal, open the View Options dialog and drag the icon size slider. As soon as you click the slider, the Finder figures out that something is amiss, changes the upper limit back to 128, and redraws the icons at a more reasonable size.

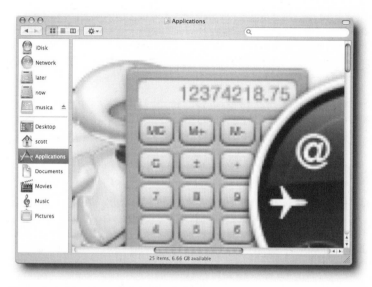

FIGURE 1-1: Giant icons! Hide the children!

Make Perfect Sidebars Every Time

Finder windows can show or hide their sidebars. You can drag the dot on the right edge of the sidebar (see Figure 1-2) to decide how big you want the sidebar to be. Drag it all the way to the left to make the sidebar vanish. The dot will still be there (in case you want to make the sidebar come back). If you want the dot to go away, you'll have to sacrifice the toolbar as well: Choose View → Hide Toolbar or click the oval in the top-right corner of the window.

FIGURE 1-2: Drag this dot
to resize the sidebar.

A couple of cool shortcuts give you control over the sidebar's size. Double-click the resize dot to make the sidebar vanish completely—except for that pesky dot. Double-click the vestigial dot to restore the sidebar to the size it was before you banished it.

This one's nifty but subtle. With the sidebar hidden, drag the dot slowly and at a steady speed. When the sidebar is just big enough to allow all its items to appear fully, with no ellipses at the ends of words, the sidebar will *stick* for a few pixels even as you drag, pinning the sidebar at its optimal size. If you keep dragging, eventually the sidebar will *unstick* and let you make it bigger.

If the sidebar is wider than necessary to display all items, you can use this trick in the other direction, as you drag to make the sidebar smaller. It doesn't work exactly as you would hope, reversing the pinning effect. Instead, when you drag within a few pixels of the optimal width, the sidebar edge suddenly jumps to the left to hit the *sticky point*, where it stays until your dragging catches up with it.

Note Each Finder window keeps its own view settings, so you can have some windows that display the toolbar and sidebar and others that hide them.

Master All the Columns

You probably know that you can resize columns in column view by dragging the divider control that appears at the lower-right edge of every column. The control, marked with two vertical bars, is easy to miss if you don't know it's there (see Figure 1-3). If you hold down Option while dragging, all the columns resize at once, making them all the same width.

FIGURE **1-3: The Resize control in the Finder column view window.**

Unfortunately, the column view people weren't talking to the list view people on this one, because this trick only works in column view.

Set Your Columns Just Right

Column view has a trick to get a column just wide enough to display all its items. If you double-click the column divider control, the column snaps instantly (or not so instantly, if there are a lot of items in the column) to exactly the right width for showing everything it contains.

Note that there's some inconsistency in what happens when you drag different user interface elements in the Finder. The sticky sidebar dragging trick described earlier in "Make Perfect Sidebars Every Time" would be handy here, but it doesn't work; double-clicking the divider control performs a very different action than double-clicking the sidebar dot.

Fun with View Options

Every Finder folder has its own collection of settings called *view options*. There are actually two sets of options for every folder: one that's used when the folder is displayed in list view and a separate set for icon view. You set view options by choosing View → Show View Options, which brings up one of the dialogs shown in Figure 1-4.

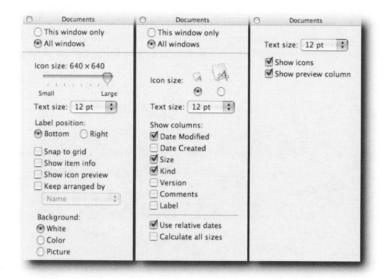

FIGURE 1-4: The View Options dialog varies depending on the current window's view type.

Note All Finder windows showing column view share common settings, and there are only two of those. They control whether the window shows icons next to the file names and whether the last column is used for a preview of the file. The main reason these options exist is so you can turn them off to speed up cruising through files in the Finder.

Note that the title bar of the view options dialog has the name of the folder, and the top section for icon and list views includes two radio buttons: This Window Only, and All Windows (for icon view and list view). If you make a change with This Window Only selected, only the current window is affected. If you change a setting with All Windows selected, you're making the change for *every window of that type*, except for those windows that already have their own custom settings.

In this section, I'll cover some of the more unusual and lesser-known features of Finder view options.

Use Background Colors and Pictures

The bottom of the View Options dialog contains the good stuff. In icon view, you get to design the background of your Finder windows. By default, windows are set to have a plain white background. To make things less boring, click Color and pick a shade you like. Your chosen color is then used to fill the window background when you're in icon view.

For more fun, use the Picture background option. Click the Picture button and then click Select. Pick your favorite picture and watch it appear as the background of the Finder window, as shown in Figure 1-5. If you've ever downloaded software that contains a disk image with a picture in its background and wondered, "How did they do that?" now you know. If you want, you can even apply the picture to every Finder window by using the All Windows button.

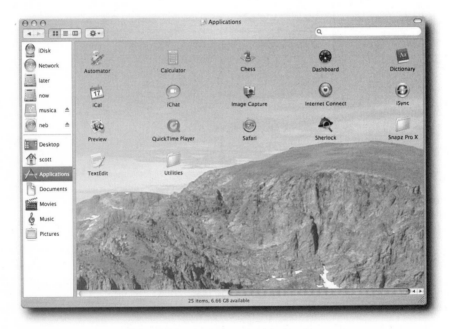

FIGURE 1-5: A custom picture background for Finder windows.

The window keeps track of your choices for color and picture, no matter which background option you're using. So if you set up a picture, switch to a color, and then decide a year later that you'd like the picture back, all you have to do is click the Picture button and you'll see that the faithful Finder remembered your choice of picture.

Show More Information

Two more view options let you control how much information you see about files in icon view. Use the Show Item Info option to learn more about every item at a glance. For example, when you turn on this nifty feature, folders display how many items they contain, images (such as JPEGs and GIFs) show their resolution, movies display their length, and all your socks are folded for you (just kidding about that last one).

The Show Icon Preview option lets you learn even more about your files just by glancing at their icons. With this setting turned on, the Finder turns the icons for image files into tiny replicas of their images.

Both of these options are nifty, but they can slow down your Finder windows, which is one good reason to keep them turned off (at least, until you get that nifty new quad-processor G6 desktop for your birthday).

Quit the Finder

You've probably noticed that the Finder has no Quit item at the bottom of its application menu, unlike virtually every other OS X program. That isn't an accident: Apple does this to prevent folks from accidentally quitting an application that should be running all the time.

But sometimes you really do want to quit the Finder as, for example, in various sections of this chapter when you work with with Finder preferences. You can always force quit the Finder by choosing Force Quit from the Apple menu, but there's a neater way. The Finder actually has its own Quit menu item, but it's disabled by default. We're going to enable it, using that classic act from the '60s, Terminal and the Defaults.

1. Open Terminal. It's usually in the /Applications/Utilities folder.

2. Type this command, then press Return or Enter:

```
defaults write com.apple.finder QuitMenuItem yes
```

3. Restart the Finder by logging out or force quitting. (The next time you need to restart the Finder, you can use the very Quit Finder item you've just enabled.)

That's it! You should now have Quit Finder as the last item in the Finder's application menu. If you ever want to remove this menu item, just repeat the command, substituting no for yes.

Be a Quitter

There are other ways to quit the Finder. In addition to the two already described (force quit and enabling the Quit menu item), another handy option is to type `killall Finder` in Terminal. You might also want to check out TinkerTool, described in Chapter 7, which lets you enable the Quit menu without any Terminal work.

Make the Default Finder Window Behave

The Finder keeps track of a default window position and size that it uses whenever you open a new window with File ➔ New Finder Window. You can tell the Finder what values to use for these settings, but there's no obvious user interface for doing it. To set up your default new window, follow these steps:

1. Go to the Finder and close all windows.
2. Chose File ➔ New Finder Window. This will be your model window. Resize it and move it until it has the size and location you want. You can also set your desired window view and toolbar/sidebar settings.
3. Close the window.
4. Open a new window to test it out. The new window should have the size, location, view, and toolbar/sidebar settings of the one you just closed.

Who's Zooming Whom?

The Finder and zooming rectangles (zoomrects) go back a long way. Ever since the earliest days of the Macintosh, the Finder has used zoomrects as an effective animation for showing that something is moving or expanding, such as a file or application opening. Even in those early days, some folks decided enough already with the zoomrects: They would rather have the zoomrects turned off so they could regain that fraction of a second spent looking at the nice animation. In today's modern, twenty-first-century world, you can turn off the zoomrects in the Finder by using the Defaults command.

1. Open Terminal.
2. Type this command and then press Return or Enter:

```
defaults write com.apple.finder ZoomRects no
```

3. Restart the Finder.

No more zoomrects will trouble you. To get them back, you can repeat the command, substituting yes for no.

 Note   The defaults command pays attention to upper- and lowercase in identifier names. For example, QuitMenuItem is not the same thing as quitMenuItem (one starts with an uppercase letter and the other doesn't). Make sure you type the identifiers just right, or stuff won't work and you'll be unnecessarily sad.

Go Directly to Secret Folders

Mac OS X is based on Unix, and lots of the system is hidden from view in the Finder. This helps prevent unhealthy poking around and any subsequent catastrophic damage that might result. Of course, you can use Terminal to see all the hidden stuff. But a trap door in the Finder enables you to look at hidden folders.

1. In the Finder, choose Folder → Go to Folder, or just press Command-Shift-G.

2. Type a directory path in the dialog box (see Figure 1-6).

FIGURE 1-6: The Go to Folder command lets you access hidden directories from the warm comfort of the Finder.

This command works for any directory, as long as you have privileges to see it. You can use it to open system directories, such as /bin and /etc, or hidden directories, like ~/.ssh.

Cross-Reference For a tip on how to make all files and folders visible in the Finder, see the section "Show Hidden Files" in this chapter.

For even more Unix fun, this command comes with autocomplete, just as in the shell. You see autocomplete work if you type a partial pathname and then press Tab (or just wait for a second or so). The Finder automatically fills in the rest of the pathname, up to the next slash. Neato!

Show Hidden Files

The Finder protects you from yourself by hiding a bunch of system files from view. But the Finder-makers included a switch in defaults that lets you turn off this protection so you can see the complete contents of disks and folders. To make all files visible in the Finder:

1. Open Terminal.

2. Type this command:

```
defaults write com.apple.finder AppleShowAllFiles -bool yes
```

3. Restart the Finder.

Now you'll see all that was previously hidden. This includes Unix directories that are deliberately kept out of sight by the Finder, such as /usr and /sbin, as well as directories whose names start with a period, the traditional Unix mechanism for hiding things. Figure 1-7 shows what a Finder window looks like with all files shown.

FIGURE 1-7: The Finder window with hidden files shown.

This trick is especially valuable when used with an iPod. Apple uses hidden folders to squirrel away music on iPods. If you want to see all the tunes stored on your iPod, just use this procedure to show hidden files. Then take a look inside the iPod_Control folder on your iPod to find folders full of music.

Fix a Frozen Archive

The Finder includes the built-in capability to create and expand ZIP archives. This is a very handy feature, especially because the ZIP format works on other, non-Macintosh operating systems as well. But every so often, the Finder gets stuck while unarchiving. You also see a progress dialog in the Finder that includes a Cancel button. But here's something funny: When you click Cancel, not only does the unarchiving process remain stuck—the Cancel button vanishes! Ha, ha. Good one, Apple.

Of course, what if you really want to cancel the unarchiving that seems to be taking forever? Here's how:

1. Open the Activity Monitor application. If you haven't moved it, you'll find it in the /Applications/Utilities folder.

2. Make sure the pop-up menu at the top of the window says All Processes (see Figure 1-8).

3. Make sure the Process Name column is selected. This causes the Activity Monitor to show the processes in alphabetical order.

4. Look for the process named BOMArchiveHelper and click to select it.

5. Click the Quit Process button in the toolbar and then click Quit in the alert box.

FIGURE **1-8: The Activity Monitor pop-up menu.**

Quitting the process with Activity Monitor should make the hung unarchive go away. Of course, you still might not be able to get the information out of your archive, but at least the hung process is gone.

Summary

The Finder is the most basic part of the Mac OS X experience, but it's also very tweakable. You can use a combination of deeply hidden features and completely buried tricks to make your Finder experience better and more interesting.

Dashboard and Dock

Dashboard is a new feature in Tiger, a way to get fast access to handy mini-applications such as a calculator, stock ticker, and dictionary. Dashboard is one of OS X's most distinctive features.

The Dock is also one of Mac OS X's most versatile and visible elements. Although it replaces a bunch of features that were in Mac OS 9 and looks kind of like a spiffier version of the Windows taskbar, there's really nothing else like it in other operating systems.

In this chapter, you dive into some of the fun and bizarre tricks you can play with Dashboard and the Dock. And if you're one of those who would rather live without the Dock and Dashboard entirely, I'll even show you how to get rid of them completely.

Dashboard

This section describes tips you can use with Dashboard and widgets, the windows that come zooming in to do their work when you summon Dashboard to the screen.

Make Widgets Go Mainstream

It's really cool how Dashboard widgets fly in when you need them and go flying away when you're done. This keeps the screen uncluttered and provides a nice visual effect. But sometimes, you really *don't* want a widget to go away. For example, maybe you'd like to keep that stock ticker on the screen all the time, or you need to use the Translation widget often while you're writing a document in Word. If you could keep widgets on the screen, it might look something like Figure 2-1.

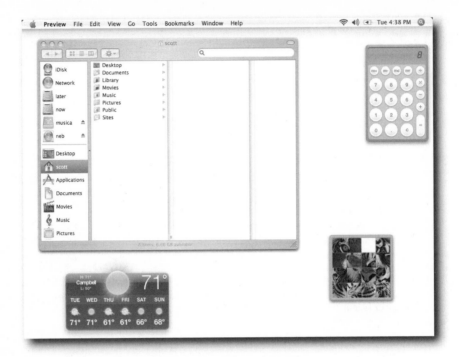

FIGURE 2-1: You can keep Dashboard widgets on the desktop.

What you really need is a way to *poke* widgets down from the Dashboard onto the regular desktop. There's no obvious way to do that in Dashboard, but Apple sneaks in the capability in the guise of a debugging feature for widget developers. Here's how to make it work:

1. Open Terminal. It's usually in the /Applications/Utilities folder. (For quicker access, you might find it handy to add an alias to Terminal in the Applications folder itself or to drag Terminal to the Dock if you're going to use it often.)

2. Type the following command, which puts Dashboard in development mode. You then press Return at the end of the line:

```
defaults write com.apple.dashboard devmode YES
```

3. Now you have to restart Dashboard to make it recognize the new setting. Dashboard is actually part of the Dock application, so what you do here is quit the Dock. Mac OS X really likes the Dock to be running so, after it's gone, OS X immediately restarts it, which is just what you want. You can quit the Dock in various ways. As long as you're in Terminal, the quickest way to restart is by typing another command (with Return at the end again):

```
killall Dock
```

Be sure to capitalize the first letter of Dock, or this won't work. If the Dock is showing, you see it vanish for a few seconds and then roll back into view. As I said, the Dashboard feature is actually part of the Dock application in Tiger, so when the Dock restarts, Dashboard restarts too.

4. With development mode turned on, you can now push widgets onto the desktop. Activate Dashboard and pick a widget that you want to keep on the Desktop.

5. Click the widget and drag it a bit—it doesn't matter how far—but don't release the mouse button when you're done dragging.

6. You're still holding the mouse button, right? Now press the Dashboard activation key (if you haven't changed it, that's F12). When you let go of the mouse button and the keyboard, Dashboard goes away, but the chosen widget stays around. It's now floating above the Desktop.

7. To add another widget to the desktop, repeat Steps 4 through 6.

Widgets behave pretty much the same on the Desktop as they do in Dashboard: You can drag them around, click the info button to set preferences, and hold down Option to reveal the close box. Because you've activated development mode, you can return a deskbound widget to Dashboard with virtually the same procedure: Drag the widget, keep the mouse button down, activate Dashboard, and then let go of all buttons and keys.

Clone Your Widgets

Widgets are like applications in many ways, but they're superior in at least one aspect: It's easy to have multiple copies of the some widget running. Not only is that fun, it's useful. For example, you can have a row of clocks with each set to a different time zone, or display several weather panels showing different cities (see Figure 2-2).

To multiply a widget, activate Dashboard and click the widget repeatedly in the widget bar. You might not notice, at first, that you've got more than one because Dashboard plops each one right on top of the last in the middle of the screen. But if you drag the top one away, you see the copies underneath.

Note

You can avoid this pile-of-widgets problem by dragging the widget out of the widget bar instead of just clicking. As you drag, you see the widget morph into its true size as soon as it departs the widget bar. Just keep dragging, and drop it wherever you want.

Get Reloaded

Many widgets draw information from the Internet, such as stock prices or sports scores. Sometimes, the connection fails and the information can become stale. If you want to force a widget to run itself again, click the widget and press Command-R. This trick shows you yet another cool visual effect as the widget's content swirls away and then swirls back as it reloads, as demonstrated by the series of images in Figure 2-3.

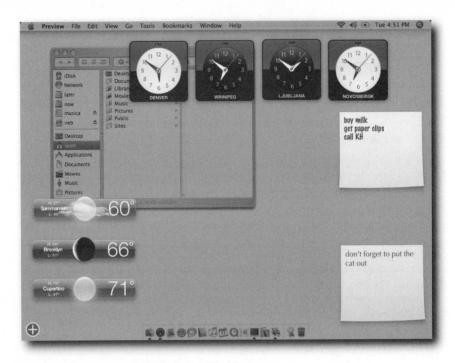

FIGURE 2-2: You can run multiple copies of widgets.

FIGURE 2-3: Reloading a widget with Command-R.

Hold a Widget Tryout

When you download and install a new widget, it won't show up in the widget bar until you put it into your Library/Widgets folder. But you don't have to move it there if you just want to try it out before deciding whether to keep it. All you have to do is navigate to the widget's file in the Finder and double-click, just as if it were an application. Tiger brings out the Dashboard and puts the trial widget in the center of the screen.

Visual Widget Fun

Some of Apple's widgets have tricks and features that are ever-so-slightly hidden. Do you want to customize the picture that appears in the Tile Game widget? Just grab an image and drag it, activate Dashboard, and drop the image onto the game window to make your custom puzzle.

Before you change the puzzle picture, make sure it's one you like: The new picture will be used every time you open the Tile Game from that point on. If you want to recover the original picture of a Tiger, you can find it at /Library/Widgets/Tile Game.wdgt/Images/game.png. Just drag the picture from there and drop it onto the game window to restore the image.

The Weather widget includes a flashy demo mode that shows off its graphical prowess. To see the demo images, open the Weather widget, and then hold down Command and Option while you click repeatedly on the picture in the center of the widget. The location changes to Nowhere, and the image flips through some wild weather, including clouds, haze, fog, and several fascinating kinds of precipitation (Figure 2-4). To return from Nowhere, press Command-R to reload the widget.

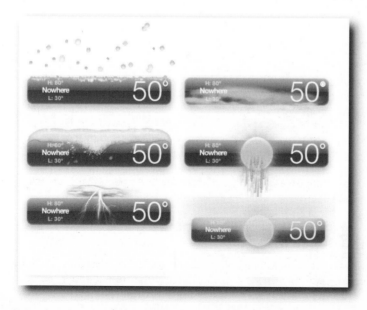

Figure 2-4: Four (or more) seasons of the Weather widget.

Dock

This section provides tips and tweaks for the Dock. You see how to move the Dock to different locations, what happens when you drag to the Dock, and how to tweak Dock options.

Snappy Dragging for the Dock

When you first started up your fresh new Macintosh, the Dock appeared at the bottom of the screen as soon as you got to the Finder. But you probably know that you don't have to keep it at the bottom of the screen. You can move the Dock to the left or right edge by using the Dock item in the Apple menu. As a shortcut to the Apple menu, you can bring up a contextual menu by Control-clicking on the little vertical divider line that separates the left side of the Dock, where applications live, and the right side, which holds documents, folders, and other icons (see Figure 2-5). If you're having trouble getting the contextual menu to appear, make sure you see the pointer change from an arrow to a horizontal line with arrows above and below, as shown in Figure 2-5.

FIGURE 2-5: The contextual menu on the Dock lets you change some settings, including the Dock's location.

Contextual menus are nice, but Mac OS X includes a super-duper shortcut for moving the Dock around. To make it work, move the mouse pointer to the divider line mentioned previously, hold down the Shift key, and drag from the divider line to the right, left, or bottom of the screen. You won't see any feedback at first, and you may wonder what the heck is going on. When you get close to the edge that you're dragging toward, however, the Dock suddenly snaps into place in its new location, and you'll get a tingly feeling and wear a knowing smile.

Note If you drag all the way to the edge of the screen and nothing happens, make sure you drag toward the center of the edge you're interested in. Stay away from the corners.

Drag Stuff to Dock Icons

Mac OS X has always let you drag documents and drop them onto applications on the Dock. This technique provides a way to open a document with an alternate application. For example, you can use this to edit a Microsoft Word document using TextEdit.

Mac OS X 10.4 Tiger adds a new capability. Now you can drag data, not just documents, to applications in the Dock. What happens depends on what you're dragging and which application you drop it on. For example, if you select some text from a TextEdit document, an e-mail, or anywhere else and then drag it to the Safari icon in the Dock, Safari does a Google search for the text you dragged. If you drag text to the Mail icon, you get a nifty new e-mail containing the text. Dragging text to TextEdit creates a new document with the words you dragged.

You can also have fun dragging and dropping pictures. Drop one onto the Safari or Preview icons in the Dock and you see a new window featuring the picture you dragged. If you drop a picture onto the Mail or TextEdit icons, you get a new document with the picture already inserted for your convenience.

Sittin' on the Top of the Screen

Apple gives you plenty of choices for positioning the Dock: You can put it on the left, right, bottom, or . . . what about the top of the screen? That's not an option, for the obvious reason that the Mac's menu bar is always there. The Dock would just get in the way.

Well, it turns out that Apple actually does provide a way to put the Dock at the top. The setting is left out of the standard user interface places, such as the Dock item in the Apple menu. But for true geeks (hello!), you can use the defaults system in Mac OS X to put the Dock up at the top.

1. Open Terminal. Remember that it's usually in the /Applications/Utilities folder.

2. Type this command:

```
defaults write com.apple.Dock orientation top
```

3. Press Return, and watch the Dock as . . . nothing happens. As with Dashboard changes, you have to quit the Dock and restart it in order to effect the change. In Terminal, type this command with Return at the end:

```
killall Dock
```

As soon as you kill the Dock process, you should see it vanish, only to reappear a moment later at the top of the screen, just as you wanted it to (see Figure 2-6). When you have had enough of this fun, you can quickly put the Dock back in a more typical location by holding down Shift and dragging the divider bar to another edge of the screen, as described in the section "Snappy Dragging for the Dock" in this chapter.

Note If your Dock is set to roll off the screen every time you move the mouse pointer away from it (that's called Dock Hiding), you won't be able to get to the Dock when it's at the top of the screen. To use your Dock-on-the-top, open System Preferences, click Dock, and turn off the Automatically Hide And Show The Dock check box.

Make the Dock Sit in the Corner

Apple thinks the bottom of the screen is a fine place for the Dock, and most people simply keep it there. If you like, you can move the Dock to the left or right sides or even, absurdly, to the top of the screen, under the menu bar.

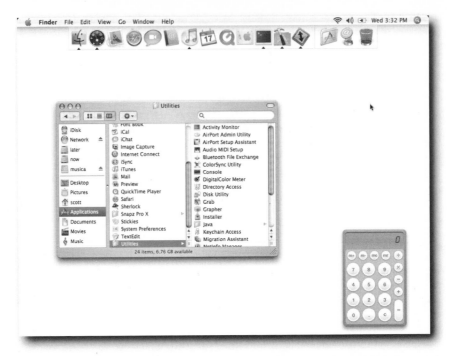

FIGURE 2-6: Amuse your friends and annoy your spouse by putting the Dock at the top of the screen.

When you move the Dock, it usually sits in the center of whichever edge you've put it on. But you don't have to settle for that. With this tip, you can move the Dock into either of the corners along its chosen edge. Here's how:

1. Open Terminal from the /Applications/Utilities folder.

2. Type the following:

```
defaults write com.apple.Dock pinning start
```

This command puts the Dock in the left or top corner of its edge. Instead of start, you can type end to stick the Dock in the right or bottom corner.

3. You probably know by now that you have to restart the Dock using killall Dock, which is described in the section "Make Widgets Go Mainstream" in this chapter.

You can use this tip along with the one described in the section "Sittin' on the Top of the Screen" to move the Dock to the top-right edge, just under the menu bar, where you might actually find it usable. Figure 2-7 shows what that might look like with the Dock cranked down to minimum size so it doesn't take up much room.

FIGURE 2-7: You can squeeze the Dock into the top-right corner
of the screen, just under the menu bar.

When you've had enough fun with the Dock in the corner, you might want to restore it to its
usual place in the middle of a screen edge. To do that, you need to change the *pinning setting* in
the Dock's preferences again. There are two ways to do this:

1. Change the pinning setting to any value other than Start or End. The Dock ignores
   the value and puts the Dock in the center, its default location. In the Terminal, type the
   following:

   ```
   defaults write com.apple.Dock pinning notStartOrEnd
   ```

   As long as you type anything other than Start or End as the value (where it says
   notStartOrEnd), the Dock returns to the center after you restart it with `killall Dock`.

2. Instead of changing the entry for pinning, you can remove it entirely from the
   Dockpreferences file:

   ```
   defaults delete com.apple.Dock pinning
   ```

   As always, follow this with `killall Dock` to complete the task. This command removes
   the pinning entry from Dock preferences. Without any entry, the Dock shows up at its
   default location in the center of its edge. This method is cleaner than changing the pinning to an unimplemented value, but if you get a little nervous when typing **delete** into
   the Terminal, you can go ahead and use the other technique instead of this one.

Yellow Means Slow Down

Apple stuff is not just functional: It's pretty. Apple's designers really sweat the visual details,
including all the cool animations in Mac OS X. When you click the yellow button at the top-
left corner of a window, the window kind of folds over on itself and slides elegantly into the
Dock in a fashion that Apple calls *the genie effect*. Clicking the minimized icon in the Dock
reverses the animation and restores the window just the way it was.

The genie effect is a great visual treat, suitable for showing off to your Mac-less friends. But to
really see what the genie effect is doing, you need to slow it down and watch the details.
Somebody at Apple must have thought the same thing because OS X has an easy built-in way
to temporarily go into slow motion. Just hold down the Shift key before you click the yellow
button, and you see the genie effect in great detail. Hold down Shift when you click the minimized icon, and you can watch the fine points of the genie coming out of the bottle.

The slow motion Shift key works on other effects as well. Open lots of applications, fill your
screen with windows, then hold down Shift before you activate Exposé. Watch in amazement
as the windows shrink down and scurry to their new places on the screen. No less impressive—
okay, actually it's much less impressive—is holding down Shift while clicking a System
Preferences panel.

Dashboard includes several nifty visual effects that can be slowed with the Shift key. Hold down Shift while you drag a widget out of the widget bar to see it morph slowly to its actual size. Shift-click a widget's close box to study closely as the window's content is sucked into the close box. And hold down Shift before showing or hiding the widget bar or Dashboard itself to watch those effects unfold.

Bottle the Genie

The genie effect is cool the first few thousand times you see it, especially in slow motion, but after awhile you start to ask "Is that all there is?" With OS X, the answer is always "No, there's more!" You can turn off the genie effect and replace it with *the scale effect,* which minimizes windows merely by shrinking their sides and moving them to the Dock. To switch to the scale effect, Control-click the vertical divider bar in the Dock and choose Scale Effect from the Minimize Using menu.

There's a more interesting item that's not available on the menu—kind of like that secret super-spicy dish at your local Chinese restaurant. You can get to it through the Terminal, as follows:

1. Open Terminal from the /Applications/Utilities folder.

2. Type this command:

   ```
   defaults write com.apple.Dock mineffect suck
   ```

3. Restart the Dock using `killall Dock`, as described in the section "Make Widgets Go Mainstream" in this chapter.

Now try minimizing some windows and restoring them. You're watching *the suck effect* in action. To observe it closely in slow motion, hold down the Shift key when you click. For the best comparison, watch the suck effect in slow motion a few times and then Control-click the divider bar to change back to genie effect. You can see the differences, and you will soon be an expert in the art of Dock minimization effects.

Dragging Docs in the Dock

The left side of the Dock is for applications, and the right side is for everything else: documents, folders, and the trash. Although these two groups of icons are fated to live apart forever, sometimes they get to meet briefly—when, for example, you drag a document from the right side onto an application on the left in order to open the document with a specific application. But when you try this, you see a problem: Dragging the document icon actually removes it from the Dock, although it zips back to its place after you drop it on the desired application icon.

But what if you accidentally let go of the document while it's on the Desktop? Poof! It vanishes, and you have to go find the original document again to put it back on the Dock. If this process of dragging a document in the Dock is too fragile for you, try holding down the Command key before you start dragging. When you do that, the document icon won't pop out of the Dock as you navigate to the left side where the applications live.

What's going on here? When you hold down Command before you start dragging, you're telling OS X to drag the *item itself* instead of the Dock icon that represents it. This means you can use the Command-drag technique as a shortcut for moving something from one folder to another or onto the Desktop. The original item is moved wherever the icon is located when you let go of the mouse button. Powerful!

Hidden Switcher Features

Switcher is not just a word for someone who upgrades from Windows to Mac OS X—it's also the name of a handy user interface feature. When you hold down the Command key and press Tab, you see the Application Switcher (Figure 2-8). You can press Tab again and again to skip along from one application to the next. When you get to the one you want, just let go of the Command key, and you're there. You probably know that you can press Shift-Tab to move to the left in the Application Switcher, going through the applications in reverse.

FIGURE 2-8: The Application Switcher shows you all running applications.

The Application Switcher has a few more interesting tricks you should know. While you're holding down Command and looking at the Switcher, you can press Q to quit the selected application without even having to switch to it. You can press H if you just want to hide an application's windows. And if you want to select an application really quickly in the Switcher, you don't have to bother tabbing to it. Just use the mouse to point to the application you want, and it is selected in the Switcher.

Did you know you can use the Application Switcher while you're dragging something? This is incredibly handy when you want to drag and drop something from one application to another. Just start the drag, and while you're holding down the mouse button with your mousing hand, use your other hand to hold down Command and press Tab. Pick the application you want to drop the object in, either by pressing Tab or by mousing there directly. When the application you want is selected, let go of the keyboard, and the application appears. Now just finish the drag, and drop the item wherever you want it.

The Bouncing! The Bouncing!

Like many other visual effects, bouncing icons in the Dock are cute for a little while. Then you just want to reach your hand into the screen to make them stop bouncing already. Dock icons bounce for one of two reasons: Either the application is starting up, or it's already running and it wants your attention (for an error message or something). Bouncing in the Dock is certainly an attention-getting device; unfortunately, there's no way to make a needy icon stop bouncing without switching to that application. But you can easily get rid of the other kind of bouncing, the kind that takes place when you launch an application.

You might be surprised to find a setting for this in the Dock panel in System Preferences. Yes, you had the power all the time. In the Apple menu, choose Dock → Dock Preferences. Look for the check box labeled Animate Opening Applications. (They had to call it that because a label like Bounce Dock Icons When Opening Applications would scare away people who fear the bouncing.) After you turn off that check box, icons will no longer bounce when you launch applications. Instead, the tiny triangle under the icons will pulse until the application is running. It's subtle, but just enough to get your attention.

Fast Folder Access from the Dock

You probably already know that you can drag frequently used folders to the Dock for easy access: Just click the docked folder to see its contents. But you might not be aware of a handy shortcut. If you Control-click a folder on the Dock, you get a menu listing everything in the folder (see Figure 2-9). The contents list is hierarchical. You can drill down into folders that are inside the primary folder until you find the item you want.

FIGURE 2-9: Control-click a folder in the dock to see and navigate to its contents.

The End

When Mac OS X first appeared, the Dock was one its most controversial features among old-time Mac folks. The Dock is very visible and provides a lot of features in novel ways, so it was probably inevitable that the Dock would take a lot of heat.

If you just can't bear having the Dock on your desktop, no matter which edge or corner you shove it into, you can get rid of it forever. All you have to do is move the Dock application out of its standard location, which is the /System/Library/CoreServices directory, and then make it quit. When OS X notices that the Dock is no longer running, it looks for the Dock application in that directory; and if it can't be found, there's no Dock.

To put the Dock out to pasture:

1. In the Terminal, carefully type the following command to move the Dock application to your Documents folder.

```
sudo mv /System/Library/CoreServices/Dock.app ~/Documents/
```

If Terminal asks for your password, go ahead and type it.

2. Force the Dock to quit with the usual command:

```
killall Dock
```

This time, when the Dock rolls off the screen, it doesn't come back. As a side effect, whether you want it to or not, this process kills Dashboard and all widgets too.

If you feel remorse and you decide you want the Dock back after all, you can easily reverse the process by typing this command:

```
sudo mv ~/Documents/Dock.app /System/Library/CoreServices/
```

To start the Dock after you've moved it back, double-click its icon in /System/Library/CoreServices.

Summary

The Dock is a frequently used, central part of the Mac OS X experience, and Dashboard is new but has already become a popular enhancement to OS X. That helps explain why there are so many tricks and mods for these features. As OS X evolves, you can expect to see even more cool stuff you can do with the Dock and Dashboard.

Now that you know how to customize your Dock and Dashboard, come back for the next chapter to see more system tricks, including the scoop on the notorious Exposé blob and how to personalize it.

Preferences and System Stuff

I n our last thrilling installment, Captain Joe was flying as fast as he could to reach little Bettina, who was hanging precariously from the Ledge of Peril as Evil Jack completed his plan for regaining . . . oh wait, that's not what we were doing at all. No, actually, you were continuing your journey through weird and useful tips for OS X system features. In this chapter, you spend time with interesting settings and tweaks in System Preferences, look at strange and useful Exposé tweaks, and explore some other fun system stuff. Hang on, little Bettina!

Fast Preferences for Sound and Screen

If you're like most users, you probably find yourself in System Preferences at least a few times a week—more, if you're a real geek or you're playing around with something new. Because System Preferences is used so frequently, it deserves a shortcut. There are several ways to get to System Preferences in a hurry. Apple includes it in the Dock, and it's also available as the fourth item in the Apple menu. But you can reach it in other ways as well.

The upper-right side of your screen is festooned with menus for various features: time and date, power, volume, and so on. These menus let you experiment with some of their features' most common settings, and most of them have an item that opens the Preferences panel for the feature (see Figure 3-1).

FIGURE 3-1: The menu bar clock with its menu revealed.

The coolest and most secret shortcuts are those available for the Sound and Displays panels. To get to Sound preferences, hold down Option and press any of the volume keys (mute, volume up, or volume down) on the top row of your keyboard. This works whether or not System Preferences is already open—if it is, the Sound panel is switched in. Similarly, if you hold down Option and press the brightness or contrast keys, the Displays panel opens. When you're in System Preferences, you can switch to any panel you want, of course, so you might want to use these as a shortcut to System Preferences in general.

Dealing in Volume

When you press the volume up, volume down, or mute keys on the keyboard, you get the really groovy transparent giant icon on the screen. And, if you're not muting the sound, you get a little *thwack* sound from the speaker so you can gauge the current volume. This sound is interesting enough, but of course, it's more fun to experiment with it. There aren't any preferences setting for changing the sound, but it's easy enough to do if you know where to look. The little noise is simply stored as an AIFF-format sound in a file. To change the sound, all you have to do is replace that file with another AIFF sound. This works best with sounds that are very short (one or two seconds, at most).

Here's how to do it:

1. In the Finder, navigate to /System/Library/LoginPlugins/BezelServices.loginPlugin/ Contents/Resources.

2. Select that folder and choose File → Get Info.

3. In the Ownership and Permissions section of the info window, click the triangle next to Details.

4. Click the padlock next to Owner: system.

5. Click the popup called *system* and choose your account (Figure 3-2). The system might ask you to type in your password at this point.

6. Navigate to the AIFF file you want to use as the new volume sound.

Cross-Reference

If you don't have any AIFF sounds you want to use, you can instruct iTunes to create one from the best moment of your favorite song. See the section "iTunes Music Processing" in Chapter 6 for details.

7. Hold down Option and drag the chosen new sound to copy it to the Resources folder. Again, the cautious and secure OS X might ask for your password because you're playing with a system folder. Drop the file in the folder to copy it there.

8. In the Resources folder, select volume.aiff, the current sound file. Rename it **volume original.aiff**. That's to preserve it in case you want to restore it later.

9. Select the file you dropped in and rename it **volume.aiff**. Make sure that you have two fs at the end—some AIFF files, such as those generated by iTunes, only have one. Without two fs at the end, you won't hear anything.

FIGURE 3-2: You must change the
file's permissions temporarily.

10. Go back to the Info window you opened in Step 2. Click the *owner* pop-up again, and
set the *owner* back to *system*. Click the padlock and close the info window.

11. Log out and log in again to test the change. When you press the volume up or volume
down keys, you should hear your funky new sound.

If you ever want to change back to the standard boring sound, just reverse the process, renaming your custom sound and restoring volume original.aiff to volume.aiff.

Mac, Build, and Serial Number

If you ever find yourself on the phone with Apple, talking about getting service for your Mac,
the technician will probably want to know your computer's serial number. For most products,
this means looking at the back or bottom of the machine, or digging around madly to find the
place you wrote it down. In OS X, there's an easier way. Just choose About This Mac from the
Apple menu. You see the familiar window that includes the version number.

Here's the trick: Click the version number, and it changes to the *build number*, a value that's sort of a subversion number. This number is generally useful only for distinguishing one pre-shipping version of Mac OS from another.

If you click again, you see your Mac's serial number. And for even more obscure information about your computer, click the More Info button. That action opens System Profiler, which provides a vast treasure of information about your hardware and software.

Note If you prefer to get your information from the command line, you can open Terminal and type **system_profiler SPHardwareDataType** to get the serial number (along with other information), or type **sw_vers** to see the OS version and build numbers.

Grow That Mouse

Mac OS X includes the Universal Access preference panel to assist anyone who has difficulty seeing, hearing, typing, or using the mouse (see Figure 3-3). Even if you're able to use these features without the aid of Universal Access, you might be interested in some of its more intriguing features.

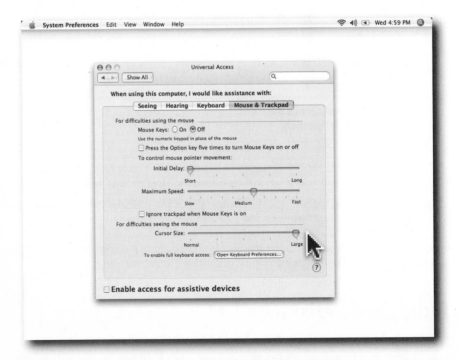

FIGURE 3-3: Universal Access lets you make the mouse pointer bigger.

You can use the Mouse & Trackpad pane of Universal Access to enlarge the mouse pointer on the screen. Just drag the slider to the right to grow your mouse. This is especially handy on laptops and on very large screens, such as the 30-inch Apple Cinema HD Display that somebody is probably going to buy you for your birthday.

Note Tiger adds a major feature to Universal Access: VoiceOver. With VoiceOver turned on, Tiger provides a spoken English interface to the system and applications. VoiceOver was designed for people with visual or learning disabilities who have trouble seeing or reading information on the screen. VoiceOver uses spoken language to guide users through the user interface and to read the text of documents on the screen. To find out more about VoiceOver, see `www.apple.com/macosx/tiger/voiceover.html`.

Hit the Big Time

The Universal Access preference panel includes a great feature that lets you easily make everything on the screen larger. On the Seeing panel, click the radio button to turn on Zoom. When Zoom is on, you can use Command-Option-= to zoom in and make everything larger (Figure 3-4). You now have more stuff than you can see at once, so just mouse around to change the part of the screen that's being enlarged. To zoom out again, press Command-Option-minus. You can hold down these keystroke combinations to zoom smoothly and rapidly.

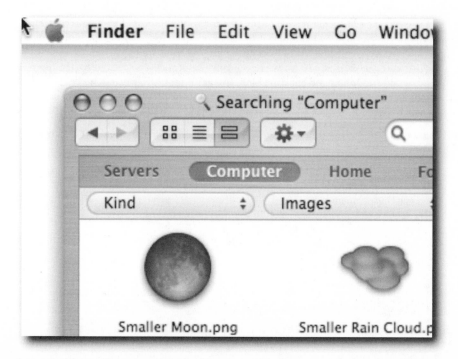

FIGURE 3-4: Zoomed screen, available via Universal Access.

Even if you have great eyesight, this feature is very handy for getting a closer look at tiny pictures and text or for showing greater detail when you're giving a presentation to a large group. It's yet another way to show off how cool your Mac is.

Beware of the Blob

Exposé is one of those awe-inspiring features of Mac OS X that you can use to torture your friends who don't use Macs. Exposé is fun to look at, and it has the added bonus of actually being useful. Apple provides a System Preferences panel with two methods for controlling Exposé: You can start Exposé by moving the mouse to a screen corner, or with a special keystroke (you can set both of these in System Preferences). But there's another, hidden way to use Exposé: the blob (see Figure 3-5).

FIGURE 3-5: The Exposé blob.

The Exposé blob is like a giant aqua button for triggering Exposé. The blob is translucent, until you hover over it, at which point it becomes opaque. You can drag the blob anywhere you want on the screen. Clicking the blob does the Exposé thing on the current application's windows, just as if you pressed F10 (or whatever other keystroke you've set in System Preferences). If you hold down Option and click the blob, you get Exposé's All Windows behavior, just as if you had pressed F9 (Figure 3-6). You might even find the blob to be a more useful and convenient way to use Exposé than the official user interface.

Wouldn't you love to have a blob of your own? After all, it's so darn cute. Here's how to unleash the blob:

1. Open Terminal from the /Applications/Utilities folder.

2. Type this command:

```
defaults write com.apple.Dock wvous-floater -bool true
```

3. Type this command to restart the Dock.

```
killall Dock
```

Enjoy your blob! When you have grown tired of having it around, go back into Terminal and type the following command to get rid of it:

```
defaults write com.apple.Dock wvous-floater -bool false
```

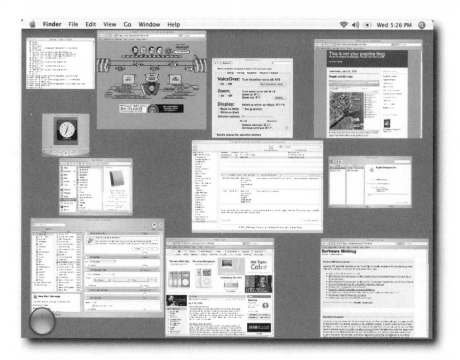

FIGURE 3-6: Using the blob to show all windows.

Pimp My Blob

After you have your Exposé blob happening, you might decide you want to customize it. That's an easy task. Mac OS X defines two images for the blob: the translucent one that appears most of the time, and the opaque version that takes over when you drag it around. By replacing these images, you can make your blob reflect your own personality by making it a different color or perhaps replacing it with the faces of your favorite politicians. You can even change the size of the blob, making it larger or smaller to be more useful to you.

Start by creating your new blob images as a pair of PNG files. You can use virtually any graphics editor for this task, or even take a screen shot with the Grab feature in Preview. After you've created your PNG files, here are the steps for customizing the blob:

1. In the Finder, navigate to /System/Library/CoreServices/ and select the Dock application.

2. From the Action menu in the window's toolbar, select Show Package Contents.

3. In the Dock contents window, navigate to Contents/Resources.

4. Select the Resources folder and choose File ➔ Get Info.

5. In the Ownership and Permissions section of the info window, click the triangle next to Details.

6. Click the padlock next to Owner: system.

7. Click system and choose your account. The system might ask you to type in your password at this point.

8. Find the files wvousfloat.png and wvousfloatselected.png and rename them **wvousfloat original.png** and **wvousfloatselected original.png**, respectively.

9. Drag the replacement files you want to use and drop them into the Resources folder.

10. In the Resources folder, select the name of the first replacement file (the one you want to use for the blob image when you're not dragging it). Rename that file **wvousfloat.png**.

11. Now select the second replacement file, the one with the image that should appear when you're dragging the blob around. Rename that one **wvousfloatselected.png**.

12. Go back to the Info window you opened earlier. Click the *owner* pop-up again, and set the *owner* back to *system*. Click the little padlock and close the info window.

13. To see your handiwork, open Terminal and type:

```
killall Dock
```

When the Dock restarts, you should see your newly designed Exposé blob on the screen. Try dragging it to make sure both your images are working. And, of course, you can trigger Exposé by clicking or Option-clicking your custom blob.

To get back your Apple-standard blobs, reverse the renaming process: Change the names of your files first; then give the files their original names back.

All My Windows

Exposé's desktop mode lets you fling all your windows aside temporarily so you can see what's happening on your desktop. But Exposé includes a wacky alternate behavior for desktop mode. In this version, instead of sliding windows aside, Exposé constructs a tiny window and slurps all your windows into that one. You can see the results of this effect in Figure 3-7.

After you're in tiny desktop mode, you can drag the little fellow around on the screen, or click it to restore everything to full magnitude. To enable this feature:

1. Open Terminal.

2. Type:

```
defaults write com.apple.Dock wvous-olddesktop -bool false
```

3. Restart the Dock.

```
killall Dock
```

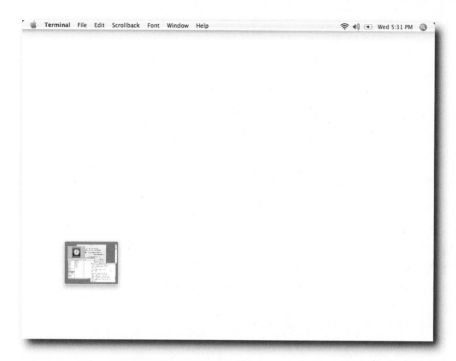

FIGURE 3-7: Exposé's alternate desktop mode.

To try it out, press F11 or use the usual command for starting Exposé's desktop mode. When you want to return to the usual behavior, type the following command into Terminal:

```
defaults write com.apple.Dock wvous-olddesktop -bool true
```

Note Mac OS X versions prior to 10.4 contained a bug that rendered the area of the tiny desktop window non-responsive to mouse clicks, even when you weren't using Exposé. This bug is partially fixed in 10.4. You can now click in the dead area; but after you do, you can't always successfully grab and drag windows. If this happens to you, turn off the feature and then trigger Exposé's desktop mode again. That should fix the problem. Because of this bug, however, it's probably best to use this mode for amusement purposes only.

Codenames Are (Sometimes) Forever

Exposé preferences start with the prefix *wvous* because at one point in its development, Exposé was known by the unlikely name *WindowVous*, as in *Rendezvous for Windows*.

Brighten a Cheerless Crash

You've seen it before, all too often: the dialog that appears when an application crashes. This is the one that says the application has "unexpectedly quit." It's not a pretty picture.

There's no easy tip I can give you to make application crashes go away, but maybe you can make them a little less painful by tweaking the text that appears in the dialog. For example, you might have it say something like "Yep, the application quit again. Are you surprised?" All you have to do is edit the file containing the text. Follow these steps:

1. In the Finder, navigate to /System/Library/CoreServices/ and select the CrashReporter application.

2. From the Action menu in the window's toolbar, select Show Package Contents.

3. In the CrashReporter contents window, navigate to Contents/Resources/English.lproj, or the folder for another language, if you're running that language.

4. Select the file Localizable.strings and choose File ➔ Get Info.

5. In the Ownership and Permissions section of the info window, click the triangle next to Details.

6. Click the padlock next to Owner: system.

7. Click the popup labeled *system* and choose your account. Type your password, if OS X asks for it nicely.

8. You might want to make a backup of the Localizable.strings file at this point, just in case something bad happens when you edit it.

9. Open Localizable.strings in TextEdit, Xcode, or any text editor.

10. At the bottom of the window you see various lovely strings defined, such as UNEXPECTEDLY_QUIT_HEADER and UNEXPECTEDLY_QUIT_ MESSAGE. You'll recognize the text they contain as those darn crash messages. Edit the ones you want to change and then close the file.

11. Now you need to put the file permissions back the way you found them. Return to the Info window you opened earlier. Click the *owner* pop-up, and this time set *owner* back to *system*. Click the little padlock and close the info window.

Now, the next time you crash, you won't be any happier than you were before, but at least you'll know that you're looking at a dialog that you helped design.

Summary

Mac OS X is complex enough and old enough now to have plenty of fascinating settings and secrets hidden away. Sometimes you find useful things by looking in unexpected places. For example, you might not have thought that the Universal Access preference panel held anything useful for you, but the Zoom feature discussed in this chapter is great for anybody. The lesson is to keep exploring—you never know what goodies you'll find.

Next, we'll ease our way from the system to the applications where you spend most of your time. To find out handy tricks for managing application windows and much more, come along to the next chapter.

User Interface

One of the great things about modern operating systems like Mac OS X is that most applications share a lot of common features provided by the system. This means that tweaks and improvements created by our friends at Apple can help you no matter which application you're using. Cool stuff with windows, menus, or dragging makes the whole experience better.

In this chapter, you'll delve into some of the fancy things you can do in applications. Although this stuff is provided by Apple in the subterranean workings of the system, not every trick works in every application. The best way to find out what works where is to try things using your favorite applications. Good luck, and have fun!

Silk Sheets

One of the cool innovations in Mac OS X is *sheets,* which are like dialog boxes that stay attached to specific windows, so you always know where they belong. Sheets also add a groovy animated visual effect to OS X's repertoire: Whenever a sheet appears, it seems to roll out from under the title bar. And when you're done, it rolls right back again. You can see sheets in action in most applications whenever you use Save As to save a document.

Ah, but perhaps you're a speed demon, and you don't like sitting there while the darn sheet unrolls. If so, you're in luck. You can set a global preference to eliminate the delay that makes the sheet slide out. Here's how to do it:

1. Open Terminal. Remember, it's usually in the Applications:Utilities folder.

2. Type this command:

```
defaults write -g NSWindowResizeTime .01
```

The new instant-sheet setting affects only applications that you open after you change the setting. If you want currently running applications to speed up their sheet appearance, you have to quit and relaunch them.

Note The –g flag in the Defaults command sets a value in the global preferences domain, which affects all applications.

When you realize you've become graphically poor and you miss the way sheets used to appear, you can go back to the old setting by typing the following command into the Terminal:

```
defaults delete -g NSWindowResizeTime
```

And if you love the sheet animation so much that you want to study it at your leisure, you can set the delay to be longer than the standard. For starters, try this:

```
defaults write -g NSWindowResizeTime 1
```

The value at the end of the command represents the delay in seconds for every 150 pixels the sheet is resized. If you never try this trick, NSWindowResizeTime is set to 0.2. You can make the value as low as zero, although numbers below .01 or so look about the same. And if you really want to test your patience (or someone else's), you're not limited to any maximum value. But have mercy!

Do All Your Windows at Once

When you're manipulating multiple windows in applications, the Option key is your friend. If you hold down Option when you click any of the *stoplight buttons* at the left side of the window's title bar, all the open windows perform the function of the button you clicked. So, if you Option-click the red Close button, all the application's windows close at once. That's handy! But there's more. Option-click the yellow Minimize button, and all the application's windows shrink down to the Dock. And, as you might have guessed, you can Option-click the green Zoom button to zoom all the windows, although that function is substantially less practical than the others.

When your application has multiple windows minimized in the Dock, you can Option-click any one of them to restore them all to full size, whether or not they got into the Dock by your Option-clicking the Minimize button.

This tip works primarily with applications written using Apple's Cocoa programming frameworks. With some applications, such as the Finder and Excel, it works most of the time; but in those programs you can't Option-click a docked window to restore them all. And it doesn't work at all in Word. Go do a few Option-clicks in your favorite application's title bar buttons and see what happens.

Note For maximum useless visual fun, hold down the Shift key while you Option-click the window button or the minimized window in the Dock. Shift slows down the visual effect, letting you watch as all the windows move hypnotically to their new positions.

Look Out behind You

As every Mac user learns quickly, when you click a window, it comes to the front. If you want to drag a window that's not active, you can click its title bar to activate it, and you can then start dragging without having to release the mouse and click again.

Occasionally, you might find yourself wanting to move a window that's not in front without making it the active window. You can do this by grabbing its title bar, dragging it where you want it to be, then clicking on the formerly active window to bring it to the front again. But there's a better way.

If you hold down the Command key when you mouse down on the title bar of an inactive window, you can drag the window around while it stays inactive (see Figure 4-1). This looks a little bit like magic the first time you do it. You find yourself dragging *through* windows that are in front of the one you're moving. But it's a nifty shortcut.

Figure 4-1: Drag an inactive window by holding down Command.

Scroll Right Here, Right Now

Scroll bars look simple, but they have lots of interesting little nuances to their behavior. You already know about the most common features: Click the arrows to scroll the document a little bit, or click in the empty space (officially called the *scroll track*) to scroll a screenful at a time.

You might not know about a couple of other scrolling tricks that can come in handy. Let's say you're looking at the top of a long Web page, and you want to get to a spot about three-quarters of the way down. You could drag the scroll bar's thumb (which Apple calls *the scroller*) to the place you want. Or, you could use this shortcut: Point the mouse at the place in the scroll bar where you want to go, hold down Option, and click. The thumb jumps instantly to the location you want, and you'll feel like you just saved a few seconds of your life that you can devote to more important pursuits.

 You can use the Appearance panel in System Preferences to reverse this behavior, so that a plain click in the scroller moves the thumb to that location, and Option-click scrolls the document by one complete screen. Look for the setting labeled Click In The Scroll Bar To.

Here's another scroll bar trick that's interesting, but somewhat less useful. If you Option-click a scroll arrow, the document scrolls one full screen in that direction, just as if you had clicked the scroll track.

Follow Your Pathname

Mac OS X does a great job of hiding Unix complexity under the hood where most users rarely have to see it. But every so often, it's handy to have quick access to those secret parts in order to take shortcuts or do other cool stuff. Usually, you have to mess with the Terminal or run a developer tool, such as Property List Editor, to dip into the system. But, in a few places, everyday applications get to interface with the underpinnings.

This tip involves one of those underground connections. In most applications, you can navigate directly to any folder, including hidden folders. You do this in the Save or Open panel. When the panel appears, type a slash (/). That's the magic incantation—after you type it, a separate Go To Folder window appears. That's where you can type any Unix path to make it appear in the Save or Open panel.

OS X even gives you some Unix-style, auto-complete help. When you type enough of the name to uniquely identify it and then press Tab, the full name fills in for you. For example, if you type **/Us**, and there's no other file or directory that starts with Us, the full name /Users appears. You don't even have to press Tab: The auto-completed name fills in if you don't type anything for a couple of seconds. And when you have a directory displayed, as in Figure 4-2, you can press Option-Esc repeatedly to cycle through all the items in the directory added to the end of the path, one by one.

Of course, you can combine these special keystrokes with typing to get the filename you want.

Like many of the other tips in this chapter, this trick doesn't work with every application. You'll find it enabled mainly in Cocoa programs, including OmniOutliner and TextEdit.

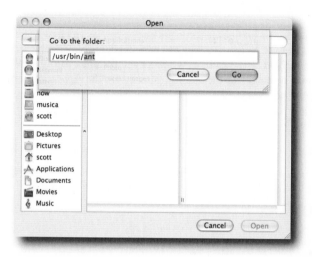

FIGURE 4-2: Navigate to hidden directories in the Open and Save panels.

Escape from Dragging

Have you ever found yourself dragging something, only to realize you don't really want to drag it after all? You haven't? Well, congratulations on your perfection—you can go on to the next section. For everybody else, here's a handy tip on canceling a drag operation while it's going on: Just press Esc. When you do, the dragged thing will float back to its place of origin, and you can safely let up on the mouse button.

Place Your Arrows

Back in the olden days, when the earth was warm and Macs were beige, scroll arrows appeared at both ends of the scroll bar: The up-arrow was at the top (or, for horizontal scroll bars, the left-arrow was at the left), and the down-arrow was at the bottom (right-arrow at the right). Then somebody decided that it might be a good idea to smoosh the arrows together at the bottom of the scroll bar. Apparently, some folks preferred it one way and some liked the other because the Appearance panel in System Preferences lets you decide which style you prefer. But, as Yoda said, "There is another." You can have double arrows at both ends (see Figure 4-3).

This option is not available with the others in System Preferences, but you can set it in Terminal with the `defaults` command:

1. Open Terminal.

2. Type this command:

```
defaults write -g AppleScrollBarVariant DoubleBoth
```

As with all `defaults` commands, the preference setting is case-sensitive, so be sure you type **DoubleBoth** with uppercase D and B. When you type the command, nothing happens right away. But the next time you launch an application, its windows will feature a pair of scroll arrows at each end. If you're ever nostalgic for the old way, you can use the Appearance panel in System Preferences to change it back.

FIGURE 4-3: Double scroll arrows at both ends of the scroll bar.

Opening Files: What a Drag

When you open a file in any application, you get some variation of the standard Open panel, which lets you find files anywhere on your Mac, including those on local and network volumes. Sometimes it takes quite a bit of navigation to get where you want to go, and you start to feel a bit like the ancient mariner after a while. In some cases, you might be staring at an Open panel, getting ready to do a bunch of clicking and scrolling to find the file you want, when you notice that you can actually see the file you want, right there in the Finder, as shown in the example in Figure 4-4.

Here's where a tip comes in handy: You can simply drag the file from the Finder and drop it onto the Open panel. When you do, you instantly navigate to the item you dragged, saving you from all that navigational tedium.

FIGURE 4-4: The file you want to open is right there on the desktop!

Menus via the Keyboard

When you're typing at the keyboard, it's often handy to issue commands without having to reach for the mouse. That's what command keys are all about. Of course, not every menu command has a keyboard equivalent. The Keyboard & Mouse panel in System Preferences goes a long way toward helping that situation. Using the Keyboard Shortcut tab of Keyboard & Mouse preferences, you can connect a menu item in any application to a command key.

That helps, but there aren't enough command keys in the world to create one for every single menu command. To remedy that situation, you can take advantage of Apple's accessibility features to happily keyboard your way through the menu bar.

Start by opening the Keyboard & Mouse preferences panel (Figure 4-5). Click the Keyboard Shortcuts tab. Scroll down to the Keyboard Navigation section. You're looking for the item that reads "Move focus to the menu bar." By default, this is set to Control-F2—look in the Keyboard & Mouse preferences to see if that's the setting on your Mac.

Note Note that the Control key is represented in the Preferences panel by a caret, which is the pointy-hat character, shown in Figure 4-5. Also, by default on PowerBooks and iBooks, you have to hold down the fn key to get any of the function keys to work, such as F2. So, to type the keystroke for Move Focus to the Menu Bar in Figure 4-5 on a PowerBook or iBook, you hold down Control and fn, and press F2. Of course, you can use the Preferences panel to change this keystroke to something else, if you like.

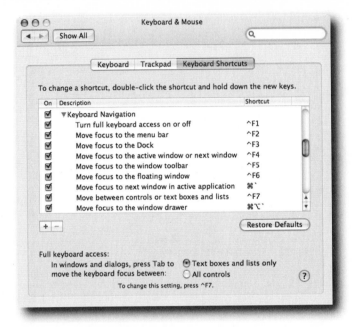

FIGURE 4-5: You can use the keyboard to navigate through the menu bar. What will they think of next?

When you type Control-F2, notice that the Apple menu is highlighted. You can then use the arrow keys to move through the menus—left and right to change menus, up and down to select menu items. You can use Option-up and Option-down to move quickly to the first and last items in a menu, or Esc to dismiss the menu. For even faster navigation in menus, you can press a letter key to go to the command that starts with that letter. To perform a menu item's command, just press Return or Enter while the item is highlighted. You can even mix mousing with your arrowing around.

Here Be Dragging

You can drag text out of almost any OS X application, although the experience can be frustrating because of a slight quirk in the user interface. You start by selecting the text. In most applications, if you then try to drag the selected text, you get a new selection, and you give up—that's the frustrating part. But here's the secret: When you mouse down on the selected text to start dragging it, pause for a moment. Some applications change the pointer, whereas others shamefully offer no feedback at all. In either case, after a heartbeat goes by, you can start dragging, and the text follows you along.

Mac OS X applications delay before dragging so that you can make a text selection even if text is already selected. Otherwise, users got frustrated when they tried to change a text selection, only to find a drag resulting instead. This scenario helps explain why designing user interfaces can be really tricky.

Can I Borrow That?

Apple's Help Viewer is useful for more than just the obvious reason (which is viewing helpful information, of course). If you see an image in Help Viewer that you like, you can use drag and drop to grab the image and use it elsewhere. For example, just drag the image to the desktop to get a GIF file, or to a new Mail message to add it to the e-mail.

Summary

In this chapter, you discovered a bunch of cool tricks for dragging, scrolling, working with pathnames, and related other goodies. These tricks prove that building useful features into the system is a wonderful way to make every application better.

Startup

chapter

5

in this chapter

☑ Streamline your login

☑ Discover special logins

☑ Seize the power of the root user

☑ Learn about safe booting

Mac OS X represents an almost magical melding of Macintosh ease of use with a strong Unix foundation. As OS X has progressed to Tiger, which is its fifth major revision, Apple has successfully been able to slide more and more Unix stuff under the rug of the graphical user interface. For most users, this is a good thing: Hide the power and complexity almost all the time, but make it available through Terminal and other techniques.

One of the best ways for curious folks like us to see what's really going on is by messing around with options at startup time. When you turn on your Mac, it's not really a Mac yet—it's just a nice computer that knows how to load an operating system. By setting some preferences or holding down certain keys, you can toss aside the beautiful Macintosh user interface and mess around deep down inside your Mac, where you can play with *two different* command lines. Check out this chapter to find out how to manipulate the way your Mac behaves at startup time.

Hide the Users

When your Mac starts up, you see the login screen with a list of the user accounts and their cute little pictures (Figure 5-1). To log in, you click the name you want and then type the password for that account.

This can get pretty tedious if you're the only user on your computer, and you're not really concerned about somebody else logging into your account. You have probably already figured out that you can easily make OS X automatically start up in your account, but if you haven't, here are the steps:

1. Open System Preferences and click Accounts.

2. If the padlock is closed, click it and enter your name and password when asked.

3. Click Login Options at the bottom of the column on the left.

4. Click the Automatically Log In As check box, and choose the account you want from the pop-up menu.

5. Type in the password for the account you picked (Figure 5-2) and click OK.

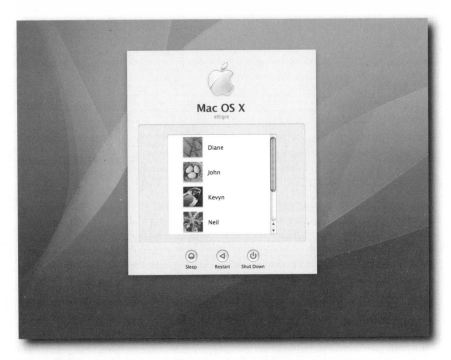

FIGURE 5-1: The login screen lists all the accounts on this computer.

FIGURE 5-2: You have to supply a password when you turn on automatic login.

The next time you start up (and the next, and the next, and the time after that), OS X won't stop to ask you which user you want. Instead, it will start directly in the user account you chose.

Warning When you turn on the automatic login option, you're trading some security for ease of use. If anybody gets hold of your computer, automatic login will allow them to see your files without knowing your password. If you want the maximum possible security for your files, you should not use automatic login.

Here's another security-versus-convenience tip you might not have thought about. An unauthorized bad person, faced with the list of users on the login screen, has to guess a user's password in order to do unauthorized bad things with the user's files. You can make this task even more difficult by hiding the list of users. System Preferences lets you turn on that feature:

1. Open System Preferences and click Accounts.

2. Click Login Options at the bottom of the column on the left.

3. On the right, under Display Login Window As, click Name And Password.

Now any intruder who gets to the login screen has to come up with the user name as well as the password (Figure 5-3). Take that, would-be evildoer!

FIGURE 5-3: With this option turned on, you have to type in both user name and password to log in.

Console Yourself

If you have Accounts preferences set to display just the name and password fields in the login window, you don't have to use one of the user accounts to log in. Instead, some hidden logins can be useful and fun to try.

The first built-in login is the >console account. If you enter **>console** in the Name field (you type the greater-than symbol followed by the word console) and then press Return or click the Log In button, your beautiful Aqua world goes away, and you are transported to a white-on-black command-line screen. Depending on your upbringing, this can be either nostalgic or terrifying. Mac OS X is now running without the trouble of a pesky graphical user interface. The first thing you see on the command-line screen is a request for you to log in using an actual user account, so you can't use this trick to bypass account security.

After you're logged in, you have full access to your account and all the services of OS X, with the rather large exception of anything that needs the graphical user interface. So what is this good for? If you ever have a corrupt system that results in the inability to boot Aqua, the OS X user interface, you might be able to use this login technique to avoid the problem and poke around, possibly deleting or reinstalling offending files. And, of course, as I said in the Introduction, merely exploring and having fun is reason enough to use any of the tricks in this book—you don't actually have to be doing something useful.

If you're curious about how to get out of console mode after you've gotten yourself in there, you just type **exit** at the command line and then press Return.

Note For more information on using console mode to fix problems and to learn much more about troubleshooting your Mac, see www.macfixit.com.

All Kids Love Logins

A few other special logins are built into Mac OS X. All of them start with >, and you use them all in the same way, by typing them into the Name box in the login window. The special logins are listed in Table 5-1.

Table 5-1   Special Logins

Login	What Happens
>console	Takes you to command-line login screen without loading Aqua user interface.
>power	Shuts down the computer. Same as clicking Shut Down button.
>restart	Restarts the computer. Same as clicking Restart button.
>exit	Relaunches the login window.

Note that >power and >restart do the same thing as clicking buttons in the login window. So what good are they, other than sheer amusement? You might remember that the Accounts pane in System Preferences includes an option to hide the Restart, Sleep, and Shut Down buttons. By using these special logins, you can still Restart or Shut Down, even if the buttons are hidden.

Root for the Home Team

Mac OS X includes a special built-in user called *root*, also known as *the superuser*. The root user is part of OS X's Unix heritage, dating from the time when every computer was shared and networked. Root is blessed with legendary powers: the capability to delete or edit any file on the computer, whether it's part of the system software or it belongs to a human user. This kind of power is obviously fraught with peril if you make a mistake or start messing around carelessly, or if you're running applications that have bad intentions. But in the age of the personal computer, the unintentional damage you can do as root is far more, well, personal. If you're willing to risk the data on your own computer, or maybe a spare Mac you reserve for experimentation, go ahead and try tricks with root.

Many Mac users from the pre-OS X days are used to running the whole show on their computers and feel a little cheated, or perhaps insulted, by the fact that the system uses security to protect files from them. If you're one of us Mac old-timers, you might want to enable root and try it out, just because you can. But in practice, you can successfully do everything you need to do without ever logging in as root.

Warning Running as root theoretically opens your Mac up to powerful attacks over the Internet. Although viruses and related programs rarely bother Macs, a nasty program that gets root access to your computer can do serious damage to your computer and can even cause problems for others on the Internet. If you're messing around running as root, be sure to study Mac and Unix security, or simply disconnect from the Internet while you're experimenting.

By default, the root user is disabled in Mac OS X. To turn it on, you have to run a curious utility program called NetInfo Manager. This program is mainly used by administrators of Mac OS X Server machines to set up users, groups, and printers; but Apple has also stashed the command for enabling the root user there:

1. Run NetInfo Manager. You'll find it in the Applications/Utilities folder.

2. Click the familiar Click The Lock To Make Changes padlock at the bottom of the screen (Figure 5-4). When you're asked, enter an administrator's name and password.

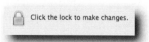

FIGURE **5-4: Click the padlock to open it so you can make changes.**

3. Choose Security → Enable Root User.

4. If you've never enabled the root user on this machine before, you get a message asking you to enter a nonblank password. Go ahead and do that.

5. Quit NetInfo Manager.

You can now log in as root from the login window. If you have the accounts displayed in a list, you won't see root among the mere mortal accounts. Instead, you see a new choice in the list: *Other*. As you know, all the best options are hidden under nondescript labels like *Other*. To log in as root, click Other, then enter **root** and your chosen password. As OS X finishes starting up, you can feel the power coursing through your veins: You can now wreak total havoc on your system. Even more ominously, applications have free reign as well. So have fun with it, and be careful.

Another way to use root access is in combination with the >console login. After you use >console on the login window, you can log in as root and have full access to your whole system from the command line.

Getting Singled Out

If you restart (or turn on) your Mac and hold down Command-S after you hear the startup chime, you see a lot of lovely Unixy status messages on the screen as your Mac starts up in *single user mode*. In this mode, you have root access to a command-line shell. Unlike logging in as the root user from the login window (see the section "Root for the Home Team"), when you boot in single user mode, no other users can log in—hence, the clever name.

When you start up in single user mode, not all system services are started. This makes single user mode an attractive option for debugging and troubleshooting problems.

Whether you're troubleshooting or just interested in pure research, single user mode is useful for running *fsck*, the standard Unix file system check and repair program. To run fsck, start up in single user mode and then type the following:

```
fsck -y
```

to check the file system. When you run fsck, you get a series of status messages on the screen as it proceeds. If something is wrong with the disk, fsck offers to repair it for you, an offer you should accept. If you receive the happy message "The volume appears to be OK," your disk is in good shape.

With single user mode, anyone can start up any Mac and gain root access. Isn't that a security risk? Yes, although not a very practical one, because the would-be attacker needs physical access to the computer. Still, if you want to plug this security hole, there are at least two ways to do it.

1. You can set an Open Firmware password. Open Firmware is the program that runs when your Mac is powered on. By setting a password, you can prevent anyone from starting your Mac without knowing the secret word. If you decide on this plan, make sure you don't forget your Open Firmware password—that would be bad. To learn more about Open Firmware, see Apple's support article at http://docs.info.apple.com/article. html?artnum=106482.

2. If you don't want to set an Open Firmware password, you can download and install an operating system patch that prevents single user mode. The patch is available at http://www.securemac.com/disablemacosxsingleboot.php.

Tell Me Everything

You can start your Mac in *verbose mode* by holding down Command-V after you hear the startup chime. Verbose mode is similar to single user mode, printing out status information and diagnostic messages as each part of the system gets started, except that unlike single user mode, the messages don't stop along the way to give you a command line—they keep right on coming until you finally see the Aqua interface. You can use this mode for its educational and entertainment value, or to diagnose problems that arise during boot. In case you can't read that fast, all the information that verbose mode spits out is stored in a system.log file that you can examine with the Console application (see Figure 5-5).

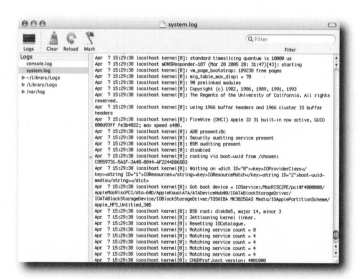

FIGURE 5-5: You can check the system.log file in Console if you can't keep up with the super-fast info that verbose mode spews out.

If you find you love verbose booting so much that you want to have it happen all the time, you can set a switch that makes it permanent. Just start Terminal and type

```
sudo nvram boot-args="-v"
```

The next time you start up, you get verbose mode, and you'll keep getting it from then on. If you change your mind and decide you want to revert to good old Macintosh-style graphical booting, use this command:

```
sudo nvram boot-args=""
```

Flip Your Lid

If you have a portable Mac, you probably appreciate the fact that it wakes up almost instantly when you open the lid. But maybe you don't: For example, if you boot from an external drive, close your PowerBook, take it somewhere, and then open it again without reconnecting the drive, your Mac gets very confused, and you probably end up rebooting.

To avoid this problem, you can tell your portable Mac *not to wake up* after you open the lid until you press a key. Here's the magic incantation in Terminal:

```
sudo pmset lidwake 0
```

To restore standard lid behavior, type this:

```
sudo pmset lidwake 1
```

For more fun with pmset, check out what else it can do: type **man pmset** in Terminal to find out.

Keep It Safe

Yet another alternate boot method in Mac OS X is *safe booting*. With this technique, OS X loads only absolutely essential kernel extensions (KEXTs) and Apple-supplied startup items. Safe booting also forces a disk consistency check, similar to that in the Disk Utility program. Safe booting is useful for debugging a startup problem that makes you suspect a third-party hardware or software add-on.

To cause a safe boot, wait until you hear the startup chime. Then, hold down the shift key until you see the dark gray Apple logo. After the disk check runs, which can take a long time, you see the familiar startup screen with the unfamiliar words Safe Boot at the bottom.

After a safe boot, you're running in safe mode (of course). In this mode, you may find that some nonessential but really important things don't work, such as sound and AirPort networking. You probably won't want to run for long in this mode. To get back to normal, you must reboot again, this time without invoking safe booting.

Get Smart

You might be surprised to learn that funky old Apple supports something called the Department of Defense Common Access Card in Mac OS X. But it's true. This feature is a secure biometric login card created by the United States military. Even if you don't have one of these cards, you can get a glimpse of how it works by following these steps:

1. Open Terminal.

2. In Terminal, type the following command:

```
sudo cac_setup
```

3. If you're asked for your password, type it in.

You should see the message Starting Smartcard Services. The next time you log in, the first item in the login window should say Please Insert A Common Access Card. If you don't happen to have your card and card reader handy, you can click Other to log in the conventional way—but first, you see a remarkable disclaimer system telling you: "This is a Department of Defense computer system. " (and lots of other stuff).

Assuming you don't really want to have this feature active on your computer, return to Terminal and type the following:

```
sudo cac_setup -off
```

That should get you back to the way you were.

More Startup Fun

There are several other keys you can hold down at startup time to perform various features. Table 5-2 lists a few of them for your amusement and edification:

Note Wait until you hear the startup chime before pressing keys.

Table 5-2   Boot-time Keystrokes

Keystroke	What Happens
(mouse down)	Ejects CD or DVD.
option	Shows System Picker (lets you choose a startup volume).
Command-option-o-f	Start up into Open Firmware interpreter.
Command-option-p-r	Zap (zero out) parameter RAM.
C	Boot from CD or DVD.
T	Start FireWire target disk mode.

For many more special keystrokes, check out Dave Polaschek's "Magical Macintosh Key Sequences" at Dave's Picks: http://davespicks.com/writing/programming/mackeys.html.

Summary

By changing startup options, you can see your Mac's Unix and Open Firmware underpinnings. This is important for two reasons: You can use these techniques to help troubleshoot tricky problems, and you can experience the fun of exploring what's happening inside your Mac.

iTunes

chapter

6

in this chapter

☑ Keep your videos around

☑ Multiply your album art

☑ Capture those hidden tracks

☑ Clean up your library

Apple has built a large chunk of its reputation by making things that are easy to use. Ease of use isn't everything, however—making products that can do a lot is important, too. iTunes is possibly Apple's most important application of the past five years or so. Apple has used iTunes and its portable cousin, the iPod, to transform the company and move into whole new markets and products.

Even though iTunes is easy to use, it's also very powerful. And with great power comes great hackability. In this chapter, you explore some of the cool advanced tricks you can use with iTunes.

Video Forever

The iTunes Music Store lists about a zillion songs for sale, but it has even more than just songs. The Store also includes hundreds of music videos from your favorite artists (and from those you despise). You can watch the videos right there in iTunes, but if you want to see them again later, you must be online to access the Store. With this trick, you can find the videos and keep them forever, or at least until your tastes change.

Here's how to download music videos that are in the Store:

1. In the iTunes Music Store, find a music video you want to download. You can see what's available by clicking the Music Videos link on the home page.

2. When you find one you want, click it. The Store will probably ask if you want the large or small version—choose the one you prefer.

3. When the video starts playing, switch to the Finder.

4. In the Finder, type Command-Shift-G to get the Go To Folder dialog. In the dialog, type:

   ```
   ~/Librarys/Caches/QuickTime/
   ```

   and click Go. (You can also navigate there manually, if you prefer clicking to typing.)

5. Now you should see the QuickTime downloads folder in the Finder. Make sure the folder appears in list view, as shown in Figure 6-1. If not, choose View → as List to get it that way.

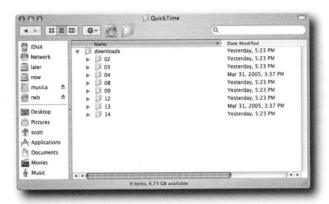

FIGURE 6-1: This is where downloaded music videos go.

6. Double-click the Downloads folder to see its contents, which should be folders that have numbers for names.

7. If the Date Modified column is not selected, click the column header to select it. Make sure the sorting triangle in the Date Modified header is pointing down—if not, click the column header again. This should leave the most recently changed folder at the top.

8. Double-click the topmost folder once to open it. This should reveal yet another numbered folder (or maybe more than one), just to confuse you further. Double-click the topmost folder to see its contents, which should be at least one file with the extension .qtch (Figure 6-2). That's a QuickTime cache file, which contains the video you're downloading.

FIGURE 6-2: The music video cached in a file.

9. Open that file in TextEdit and take a look. Control-click on the file and choose Open With. If TextEdit appears in the submenu that pops up, select it. If not, choose Other, pick TextEdit from the dialog that appears, and click Open. You'll see something that looks like Figure 6-3.

FIGURE 6-3: Music video file displayed by TextEdit.

Note

Music video files can be big, especially if you choose the large version. TextEdit sometimes struggles a bit when opening one of these big files, so don't be surprised if TextEdit seems unresponsive for up to a minute while it sorts things out.

This file contains some header information, followed by the actual video data—as much of it as has been downloaded when you open the file. You can't really do anything with the data, but the header contains vital information: a URL for the video itself. To find the URL, look at the first line of the file, right after the letters *url*—what a giveaway! You see text starting with *http* and ending with *.mov*. (More text may be tacked on immediately after the *.mov*, but that's not part of the URL, and you don't want it.)

10. Select the text of the URL. That's everything from *http* to *.mov*, inclusive. Choose Edit ➜ Copy.

11. Switch to Safari. Select the Downloads window: Choose Window ➜ Downloads. Then paste the video URL with Edit ➜ Paste.

After you paste the URL, you see the QuickTime movie start to download in Safari. When it's done, you can click the magnifying glass next to the file in Safari's Downloads window to see your video in the Finder, and then play it in the QuickTime Player or preview it right there in the Finder. Sweet!

Back Up the Trailer

The iTunes Music Store has a large and ever-changing collection of movie trailers for your perusal. You can find them via the Movie Trailers link on the Store's home page. You can keep a copy of a movie trailer using the same technique described in the preceding paragraphs.

If you have QuickTime Pro, there's usually an easier way. After the trailer loads, you can click the down-pointing triangle in the lower-right corner of the movie window. You see a menu that lets you save the trailer as a QuickTime movie, and that's all there is to it.

You can use the Save As feature in the same way when you watch a trailer from Apple's site at www.apple.com/trailers or for virtually any other QuickTime movies on the Web. Sometimes you'll find movies that have the Save As item disabled. If you run into one of those, you can use the more complicated ferret-out-the-URL technique you went through earlier.

More for Your Money

When you're looking at your library or a playlist in iTunes, notice that every song, artist, and album name has a tiny right-pointing arrow next to it. Because you're the curious type, you have no doubt clicked one of those arrows and discovered that iTunes takes you to the Store and shows you the album that holds that song. That's useful if you want to see the other contents of the album in the Store. Clicking on the arrow next to the artist is slightly more useful, because it takes you to the artist's page in the store.

You might find it more useful if clicking the name of a song or album showed you that album *in your library*. And you can do that: Just Option-click the arrow to see the album. If you find that you prefer this behavior, you can reverse the meaning of the Option key with a short trip to the command line.

1. Open Terminal. Remember, it's usually in the Applications:Utilities folder.

2. Type this command:

```
defaults write com.apple.iTunes invertStoreLinks -bool YES
```

After that's done, the result of holding down the Option key when clicking the arrows is switched. Use Option to go to the Store; no Option means stay in your library. If you want to change the behavior back to the usual, just repeat the Defaults command with NO instead of YES.

Note that this setting only changes what happens when you click arrows next to your own songs. Arrows in the store always take you to other Store pages without Option and to your library when you hold down Option.

There's one more thing to say about these handy arrows: If you would rather not be bothered by them at all, open iTunes preferences, click the General panel, and turn off Show Links To Music Store.

Seeing Double

You have probably noticed iTunes' album art feature, which lets you add a picture to every song and then see the art while the song is playing. When you buy music from the iTunes Music Store, you get a picture of the album cover, of course. Well, it turns out that you can have more than one picture associated with every song. These additional pictures can include an interior view of the album, a fond photo of the lead singer, or anything else you want. Here's how you do it:

1. In iTunes, pick the song that's going to get a second picture and select it. If you want, you can select multiple songs or an entire album.

2. Make sure the album art panel is showing at the bottom of the Source column. If it's not, choose Edit → Show Artwork.

3. If the title bar of the album art panel reads Now Playing, click it to change it to Selected Song.

4. If the selected song or album already has artwork, it's displayed in the art panel. To add another picture, just drag it into the art panel and drop it.

After you've added the second picture, you see that the album art panel's title bar has now acquired next and previous arrows (Figure 6-4). Click these to select the art you want to see.

FIGURE 6-4: You can have multiple pictures for every song, and choose the one you want to see.

Outsmarting a Playlist

Smart Playlists, a nifty iTunes innovation, don't contain a static list of songs—instead, they're made up of a set of rules and conditions that are evaluated by iTunes and applied to your library.

Note You can construct smart playlists that never reevaluate their rules and never change. To freeze a smart playlist, uncheck the Live Updating box in the smart playlist's info window.

When you try to delete a song from a smart playlist by selecting it and pressing Delete, nothing happens. That's because a smart playlist is based on rules, not an actual list of songs. The songs are just the result of the rules—if a song matches the rules, it's in the playlist, and you can't delete it. Apparently.

But there is a way. If you hold down Option and press Delete, you see the dialog shown in Figure 6-5. You can't remove the song from the smart playlist, but iTunes is offering to remove it from the library. If the song is not in the library, it becomes unknown to iTunes, and so it vanishes from the smart playlist (and any other playlists it belongs to).

FIGURE 6-5: You can remove a song from the library via a smart playlist.

This trick works on regular playlists, too. You can use the Option-Delete trick to *punch through* the playlist and delete a song from the library.

Removing a song from the library doesn't affect the music file itself on disk—it just makes iTunes forget about the song. But iTunes gives you a chance to delete the file from disk, too, If you answer Yes to the confirmation dialog in Figure 6-5, you get another dialog asking if you just want to go all the way and trash the song file from the disk as well.

Words and Music

iTunes is more than a mere music player. Among its many skills, iTunes is a powerful database program that keeps track of all your music and lots of data that goes along with your tunes, such as album and artist names, play counts, and album art.

In iTunes 4.7, Apple taught iTunes how to keep track of a whole new kind of data: PDF files, the kind that Preview and Adobe Acrobat Reader normally handle. This iTunes update appeared at the same time as the introduction of the U2 iPod, when the iTunes Music Store started selling "The Complete U2," a huge set of U2 songs that come with a *digital booklet* – basically, super-duper liner notes delivered as a PDF file. When you buy the U2 collection, you get the PDF delivered into your library along with the tunes. If you try to play it, iTunes does nothing but silently mock you. But if you double-click it, the document appears in Preview. Since "The Complete U2" came out, other albums, such as Jack Johnson's "In Between Dreams," have shipped with PDF digital booklets.

If you like, you can store PDF documents in iTunes right now, using the info tags (artist, album, comments, and so on) however you want, taking advantage of the database aspect of iTunes' personality. In the future, you are likely to see more PDFs coming from the Store, containing liner notes, lyrics, and other goodies, and more advanced PDF handling in iTunes itself.

Secret Messages

Lots of artists include *hidden tracks* on CDs. These are extra songs, both good and not so good, placed on the CD without any listing on the package. Sometimes, the song is extra-secret: Instead of giving the hidden song its own track, it's buried at the end of another track, usually after minutes and minutes of silence.

What if you want to play just the hidden track without waiting for the silence to pass? iTunes provides a solution by letting you set a start and stop time in the track's info tags.

If you have one of those tracks that features a regular song as well as a hidden song at the end, here's the procedure for giving the bonus tune its own entry in your music library.

1. Play the track that has the hidden song at the end. Note the time the regular song ends and the time the hidden part starts, as given in the Elapsed Time display. If the hidden track ends before the track is all the way done, write down that time, too.

2. You're going to make a copy of the file that contains the two songs, so that you can deal with them separately. In iTunes, make sure the song is selected, and then choose File → Show Song File.

3. With the song now selected in the Finder, choose File → Duplicate to copy it. The new copy should appear in the Finder, right next to the original.

4. Drag the new copy and drop it on the Library icon in the iTunes source list. iTunes will add the new copy to the library.

5. Back in iTunes, select Library. Click the Song Name column header to sort the list by name. If the triangle in the Song Name header is not pointing up, click it again to reverse the direction. That will make sure the list goes from A to Z.

6. Find and select the song in the library (if it's not already selected). You should see two copies side by side with the same name (Figure 6-6). Select the first one listed (that's the original).

FIGURE 6-6: There are now two copies of the track in our library.

7. Choose File ➜ Get Info and click the Options tab.

8. Fill in the Stop Time box with the time the regular (not hidden) song ends (which you noted way back in Step 1) and then click OK.

9. Now select the new copy of the file, which should be the second one listed. Choose File ➜ Get Info again.

10. This time, fill in the Start Time box with the second when the hidden track starts. If necessary, fill in the Stop Time for the hidden track, too. Click OK.

Note

In this section, you've changed the Start and Stop Times for the tracks. This information is kept by iTunes in the iTunes Music Library, not in the files that contain the songs. So if you were wondering about keeping a copy of the original file that contains both songs, don't worry—the song file itself is unaltered.

11. Now the first track will play just the regular song, and the second will play only the hidden track. You'll probably want to rename the hidden track to better indicate what it actually contains.

You can stop at this point and go get a cup of coffee if you want. You have successfully split the hidden track into its own song, and it will play fine. However, if you're short of disk space, or you're just the tidy type, you might also want to use iTunes to snip away the excess part of the tracks that you're no longer using. To do the trimming, follow these additional steps:

1. In the Library, select both the regular song and the hidden track you just unveiled. (Use Command-click or Shift-click to get them both.)

2. Now you're going to trim the unused parts by re-encoding the songs. To do this, choose Advanced ➔ Convert Selection.

Note

The item in the Advanced menu ends with the name of the format you're converting to: typically MP3, AAC, or Apple Lossless. You can change this format in Preferences on the Importing tab. Re-encoding music like this can cause the quality to deteriorate. For best audio quality results, use Apple Lossless. For more on this feature, see the following section, "iTunes Music Processing."

3. You now have two new library entries, one for each of the trimmed songs. You can go ahead and delete the untrimmed versions from your library and the disk.

You can use this trick any time you want to split a track into two (or more) pieces, or whenever you want to simply get rid of part of a track for any reason.

iTunes Music Processing

One of the best secret tricks in iTunes is the capability of converting songs from one format to another, a process called *transcoding*. You can use this to convert songs from AAC to MP3 for non-iPod music players, or to change a tune to AIFF if you want to use it as a system sound, as described in Chapter 3.

Here's how to transcode a tune:

1. Make sure the song you want to transcode is already in the iTunes Library. If not, add it by choosing File ➔ Add to Library.

2. Next, choose the format you'll be converting to. Choose iTunes ➔ Preferences and click the Importing tab.

3. From the Import Using menu, choose the format you want to convert to. Your choices are AAC, AIFF, Apple Lossless, MP3, and WAV.

4. In the Library, select the song you want to convert.

5. Choose Advanced ➔ Convert Selection to. The last part of the menu item reflects the name of the format you're converting to.

iTunes then converts your song. After the conversion, it plays its jaunty *I'm Done* jingle, and the new file is ready in the Library.

Dump Your Dupes

As your digital music collection grows, you're bound to find yourself with multiple copies of the same tracks. There are lots of ways this can happen: You might rip the same CD more than once, or maybe you ripped on different computers or hard disks and now you're combining the collections. In any case, now you have lots of duplicates, and you'd like to get rid of them. Not only is this useful for freeing up disk space, but multiple copies of songs and albums tend to mess up smart playlists.

If your multiple copy problem isn't too severe, you can take advantage of iTunes' built-in duplicate detector. To see how it works, select the library or any playlist, then choose Edit ➔ Show Duplicate Songs. You'll see your song list reduced to just duplicates—that is, songs that have the same title and artist (Figure 6-7). You can go through the list and delete or otherwise handle your duplicate copies.

FIGURE 6-7: iTunes includes a basic feature for displaying duplicate songs.

If you have a complex library with a large number of duplicates, the Show Duplicate Songs feature is less useful. Its biggest drawback is that it doesn't automate the process of removing duplicates—it only displays them. With hundreds of duplicates, that leaves you with a lot of dirty work to be done by hand. A better way to deal with your duplicates is a utility called iSweep, available as shareware for $15 from www.davtri.com.

iSweep adds several indispensable features you can't get with Show Duplicate Songs in iTunes. For example, iSweep lets you decide what constitutes a duplicate song. In iTunes, songs are duplicates if their titles and artists match, even if they're on two different albums. iSweep lets you decide whether to consider same-named songs on different albums are duplicates (Figure 6-8). You can consider other criteria as well, including track length, bit rate, and others.

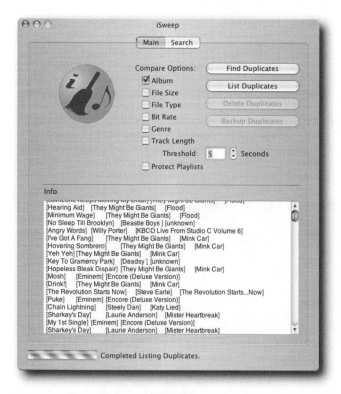

FIGURE 6-8: iSweep detects and handles duplicates in your iTunes library.

Most important, iSweep removes duplicates for you automagically. You can ask iSweep to delete duplicates from your disk and remove them from your library, or if you want to be a little more cautious, iSweep will move the duplicates to another location rather than deleting them. You can also instruct it to be sure not to remove any songs that are part of a playlist.

Getting rid of duplicates is the reason to buy iSweep, but it has a few other useful features as well. If you have music scattered around your disk and not included in your iTunes library, you can ask iSweep to find these stray tunes for you and even consolidate them in one place.

If you're not sure whether you want to buy iSweep, you can download and try it out for free. The limited tryout version lets you find and list duplicates, but not delete or move them.

Shoot the Screen

If you run iTunes on a Mac that's dedicated to music, or if you have plenty of screen real estate, you're likely a fan of the iTunes Visualizer and its psychedelic, hypnotic display. Visualizer displays are always changing, but if you happen to see one that's totally awesome, there is a way you can record it for posterity.

To capture the screen, just press Command-Shift-3, the Mac's standard screen-shooting keystroke. You'll get a file named Picture 1 (or some larger number) on your desktop that you can open in Preview or otherwise fool around with. This even works if you're watching the Visualizer in full-screen mode, as demonstrated by Figure 6-9.

FIGURE 6-9: You can take a screen shot of a full-screen Visualizer effect.

Summary

More than any other user application, iTunes gets poked and prodded by folks who use it, probably because it's so popular. iTunes does a great job of playing music, but it has so many features that tricks and shortcuts are inevitable. This chapter introduces some of those. And if you'd like to learn more about practical tips for iTunes, check out the iTunes and Music Store Help item in the iTunes Help menu. On the other hand, for less practical and more fun iTunes and iPod tricks, you might enjoy my previous book, *Hacking iPod + iTunes* (Wiley Publishing, Inc., 2004), available from the usual fine booksellers.

Nifty Utilities

From the very first days of the Macintosh, Apple has provided tools that help outside developers create great software. Now that we live in the world of Mac OS X, the full power of Unix is available in addition to the Macintosh magic provided by Apple.

Most Mac users know about popular applications like Microsoft Word and Adobe Photoshop. Less well known, but at least as important, are the clever utility programs from small, smart developers you might not have heard of. In this chapter, I'll discuss a few of these great utilities that can make your Mac even more of a joy to use.

Time to Tinker

TinkerTool is a wonderful utility for playing with all sorts of preference-type settings. Most of the options available in TinkerTool can also be set from Terminal or with specialized command-line tools, but TinkerTool puts a lovely Mac-like face on everything. It's far from the only utility around for doing this kind of thing, but it's probably the most thorough and friendly, and it's free (from Marcel Bresink Software-Systeme, www.bresink.de/osx/TinkerTool.html).

TinkerTool's user interface is a preferences-like window with controls that take you to various panels, as shown in Figure 7-1.

Here's a brief guide to some of TinkerTool's coolest features, organized as they are in the program itself.

Note   When you run TinkerTool, it figures out which version of Mac OS X you're running and only displays features that are appropriate to your version. As you read the next section, you might find that you don't see some of the tweaks listed here. That's probably because they're not compatible with the version of Mac OS X that you're running. The author keeps TinkerTool fresh with periodic updates. You can always make sure you have the latest version by choosing TinkerTool ➜ Check For Updates.

FIGURE 7-1: TinkerTool's main panel.

Finder Settings

The Finder panel of TinkerTool lets you change some of the same settings covered in Chapter 1.

- Show Hidden and System Files makes all files visible in the Finder. This is useful for examining the contents of iPods or for looking in folders like /bin and /tmp.

- Add "Quit" Item To Finder Menu makes it much easier to restart the Finder so you can see changes after you fool around with Finder preferences.

- You can turn off the zooming rectangles you normally see when opening a document by unchecking the Show Animation Effect When Opening Files box.

- Two more settings help you speed up the apparent performance of your Mac at the expense of nice visual effects. If you turn off Animate Opening Info Panels and Desktop Icons, you lose the zooming effect that usually happens when you select an icon and choose File ➔ Get Info. The Animate Selecting Info Panel Categories setting controls whether you see a smooth animation when you click one of the triangles to open part of an information window.

- If you don't like to store things on it, you can convert the Desktop into an inert back-drop by turning off Use The Desktop. If you do this, you won't be able to click the Desktop to activate the Finder, and files you've placed on the Desktop will not be visible. (Don't worry—you can still get to them by looking in the ~/Desktop/ folder.)

Dock

TinkerTool's Dock settings give you direct access to preferences that are usually hidden. I dis-cussed command-line access to many of these settings in Chapter 2.

- Use the Dock Options settings to perform Dock tweaks that aren't available in the standard Dock preferences. You can tell at a glance which applications are hidden by turning on the Use Transparent Icons For Hidden Applications setting. Enable Dock Shadow produces a subtle shadow around the Dock's edges—barely visible on some backgrounds—that softens the Dock's sharp edges.

- The Position settings are exactly the same as those in Dock preferences, except for the addition of Top, which lets you place the Dock in the rather unwieldy location under the menu bar. Think different, indeed!

- Use the Placement setting to make the Dock stick to one of the corners of the screen instead of keeping it in the center. Check out Figure 7-2 to see what the Dock looks like at the top-right edge of the screen.

- Play around with the Minimizer Effect to change how windows animate when you minimize them to the Dock and expand them again.

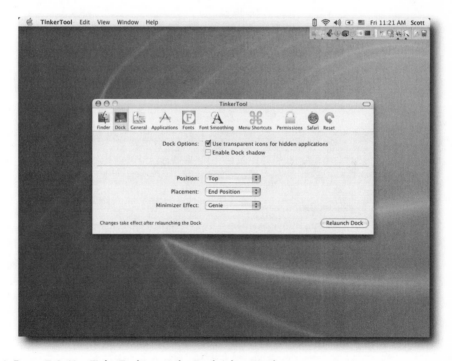

FIGURE 7-2: Use TinkerTool to put the Dock (almost) wherever you want.

General

The General panel includes settings that don't fit anywhere else, including Place Scroll Arrows for controlling whether your scroll arrows appear at one end or both ends of the scroll bar, Exposé Window Hiding to enable the *miniaturized Desktop* mode of Exposé (see Figure 7-3), and Display Of Sheets to make sheets (like save and open panels) roll out faster, if you're that impatient.

FIGURE 7-3: Exposé miniature desktop mode.

Applications

TinkerTool crams settings for various applications into this panel. You can find tweaks for the Address Book, Terminal, and disk images here, along with a way to control what you see when an application crashes. Here are some sample settings:

- In Terminal, you can make windows active just by mousing over them, without having to click.

- You can speed up the processing of disk images by telling the system to skip the checksum verification phase, which rarely fails anyway.

- You can turn on the diagnostic menu for additional features in Address Book.

Fonts

Use TinkerTool's Fonts panel to change just about any system-wide font setting you're interested in, including the system font itself and the font used in window title bars. You can really have some atrocious fun with this one.

Permissions

Mac OS X uses the powerful and complex Unix permissions model to determine which users are allowed to access each file and folder. You can use TinkerTool's Permissions panel to specify default permissions settings for new files and folders, a task that usually requires noodling around on the command line. For example, you can use this feature to allow only the owners of newly created files to be able to read them.

Permissions and privileges are a big topic, worthy of whole books on the subject. For an introduction to the basic features of Mac OS X permissions, see www.gideonsoftworks.com/macosxprivileges.html.

Safari

If you're a Safari fan, you can use TinkerTool's Safari panel to change some hidden options in Apple's Web browser, such as enabling Safari's debug menu and increasing the number of items remembered in the History menu.

TinkerTool also includes a handy Reset command, just in case you go a little crazy and make some changes you wish you hadn't. You can put everything back the way it was before you ran TinkerTool, or revert all the way to system defaults.

Two Versions of TinkerTool

TinkerTool comes in two flavors. So far, I've been talking about the standard, free version, which provides access to features in your own user domain: settings that affect the way the Mac works when you alone are logged in. Another version, called TinkerTool System, lets you fool around with system settings, which change the way things work for every user on the computer. This advanced version costs 7 Euros, which is about $9 US. The features you get with TinkerTool System include the following:

- To decide when to run periodic maintenance scripts.
- To reset permissions on system files.
- To remove lots of files you might not need, or that might be causing problems, such as caches and log files.
- To trash or delete files the Finder stubbornly refuses to trash or delete.

- To change the startup language or mute the startup sound.

- To remove languages you're never going to use (Kinyarwanda, anyone?).

- To find out more information about your computer, even the time and place it was manufactured (Figure 7-4).

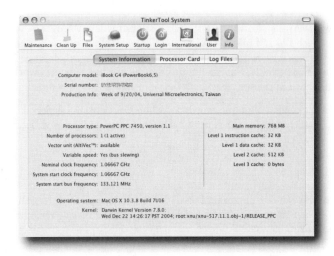

FIGURE 7-4: TinkerTool System's info panel tells you things about your computer that you probably didn't know.

By Any Other Name

The Finder makes it easy to manipulate files: move them from place to place, double-click to open, or drag them to the trash. You can rename a file in the Finder by selecting its name and typing the new name. Where the Finder (and graphical user interfaces in general) tends to slip is when performing repetitive, automated kinds of tasks, such as renaming a whole bunch of files in the same way—stripping out a date or adding a prefix, for example.

One answer for handling these situations is writing a shell script and running it in Terminal. Another technique is to write an AppleScript. But if you're not yet a scripting whiz, you can take advantage of a terrific shareware utility called A Better Finder Rename ($20, publicspace.net). After you install A Better Finder Rename, it insinuates itself into contextual menus in the Finder. To make it work, you select the files you want to process, Control-click, and then choose A Better Finder Rename (Figure 7-5).

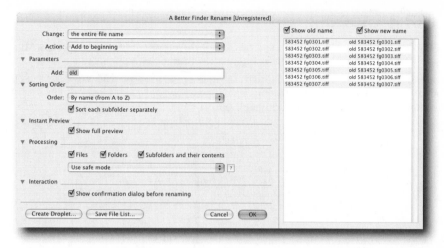

FIGURE 7-5: A Better Finder Rename's main screen appears when you Control-click in the Finder.

A Better Finder Rename presents a rather mind-boggling array of options. You can do simple operations, such as changing one string of characters to another. But you can also take advantage of many choices, including these:

- Change the whole filename or just the extension.
- Rename files in subfolders.
- Match characters only at the beginning or only at the end.
- Remove trailing spaces.
- Add sequential numbering to the files at the beginning or the end.
- Rename files according to their creation time and date.
- See a preview of what will happen to each file before you actually change it.
- Rename music files according to their MP3 tags.
- Rename files to legal Windows names, so you can move them to a Windows volume.
- Rename files according to a regular expression.

One of the coolest features of A Better Finder Rename is the capability to construct a renaming task—such as changing .htm files to .html—and save it as an application. Then, the next time you need to perform the same task, you can simply drag your files or folders and drop them on the application. A Better Finder Rename will then perform its magic.

Leave Me a Clone

You know it's important to back up your work, right? And you do it frequently, right? If not, maybe it's because you're daunted by the complexity of the task. Well, there are plenty of programs that can help you back up your data. In this section, I'll focus on Carbon Copy Cloner, a popular free utility (Bombich Software, `www.bombich.com/software/ccc.html`). Carbon Copy Cloner is pictured in Figure 7-6.

FIGURE 7-6: The Carbon Copy Cloner main window.

Carbon Copy Cloner makes it very easy to simply replicate your disk onto another, which is a great way to back up your data. You can tell Carbon Copy Cloner to ignore certain folders if you don't want to bother backing them up, and you can automatically maintain synchronized copies between the source and the backup.

Carbon Copy Cloner can create bootable backups. This means that if you're ever so unfortunate as to need your backup, you can simply boot from it and operate just as you were—at least at the time of the last backup.

Carbon Copy Cloner has a bunch of other awesome features, too, such as a built-in task scheduler and hooks for pre-backup and post-backup shell scripts.

Note For more information on options for backing up your Mac, see the ebook "Take Control of Mac OS X Backups," available for $10 at www.tidbits.com/takecontrol/backup-macosx.html.

For the curious geeks reading along, you might be interested to know that Carbon Copy Cloner is basically a nice interface on a command-line utility called ditto. You can find out more about ditto, and see how much complexity Carbon Copy Cloner is saving you from, by going to Terminal and typing **man ditto**.

Making a Batch

Mac OS X brings the wonderful world of Unix file ownership and permissions to the Macintosh, along with all its power and pitfalls. There are tools for changing permissions in the Finder and in Terminal, but as with A Better Finder Rename, sometimes you need a program that's easy to use but powerful enough for repetitive tasks. The free utility BatChmod (Renaud Boisjoly, www.macchampion.com/arbysoft) is just what you're looking for. Figure 7-7 shows BatChmod's window.

FIGURE 7-7: BatChmod's window looks like this.

You can use BatChmod to change the permissions on a bunch of files all at once. As you might guess, all you have to do is drag the files to the BatChmod window, then use the pop-up menus to change the permissions you want to new settings. You may be asked to authenticate yourself, of course—this ain't no security hole.

For more information on permissions, see the "Permissions" section under "Time To Tinker" earlier in this chapter.

Watching Memory

MemoryStick is a nifty free utility (Matt Neuberg, `www.tidbits.com/matt`) that lets you keep an eye on memory usage in your Mac. MemoryStick, pictured in Figure 7-8, is designed to provide an unobtrusive monitor on various aspects of OS X virtual memory management.

FIGURE 7-8: MemoryStick's minimalist display.

MemoryStick gives you a fast look at five pieces of information:

- The amount of *wired* memory and the percentage of total memory it occupies. This memory contains basic resources that OS X needs all the time, so this value should always be the same.

- The amount and percentage of *active* memory. This denotes memory currently being used by applications. Mac OS X uses *virtual memory*, a system in which data in memory is periodically saved to *swapfiles* on disk and then reloaded when it's needed. Blocks of memory in this active area are not candidates for being swapped out to disk, because they're in use.

- The *inactive* memory region. This part of memory contains objects that are more likely to be swapped out—that is, saved to disk—or released.

- *Free* memory. This is memory that's just waiting around for somebody to use. This section gets really small if you start opening lots of applications.

- The number at the left of the bar, which shows how many swapfiles you're using. This is a general indication of the amount of disk swapping you're doing. In general, the higher this number, the more disk space is consumed, the more swaps you have, and the pokier your performance gets.

You can set MemoryStick to tell you more about virtual memory. You can turn on the Signal Pageouts and Signal Swapfiles options to have MemoryStick make a sound every time Mac OS X swaps memory or creates a new swapfile. If you would rather keep MemoryStick silent, you can enable the Log Events option to write information to a logfile instead of sounding the alarm. You can use Console to examine the log whenever you want to study your memory usage.

The help file that comes with MemoryStick contains a nifty description of how memory usage works on Mac OS X. You can read this file by choosing Help → MemoryStick Help in the application, or by looking for the Resources/help.html file in MemoryStick's application bundle.

Staying Punctual

Unix includes a handy tool called *cron* that's useful for performing tasks on a schedule. In typical Unix fashion, it includes a beautifully nerdy table structure, called the *cron table*, or more commonly *crontab*, for specifying the commands you want to run and the times you want to run them. The format of the cron table is just simple enough for many folks to be able to figure it out, and just tricky enough that you can make little mistakes without realizing it.

Cronnix is a free utility (abstracture IT-Beratung GmbH, `www.abstracture.de/cronnix`) that fills this gap by providing a nice Mac-like interface to cron. With Cronnix, (Figure 7-9), you add entries to a list in order to create cron tables.

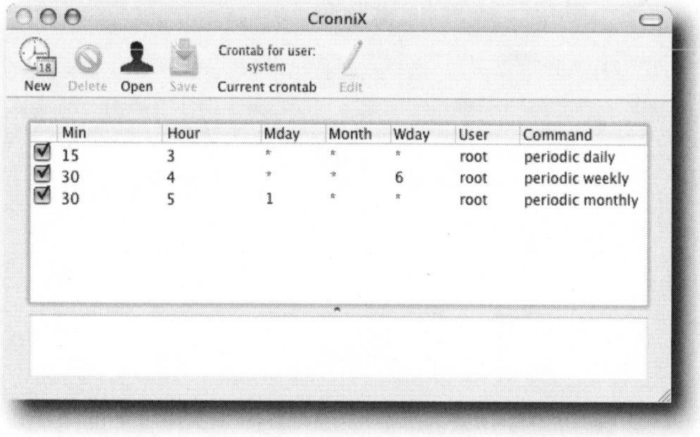

	Min	Hour	Mday	Month	Wday	User	Command
☑	15	3	*	*	*	root	periodic daily
☑	30	4	*	*	6	root	periodic weekly
☑	30	5	1	*	*	root	periodic monthly

FIGURE 7-9: You can add cron entries by clicking New and then filling in details.

Because Cronnix creates standard crontabs that are used by the actual cron tool, you can switch freely between Cronnix and cron if you want to use Cronnix as a tool for learning how the whole thing works.

Summary

Mac OS X is a wonderful platform for adding software, and thousands of developers large and small have taken advantage of this fact to give us great applications and cool utilities. I've only been able to scratch the surface in this chapter. There are a few good sources of more, including `www.versiontracker.com`, `http://macupdate.com`, and Apple's own downloads page at `www.apple.com/downloads/macosx/`. Check these frequently and find your own hidden treasures.

Running Unix Applications

For the first 15 years of its digital life, Macintosh was basically an island of its own compatibility. The release of Mac OS X—based on the Unix operating system, a non-proprietary technology—changed everything, promising to open the Mac up to a much larger world.

Now that Mac OS X has reached maturity, having had five major releases, what has happened to the notion of running Unix applications on the Mac? Can it really be done? Do you have to be a super-ultra-techno expert to do it? Yes, it can be done and, in most cases, a savvy Mac user like you can do it. In this chapter, you take a look at how you can run popular (and unpopular) Unix applications on your Mac. It's generally not as easy as double-clicking a true OS X application, but it's far from impossible, as you'll see.

Overview

In this overview section, I'll discuss the vast alternate universe of Unix software, how you can get it to run on your Mac, and why you would want to. I'll also cover expectations you should have for Unix software, and I hope you'll realize just how good we have it as Mac OS X users.

Mac OS X Is Unix

Mac OS X is Unix. It's not *sort of* Unix, not a Unix emulator, not a toy Unix. Yes, an awful lot of wonderful non-Unix stuff is layered on top, such as the Aqua user interface, but underneath it all is an actual, solid Unix base. In fact, with more than 10 million Mac OS X users, Apple is among the leaders in shipping Unix.

Why Did Apple Use Unix As the Base for OS X?

At the end of 1996, Apple acquired NeXT, the company Steve Jobs founded after being ousted from Apple. (Because Jobs wound up in charge of the combined companies, and because many NeXT people and technologies soon occupied prominent positions at Apple, some people joke that it was actually NeXT that acquired Apple, rather than the other way around.) Along with the company, Apple acquired NeXTSTEP, a Unix-based operating system that morphed into OS X. NeXT had used Unix because it was the standard operating system for its original target— customers in higher education—and because it was easier and cheaper than developing a new OS from scratch.

This Unix heritage isn't a secret, either. Apple likes to brag about it, as shown in this passage from the Apple Web site:

"Don't let its elegant and easy-to-use interface fool you. Beneath the surface of Mac OS X lies an industrial-strength Unix foundation hard at work to ensure that your computing experience remains free of system crashes and compromised performance. With its advanced virtual memory, you don't have to concern yourself over the number of applications you have open — just continue working. If an application should ever crash, the system's memory protection prevents it from taking the rest of the system down with it. And the time-tested security protocols in Mac OS X keep your Mac out of harm's way."

To find out much more about Apple's implementation of Unix in Mac OS X, see the document "Mac OS X for Unix Users Technology Brief" at http://images.apple.com/macosx/pdf/Panther_Unix_TB_10082003.pdf.

Tower of Babel: Various Unixes and Linux

OS X is based on FreeBSD 5, one of many varieties of Unix that are loose in the world. Thousands of applications are written for Unix, and many of them can run on OS X. Before you get too excited about this prospect, you should understand that we Mac users are spoiled by easy-to-use software. If you ever use Windows, you probably already think we're spoiled, but most Unix systems are even more challenging. Instead of one standard set of user interface conventions, like Apple's Aqua, there are several competing varieties, all of them somewhat Mac-like, but just unpolished enough to prove maddening to folks who don't use them all the time. Many applications don't have a graphical interface at all, instead they interact when the user types in the command-line shell in Terminal.

Given the dire condition of user interface in most Unix applications, why on earth should Mac users be interested in acquiring and running them? There are a few reasons:

- The most important characteristic of an application is its list of features. If the program does something you really need to do, you're likely to put up with a clumsy or inconvenient user interface in order to get it done. Unix is particularly strong in the area of scientific applications, although it also has some cool games.

- Many Unix programs are available for free. *Freeness* is a very popular feature. Some of these are even reasonable alternatives to commercial software.

- Unix applications often are open source, which means you can get source code. If you're handy with a compiler, you might want to add features, fix bugs, or otherwise customize or advance the state of your favorite application.

The spirit of hacky exploration and fun demands that you investigate this fascinating corner of the Mac universe.

Linux is an operating system that's similar to Unix, but not exactly the same. Linux was created by a legendary programmer named Linus Torvalds, who coordinated the work of hundreds of developers worldwide in building a non-proprietary alternative to Unix. Because nobody owns Linux, it's distributed freely, and it's available in versions for many different kinds of computers, including Macs. Most Macintosh users have no reason in particular to try Linux, because every Mac comes with Mac OS X, but if you're curious you might want to check it out. For more information, see www.linux.org.

X Window System

The idea of using pointing devices, windows to display information, and menus to command programs was pioneered by Xerox, shipped by Apple, and commoditized by Microsoft over the past 20 years. After the Unix world got a look at the success of graphical user interfaces, it was inevitable that various window-based interface projects would start up. One of the most popular of these is the X Window System, also known as X11, XWindows, or simply X (see Figure 8-1).

Apple has its own implementation of X11. This is X11R6.6, which is based on the open source XFree86 project. Apple's X11 is integrated with other system software, such as Quartz and Aqua, so that X11 windows can exist alongside more familiar OS X-native applications. I'll spend a lot more time and space later in this chapter discussing X11, in the section cleverly entitled "X11 (X Window System)."

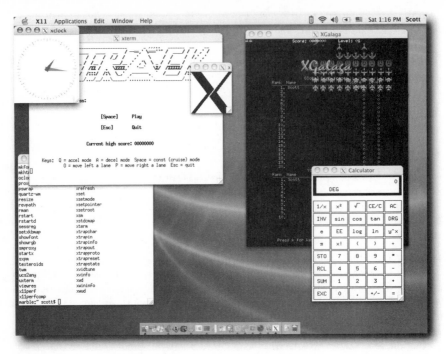

FIGURE 8-1: X11 applications running with Mac OS X.

How to Get, Install, and Run Unix Apps

As a Mac user, you're probably used to buying software at your local Apple store, ordering packaged products online, or downloading applications from developers' Web sites. You might get links to downloadable software from sites like VersionTracker and MacUpdate. These downloads typically come with lovely installers that work in Aqua and install programs with nice user interfaces. I've already established that the Unix world is usually a little more wild than that. You can use various strategies for jumping into the world of Unix applications, from least convenient to most convenient:

- **Build from sources**. As I mentioned earlier, many Unix applications are open source and freely available. You can download source code and build these yourself using Xcode, Apple's developer software, which comes along for free when you buy Mac OS X and are available for download at http://connect.apple.com. The best sites for finding open source projects are SourceForge, www.sourceforge.net, and freshmeat at `http://freshmeat.net`. If you're building X11 applications, be sure you install the X11 SDK from the Developer Tools installer.

- **Install binaries.** If you're not interested in modifying or building the application yourself, and you have access to prebuilt binaries that are set up for OS X, you can install just binaries to get the program running. This method has advantages over building it yourself: You don't have to worry about whether the build will work, and you don't have to wait while all that compiling takes place. On the other hand, you don't get that built-in programmer's coffee break that comes when you build a large project.

- **Use X11.** If the application you want has been built to run under X11, you can get that version and run it under Apple's implementation of X11.

- **Use a package manager.** Fink is a command-line application that automates the process of seeking, downloading, and installing Unix software. Fink comes with a companion program, FinkCommander, an OS X-native application that greatly simplifies the work that Fink does. FinkCommander makes it so easy to install Unix applications that it almost brings a tear to the eye of Unix purists who are used to suffering for their software. To get Fink and FinkCommander, visit `http://fink.sourceforge.net` and `http://finkcommander.sourceforge.net`. Other package manager projects are less mature than Fink, but some are promising. These include DarwinPorts (on the Web at `http://darwinports.org`) and the GNU-Darwin Distribution (`http://gnu-darwin.org`).

- **Install the application with a Mac OS X installer package.** Most of us Mac users would be thrilled if we could install all Unix applications by using Apple-style Installers. Few Unix applications are available with Mac OS X installers, but there are some, and there is (of course) an open source project to gather more. For example, you can download an OS X installer for OpenOffice software at `www.openoffice.org`, and you can get an easy installer for the GNU Image Manipulation Program (better known as The GIMP) at `gimp-app.sourceforge.net`. You might also want to take a look at the GNU Mac OS X Public Archive at `www.osxgnu.org`. This site has the goal of providing OS X installers for as much Unix software as possible.

Think Different

Even if you're fortunate enough to find a Mac installer for the software you want to use, don't expect a full-on Mac-like experience. After the installer completes its task and you start using OpenOffice, The GIMP, or other packages, you'll find yourself inside X11 or some other non-Mac environment. Have no fear and just move ahead slowly. You might not find the environment as friendly as the usual Aqua-based Mac applications, but you'll figure out how to get by.

When All Else Fails

Some Unix applications resist all attempts at running under Mac OS X, even if you build from sources. If you encounter one of those, maybe you will be the one to make it work on the Mac. Study Apple's porting guide at `http://developer.apple.com/documentation/Porting/Conceptual/PortingUnix`, use your favorite search engine to scour the Web for clues, or contact the developer or project lead to learn what you need to know.

X11 (X Window System)

Apple ships X11 as part of the standard OS X 10.4 package. So why don't you have it installed? Although it's on the install disks, X11 is clearly a second class citizen: It's not part of the standard *Easy Install*. To install X11, you have to visit a little-used screen in the installer. To get there, click the Customize button on the Easy Install screen of the installer. When you see the Custom Install screen, make sure the X11 item is checked (Figure 8-2).

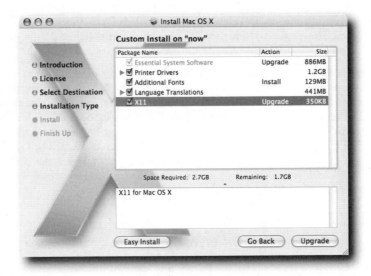

FIGURE 8-2: Custom Install options in Mac OS X installer.

Of course, this only works if you're freshly installing 10.4. In the more likely event you've already got a 10.4 system and you simply want to add X11, you can download an X11 installer from Apple at `www.apple.com/macosx/features/x11/download/`.

Shibboleth

Although many folks use the term *X Windows,* the correct name is actually *X Window System,* without a plural main noun. This is reportedly because of some real or perceived conflict with another bunch of folks who are fond of the term Windows as it applies to personal computer operating systems. Because many people in the open source crowd are an independent bunch with no love lost for Microsoft, some folks insist on saying *X Windows,* not because they're ignorant of their mistake, but precisely because it irritates certain other people.

No matter which route you've taken to install X11, if you're successful, you'll find an application named X11 inside your /Applications/Utilities folder. Just double-click this icon and you enter the wonderful world of the X Window System. When you first start X11, you see something like Figure 8-3.

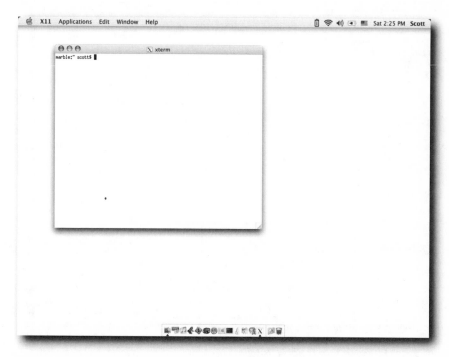

FIGURE 8-3: X11 looks like this when you start it up.

When you see X11, you might be filled with questions. Isn't this just some other version of Terminal? Where are all the cool graphics applications? Is X11 just a big lie?

The answers to those questions are yes, hang on, and no, respectively. When X11 starts, it opens an application called *xterm*, which is a lot like Terminal: It runs a Unix shell in a window. But there's more. The standard install of X11 includes the xlogo application, which proudly displays the logo of the X Window project (Figure 8-4). You can see that one by choosing Applications ➔ xlogo.

Pretty cool, huh? Well, it would be if you had been using text-based Unix systems all your life. There's more: The logo window is resizable. Just stretch it out to see an even bigger X. Are you impressed yet? If not, don't worry. X11 can do *even more* than display its logo in a window. For example, X11 comes with a famous graphical clock program. To see the clock, just type **xclock** into the xterm window. The xclock program (are you sensing a trend in the names of X11 applications?) appears, as shown in Figure 8-5. For geekier fun, check out xload, which uses nostalgic 2D black and white graphics to show how busy your system is.

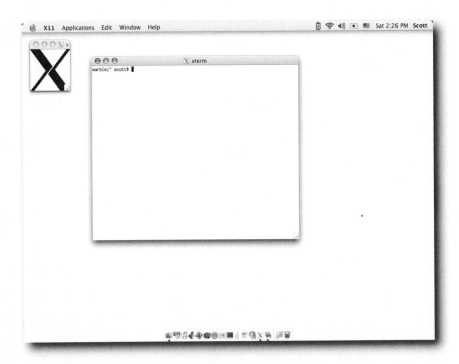

FIGURE 8-4: X11 knows how to show its logo.

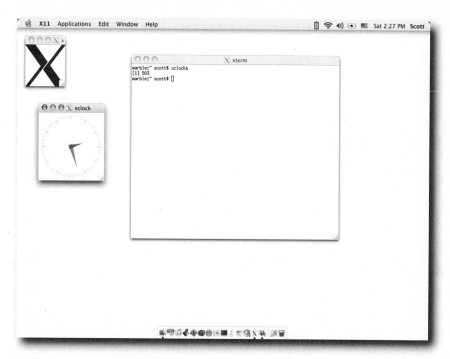

FIGURE 8-5: The xclock application is a standard part of X11.

Note When you run an X11 application by typing its name into xterm, the application takes control from the shell, just as any shell command does. If you want to start the application and return control immediately to the shell so you can continue with more commands, add an ampersand after the command, like this: **xclock&**.

By default, X11 looks for its applications in the /usr/X11R6/bin/ directory. This location is defined by the $PATH variable. You can take a look in /usr/X11R6/bin/ to see what other programs are available. Most of them have inscrutable names, but a few are immediately interesting. For example, if you run xwininfo, you are asked to click in a window, and you then get a table of information about the window, including its X-Y location and other esoteric data. You might also want to try xcalc, a scientific calculator shown in Figure 8-6.

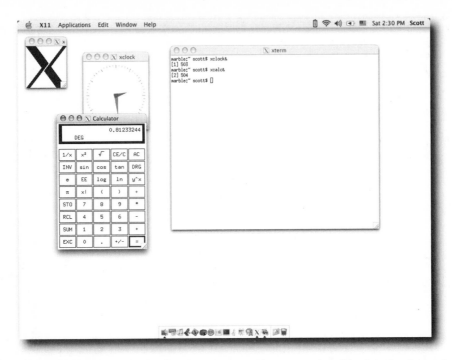

FIGURE 8-6: X11 comes with a scientific calculator. This was cool stuff back in the day, and it's still pretty neat.

Installing More X11 Applications

Geeks cannot live by xcalc alone, so you'll probably want to get more applications to try in X11. The easiest way to do this is with FinkCommander, which I mentioned earlier. Many of the graphical applications available from FinkCommander run in X11. When you install applications with Fink or FinkCommander, they're stored in the /sw/bin/ directory. So to run them, you can type **/sw/bin/applicationName** into xterm.

Customizing X11

If you're going to be spending some time running X11, you might be interested in how you can customize it. To see some of your options, choose X11 ➔ Preferences. One of the options on the Output panel of X11 Preferences is whether to enable full-screen mode. If you turn this check box on, the X11 menu enables the Enter Full Screen item. Choosing this item causes all other applications and windows to go away, leaving just the X11 windows to play with. You can use the command-key shortcut, Command-Option-A, to switch out of full-screen mode (and into it again).

X11 ships with three programs on its Applications menu: Terminal (xterm), xman, and xlogo. You can add your favorites by choosing Applications ➔ Customize Menu, which produces the window shown in Figure 8-7.

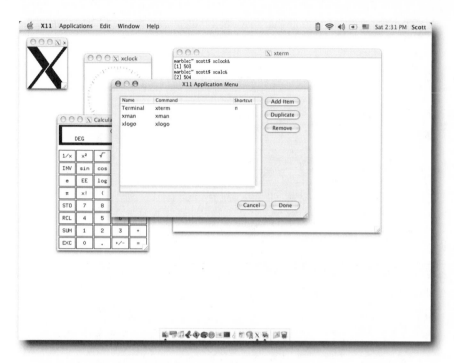

FIGURE 8-7: The X11 window for customizing the Application menu.

Running Applications Remotely

Although it's not often used this way now, X11 was originally designed for running graphical applications across a network. In that scenario, the application lives on a computer somewhere else on the network, but you see its windows and interact with it on your own computer.

If you're interested in checking out this feature of X11, here are the steps to get it going:

1. To make X11 work remotely, you first have to enable a feature on the remote machine called *X11 Forwarding*. You do this by editing the file /etc/sshd_config, changing a line that includes the line #X11Forwarding no to read X11Forwarding yes. The easiest way to do this is with a couple of Terminal commands. Type the following into Terminal:

```
sed 's/#X11Forwarding\ no/X11Forwarding\ yes/'
/etc/sshd_config > /tmp/sshd_config
sudo mv /tmp/sshd_config /etc/
```

The first line searches for the desired text and changes it (using the sed command), and then puts the result into a temporary file. The second line uses root privileges (using the sudo command) to replace the actual file with the temporary one you just created. You'll be asked for your password in order to complete the command.

2. Still working on the remote machine, open Preferences, choose Sharing, and select the Services tab.

3. Make sure the check box for Remote Login is turned on (Figure 8-8).

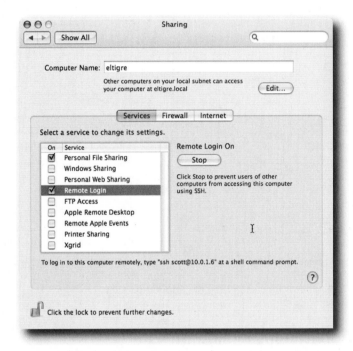

FIGURE 8-8: You must turn on Remote Login to use X11 applications remotely.

4. Now the action moves to your local machine. First, you're going to log in to the remote X11 system. Run X11 on your local machine. In xterm, type the following:

```
ssh -X -l username remoteMachineName
```

(Just to be clear, that second option after the dash is the letter that comes between k and m, not the integer that comes before 2.) I'm sure I don't need to tell you to replace username and remoteMachineName with actual values for the remote computer. So I won't. When xterm asks for your password in order to log in, go ahead and provide it.

5. Type the name of an X11 application to run it. For example:

```
/usr/X11R6/bin/xcalc&
```

or, if you've been fooling around with Fink and FinkCommander on the remote machine:

```
/sw/bin/someDownloadedXApp
```

You should see the window running on your machine, although the application itself is on the remote machine. This is pretty cool. By the way, note that X11 doesn't even have to be running on the remote computer. When you're all done, you can log out of the remote machine, although you should quit any running X11 applications to complete the logout.

Note If you study X11 further, you'll find that X11 reverses the usual terminology for *client* and *server*. In the world of X11, the *client* is the application running on the remote system, and the *server* is the local computer which is providing the display device. Go figure.

Summary

There are thousands of Unix applications in the world, so it's likely that you'll be interested in at least some of them. Using the information in this chapter, you can go fishing for interesting Unix software and give it a try. The price of most Unix software—free—makes it even easier to dip your toe in this ocean. To dive in even deeper, you might want to look up a local user group: See www.bsdusergroups.org or www.linux.org/groups to find a group near you.

There are already tens of millions of Macs running OS X, with millions more every year. Nobody sells as many Unix computers as Apple, which creates tremendous gravity pulling Unix applications toward OS X. In the coming years, you're likely to see more and more Unix software appearing on the Mac. So get ahead of the trend! Be the first one on your block to run a Unix application.

Terminal

Terminal is your ticket to the strange and wonderful Unix underpinnings of your Mac. Although you can accomplish a tremendous
amount of work and play without ever using Terminal, no discussion
of cool Mac tricks would be complete without a tour of this vital tool.
In this chapter, you'll explore some of the ways you can fool around with
Terminal, ranging from customizing how Terminal looks and behaves to
interesting and amusing tips about getting to stuff hidden inside your Mac.

What Is Terminal?

Every copy of Mac OS X includes the Terminal application tucked away
in the Utilities folder inside the Applications folder. Terminal provides
you with a *command-line interface* for communicating with your computer.
When you start Terminal, a window opens and Mac OS X runs a program
called a *shell*. The job of a shell is to take commands that you type and
send them along to the Unix kernel. For example, you can see a list of files
by typing `ls` in Terminal. This issues the text `ls` to the shell, which interprets that as a command meaning "List files in the current directory." If you
start Terminal and type **ls**, you'll see something like the screen shown in
Figure 9-1.

Guess what? You're speaking Unix now. Don't worry—I won't tell anyone.

Most shell commands can have *arguments*—additional values that provide
more information about what the command is supposed to do. For example,
you can list the files in a different directory by using an argument with `ls`,
like this:

```
ls Desktop
```

in this chapter

☑ Learn the power of
the command line

☑ Use the shell's
command history

☑ Play hidden Unix
games

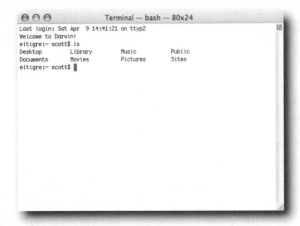

FIGURE 9-1: Terminal window with a command sent to the shell, and its output.

You can see the result of this command in Figure 9-2.

FIGURE 9-2: The ls command can take arguments.

Most commands support a special set of arguments called *options*, which tell the command to behave in a certain way. Options usually start with a hyphen. For example, the −a option tells ls to list all files, including those that start with a period, which is a Unix convention for hiding files. Figure 9-3 shows what happens when you give the ls −a command.

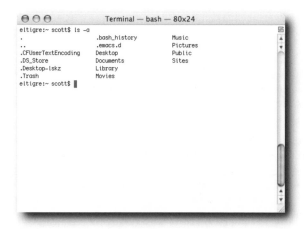

FIGURE 9-3: The ls command with -a option.

Most users rarely have to use Terminal, just as most drivers rarely pop the hood of their cars. But of course, just as you can accomplish a lot when you get down into your car's engine, Terminal is the gateway to a great deal of Mac OS X power.

Warning

I know I've said this before, but it's worth repeating: Be careful in here. In Terminal, you're typing commands to the shell, and you can do serious damage to your system if your adventurous nature takes hold. Type examples carefully, because in Terminal, typos can have consequences. For example, if you remove a file in the Terminal, it's gone instantly —no pulling it out of the Trash later. As always, the best idea is to back up frequently, or experiment on a Mac you have set up just for fooling around.

See Shells

The first Unix shell was called the Bourne Shell. Nowadays, many different shells are available. The default shell for Tiger is called *bash,* which stands for "Bourne-Again Shell." Mac OS X 10.2 used the *tcsh* shell. Most shells have a lot in common, so even if you're stuck with an alien shell, you can usually perform the basic commands.

Everyday Terminal Tips

As you try the tweaks in this chapter and advance your knowledge from there, you'll get to know Terminal much better. In this section, I'll discuss some tips you can use for becoming a more productive geek.

Drag and Drop

Even though you're running a Unix shell, remember that the shell is inside a nice Aqua window in OS X. One great way you can take advantage of this fact is by using drag and drop. Let's say you want to use the ls -a command described previously to get a listing of a particular folder on your hard disk. The folder is deeply nested inside other folders, so you have to type a long pathname in order to see what's inside the folder.

This is where drag and drop comes in. When you drag a folder out of a Finder window and drop it into a Terminal window, Terminal figures out the pathname of the file and enters it at the current insertion point. So, just start by typing **ls -a** in Terminal (be sure to type a space after the -**a**). Then, in the Finder, navigate to the folder you want, drag it, and drop it into the Terminal window. You see the pathname for the folder added to the command line. Just press Return to run your ls command.

Note
If your folder name contains any spaces or punctuation marks, Terminal puts a backslash in front of them when its pastes in the text. That's because such characters are often treated as variables or other special characters by the shell. Putting the backslash in front of them—a process called *escaping* the characters—informs the shell that they're to be taken literally.

Sometimes it's handy to be able to perform this escaping function automatically on text before you send it off to the shell. To do that in Terminal, copy the text that has to be escaped, and then choose Edit → Paste Escaped Text.

Command History

Your shell has a long memory. Every time you type in a command, it remembers and keeps track of what you typed. This is a good thing, because if you ever need to repeat a command, it's still in there. To see your previous commands, press the up-arrow key. The last command you typed appears on the current line, replacing anything you've already typed there. Press up-arrow again to go further back in time, or down-arrow to move forward. When you find the command you want, just press Return and the command is carried out.

Instead of using the arrow keys to cycle through your previous commands one at a time, you can use the `history` command to get a complete list, as shown in Figure 9-4.

```
Terminal — bash — 84x40
49  blah
50  history
51  killall Finder
52  killall Dock
53  defaults write com.apple.Dock pinning start
54  killall Dock
55  defaults write com.apple.Dock pinning end
56  killall Dock
57  history
58  defaults write com.apple.Dock orientation top
59  killall Dock
60  defaults write com.apple.Dock vvous-floater true
61  killall Dock
62  defaults write -g AppleScrollBarVariant DoubleBoth
63  killall Dock
64  killall Finder
65  cd ~/Library/Preferences/
66  plutil -convert xml1 com.apple.Preview.plist
67  open -e ~/Library/Preferences/com.apple.Preview.plist
68  defaults find 'yesterday'
69  man mdfind
70  mdfind 'blow'
71  man mdfind
72  mdfind krapmeier
73  mdfind jungle
74  mdfind jungle -live
75  mdfind jungle -live
76  man mdutil
77  ls /usr/include/
78  ls /usr/lib
79  mdimport -L
80  mdimport -L
81  man mdimport
82  mdimport -r ~/Library/Spotlight/XMLImporter.mdimporter/
83  man screencapture
84  sudo screencapture -w /Users/scott/desktop/
85  ls /Users/scott/Desktop/
86  ls /Users/scott/desktop -a
87  history
eltigre:~ scott$
```

FIGURE 9-4: The history command shows all the shell commands you've used.

Notice that items in the history list are nicely numbered. That's not just for show. You can use those numbers to issue any of the commands again. Just enter a line with an exclamation point (!) followed by the number of any command and then press Return. The shell executes the command again. To execute the last command again, you can type !! and press Return.

Terminal remembers your history even when you open a new window or quit the application. The command history is stored in a file named .bash_history in your Home directory so it can stay around until you need it again.

Word Completion

Another magic feature provided by the shell is the capability to automatically complete words before you finish typing them. Specifically, when you're typing the name of a command or a path, you can press Tab and the shell finishes the rest of the name. This works only if you've typed enough of the name to distinguish it from any other possibility; if you haven't, you hear an alert sound, and nothing else happens. But more help awaits you. If you then press Tab again, the shell shows you all the possible matches for what you've typed so far. For example, if you type this:

```
ls /Applications/i
```

and then press Tab, you'll hear the alert sound. If you press Tab again, you get a list of all possible matches for your command, like this:

```
iCal.app    iMovei.app    iSweep.app    iTunes.app
iChat.app   iPhoto.app    iSync.app
```

After displaying the list, the shell thoughtfully retypes your command line for you, so you can continue typing, picking up right where you left off.

Just for Fun

Unix systems (like Mac OS X) have been maintained lovingly by thousands of geeks over the past 30 years, so it's probably not surprising to find a full complement of cool Easter eggs inside. In this section, we'll take a look at some of the fun and bizarre hacks you can access inside your Mac. Impress your friends! Frighten your family!

Play Tetris

Mac OS X includes a legendary Unix program called emacs (not to be confused with eMac, Apple's education computer). Emacs started life as a humble text editor more than 20 years ago, and while it's still primarily used for that purpose, it has grown to become an environment of its own, performing not only text editing tasks but all sorts of integrated functions that include e-mail and Web browsing.

Along with all the other features inside emacs, you can find a collection of games. The suite of games available and the simple graphics they use create a strong sense of the 1980s when you play them. For example, one of the games in emacs is the classic Tetris. Here are the steps for playing Tetris:

1. You use Terminal to get emacs running, so start Terminal if it isn't already running.

2. In Terminal, type **emacs** and press Return. You should see the emacs screen inside your Terminal window, with a white-on-black menu bar at the top and a white-on-black status bar near the bottom.

3. Press Esc and then type an **x** to get into the emacs extended command mode. The block cursor moves to the bottom of the screen.

4. Type tetris and press Return. You should see something like Figure 9-5.

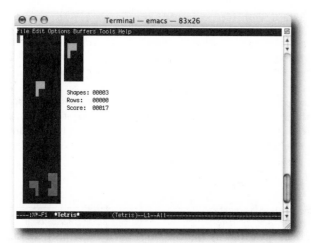

FIGURE 9-5: Play Tetris in emacs.

Yes, kids, this is what video games used to look like. To play the game, use the right- and left-arrow keys to slide the puzzle piece, up- and down-arrows to rotate, and space bar to drop. When you're done, you see a list of high scores. To get out of emacs at that point, you can type Control-X followed by Control-C. If all else fails, you can simply close the Terminal window.

Tetris is not the only game inside emacs. There are enough of them there to waste hours and hours of your precious time. You use the same steps to start any of the emacs games. Just follow the instructions listed above, changing only the name of the game. Some of the other games you can play:

- Pong, a replica of the ancient home video game, for two players. Use the 4 and 6 keys to move the left paddle up and down. To move the right paddle, use the up- and down-arrow keys. Have fun!

- For a change of pace, try Doctor. This is an implementation of Eliza, one of the first demonstrations of artificial intelligence, a discipline of computer science. The first version of Eliza was created in 1966 and was pretty darned impressive at the time. You can talk to Eliza for as long as you want—she'll be your special friend and helper.

- Dunnet is a textual adventure game, similar to those that were all the rage in the late 1970s. You use a basic vocabulary to move around the world, work with various objects you find, and try to accomplish the object of the game, after you determine what the object of the game is.

When you get tired of these, there are more. Emacs keeps its fun stuff in /usr/share/emacs/ 21.2/lisp/play. Just take a look in there and see what else you can fool around with. In the Finder, you can see this folder by typing Command-Shift-G and then entering the pathname. In Terminal, type `ls /usr/share/emacs/21.2/play/` .

> **Note** In the pathname above, the *21.2* refers to the version of Emacs installed. This number is sometimes different across various versions of Mac OS X. If you can't find a directory named 21.2 in that location, look for a folder with a slightly higher or lower version number.

Lest you think emacs is just for games, you should remember that it's a powerful and popular text editor. To find out more about how it works, you can run the tutorial right inside emacs itself: start emacs, type Control-h, press t, and you see the emacs tutorial. You can find much more information in the emacs wiki at `www.emacswiki.org`.

See "Lord of the Rings" Events

Movie audiences recently discovered J. R. R. Tolkein's *The Lord of the Rings*, but savvy computer geeks have been Rings fans for decades. For proof, you can check out a file inside Mac OS X's Unix world that provides a chronology of historical events from Middle-Earth. To see these events, go to Terminal and type:

`cat /usr/share/calendar/calendar.history | grep "LOTR"`

Your geeky typing will be rewarded with a Tolkein treasure.

Watch Star Wars in ASCII

A long time ago, in a galaxy far way, one movie was the most popular among geeks everywhere: *Star Wars*. No doubt you've seen this classic film many times. Now you can experience it as you've never seen it before, using the incredible ASCII text technology. Is this what George Lucas had in mind?

To see ASCII Star Wars:

1. Start Terminal, if it's not already running.

2. In Terminal, type `telnet towel.blinkenlights.nl` and press Return. After a few moments, you should see your computer connecting to the remote machine. It looks something like Figure 9-6.

After you get past the credits (just like in the theaters), you can watch ASCII Star Wars. Strictly speaking, ASCII Star Wars isn't an Easter egg inside your computer. It's being transmitted from the remote computer at `towel.blinkenlights.nl`. You're using Telnet, a standard Unix program that lets your Mac act like a terminal to the remote computer, to get the text displays that make up the movie. So this one technically isn't a Mac hack or even a Unix one, because Telnet runs on Windows as well, but it's just too cool to leave out.

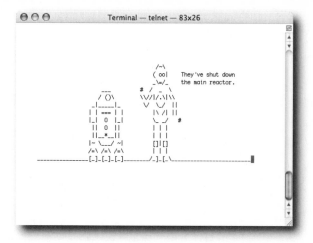

FIGURE 9-6: Perhaps you find this scene strangely familiar.

Summary

Terminal is your gateway to the Unix command line and all the goodness it provides. You could spend years just studying the Unix features inside your Macintosh, and learning how to use a command shell is a vital step in understanding and playing with the Unix core inside Mac OS X. If you're interested in finding out more about Unix, be sure to check out the next chapter on command-line tools and shell commands.

Shell Commands

Y ou can't truly unlock Mac OS X without Terminal, and after you're in Terminal, it's handy to know a few shell commands. In this chapter, you'll learn a few commands that are useful, some that have practical value but are also entertaining, and a few more that are definitely designed to help you have fun.

Practical Tips

In this section I'll provide some tips and tricks that come in handy all the time. You can probably use the tips in this list every day—or every day that you find yourself in Terminal, at least.

Monitor Your Processes

Mac OS X is based on Unix, which means there are zillions of processes running around your machine at any one time. Some of these processes are obvious: The big GUI applications like the Finder and iTunes are processes. But lots of other faceless processes are going on all the time. Applications sometimes spin off other processes to perform specific tasks, and the system itself runs invisible processes to do various jobs.

The shell provides commands, such as `top`, that you can use to see what the heck is going on with all your computer's running processes. After all, it's your computer, and you have a right to know. This kind of information can be especially useful if your Mac seems to have slowed to a crawl, and you suspect an application is taking more than its share of your CPU time.

To use `top`, just type **top** at the shell prompt. You see (Figure 10-1) a constantly updating table that gives various information about each running process, including its name, process ID number (PID), and the percentage of the CPU's time that's currently devoted to it.

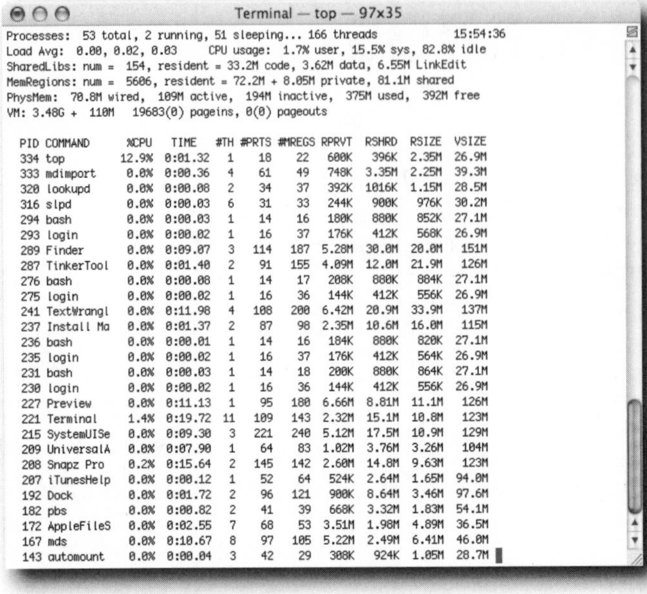

```
● ○ ○              Terminal — top — 97x35
Processes:  53 total, 2 running, 51 sleeping... 166 threads          15:54:36
Load Avg:  0.00, 0.02, 0.03    CPU usage:  1.7% user, 15.5% sys, 82.8% idle
SharedLibs: num =  154, resident = 33.2M code, 3.62M data, 6.55M LinkEdit
MemRegions: num =  5606, resident = 72.2M + 8.05M private, 81.1M shared
PhysMem:  70.8M wired,  109M active,  194M inactive,  375M used,  392M free
VM: 3.48G +  110M  19683(0) pageins, 0(0) pageouts

PID COMMAND      %CPU   TIME   #TH #PRTS #MREGS RPRVT  RSHRD RSIZE VSIZE
334 top         12.9% 0:01.32  1   18    22    600K   396K  2.35M 26.9M
333 mdimport     0.0% 0:00.36  4   61    49    748K   3.35M 2.25M 39.3M
320 lookupd      0.0% 0:00.08  2   34    37    392K   1016K 1.15M 28.5M
316 slpd         0.0% 0:00.03  6   31    33    244K   900K  976K  30.2M
294 bash         0.0% 0:00.03  1   14    16    180K   880K  852K  27.1M
293 login        0.0% 0:00.02  1   16    37    176K   412K  568K  26.9M
289 Finder       0.0% 0:09.07  3   114   187   5.28M  30.0M 20.0M 151M
287 TinkerTool   0.0% 0:01.40  2   91    155   4.09M  12.0M 21.9M 126M
276 bash         0.0% 0:00.08  1   14    17    208K   880K  884K  27.1M
275 login        0.0% 0:00.02  1   16    36    144K   412K  556K  26.9M
241 TextWrangl   0.0% 0:11.98  4   108   200   6.42M  20.9M 33.9M 137M
237 Install Ma   0.0% 0:01.37  2   87    98    2.35M  10.6M 16.0M 115M
236 bash         0.0% 0:00.01  1   14    16    184K   880K  820K  27.1M
235 login        0.0% 0:00.02  1   16    37    176K   412K  564K  26.9M
231 bash         0.0% 0:00.03  1   14    18    200K   880K  864K  27.1M
230 login        0.0% 0:00.02  1   16    36    144K   412K  556K  26.9M
227 Preview      0.0% 0:11.13  1   95    108   6.66M  8.81M 11.1M 126M
221 Terminal     1.4% 0:19.72  11  109   143   2.32M  15.1M 10.8M 123M
215 SystemUISe   0.0% 0:09.30  3   221   240   5.12M  17.5M 10.9M 129M
209 UniversalA   0.0% 0:07.90  1   64    83    1.02M  3.76M 3.26M 104M
208 Snapz Pro    0.2% 0:15.64  2   145   142   2.60M  14.8M 9.63M 123M
207 iTunesHelp   0.0% 0:00.12  1   52    64    524K   2.64M 1.65M 94.0M
192 Dock         0.0% 0:01.72  2   96    121   900K   8.64M 3.46M 97.6M
182 pbs          0.0% 0:00.82  2   41    39    668K   3.32M 1.83M 54.1M
172 AppleFileS   0.0% 0:02.55  7   68    53    3.51M  1.98M 4.89M 36.5M
167 mds          0.0% 0:10.67  8   97    105   5.22M  2.49M 6.41M 46.0M
143 automount    0.0% 0:00.04  3   42    29    308K   924K  1.05M 28.7M
```

FIGURE 10-1: Display from the top command.

The processes are listed in the order they were started, with the most recent ones first. When you start `top`, you can use options that let you see the processes displayed in any order you want. Probably the most useful view is to see them in order of CPU usage, from most to least piggy, which you can get by typing `top -u`. For more about what you can do with `top`, see its manual page by typing **man top**.

If you prefer a more graphical display, check out Activity Monitor, which you can find in the Applications/Utilities folder. (You might recall that you used Activity Monitor briefly back in Chapter 1.) This program performs many of the same functions as `top`, but with nice pictures (Figure 10-2).

Activity Monitor does a great job in most process-watching cases. It even has a literal killer feature: You can select any process and click the little stop sign to terminate the process, even force-quitting if necessary. This is a great way to handle applications that are frozen or otherwise stubbornly misbehaving. Quitting an application from Activity Monitor is similar to using the `kill` or `killall` commands from Terminal, as you did in earlier chapters.

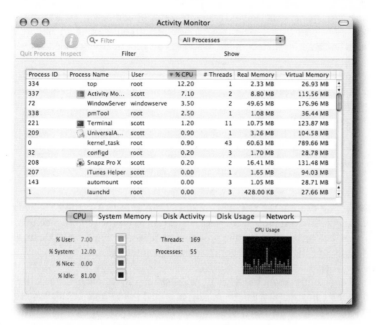

FIGURE 10-2: Activity Monitor is like a better-looking top.

One thing that Activity Monitor can't do is help you when you're logged in remotely to another machine, as described in the next section. That's when top comes out on top.

Remote Login with ssh

One of the cool things about having Unix is that you can use the ssh (secure shell) command to access your computer remotely and do real command-line work on it. This is great for practical work, and it's even niftier if you're the master of your home network. Here's how you can log in to your Mac remotely:

1. On the machine you want to access remotely, open System Preferences, go to the Sharing panel, and make sure Remote Login is turned on.

2. While you're there, check out the machine's IP address by looking at the bottom of the Sharing panel. You should see a statement like this: To log in to this computer remotely, type "ssh scott@a.b.c.d" at a shell command prompt. The "a.b.c.d" part is the machine's IP address.

Note

If you're using NAT, or network address translation, for IP addressing, you can use this technique only from your local subnet. NAT is common if you're using an AirPort Base Station or other hardware to share a single IP address on your Internet connection.

3. On the machine that you're using to do the accessing, start Terminal and type **ssh scott@ a.b.c.d**, except instead of **scott@a.b.c.d**, type the user name and IP address of the remote machine that you learned in Step 2. Instead of an IP address, you can use the name of the computer, as defined in the Sharing preference panel.

4. When you're asked if you want to continue connecting, say yes, of course!

5. Type the password of the remote account when you're asked for it. (If you don't know the password, what are you doing trying to log in to that remote machine?)

After you're logged in, you can run the remote computer from Terminal just like you would the local one. Commands that you type to the shell are executed on the remote machine. Pretty cool! Unfortunately, you can't run Aqua programs this way—you can start them, with the open -a command, but their windows appear on the remote machine.

Cross-Reference

You can run graphical applications using the X Window System on the remote machine while you interact with them on the computer that's right in front of you. It's not Aqua, but it's something. For much more on this subject, see Chapter 8.

One of the most useful features of remote login is the capability to recover when an application—or, on rare occasions, the whole machine—gets hung up trying to do something. If you have a process that you want to terminate remotely, you can perform the assassination in two ways: by process ID (PID) or by name. If you know the PID, because you saw it in Activity Monitor or in top, you can type **kill xxxx**, where **xxxx** is the ID of the doomed process. You can also get rid of the process by typing **killall ProcessName**. If you use **killall**, be sure to enter the right capitalization for the process name or it won't work.

Warning

It's easy to get confused by multiple Terminal windows when one is logged into your local machine and the other is talking to a remote computer somewhere. Be sure you know which machine you're talking to when you enter shell commands, or you might do something you didn't really want to do. A good trick is to color-code your Terminal windows: Choose Font → Show Colors, pick a color you like, and then drag the color out of the Colors window to the Terminal window. You can use a red background to mean *be very very careful,* for example.

Searching with man

If you've used Unix at all on your Mac, or any other computer, you have probably learned about the man command, short for *manual*, which provides online documentation inside the shell. You might not know, however, that man has its own built-in search facility, which you can access by using its −k option. For example, if you want to search for commands that include the word *Apple* in their short description, you can type man −k Apple. You get results like the ones shown in Figure 10-3.

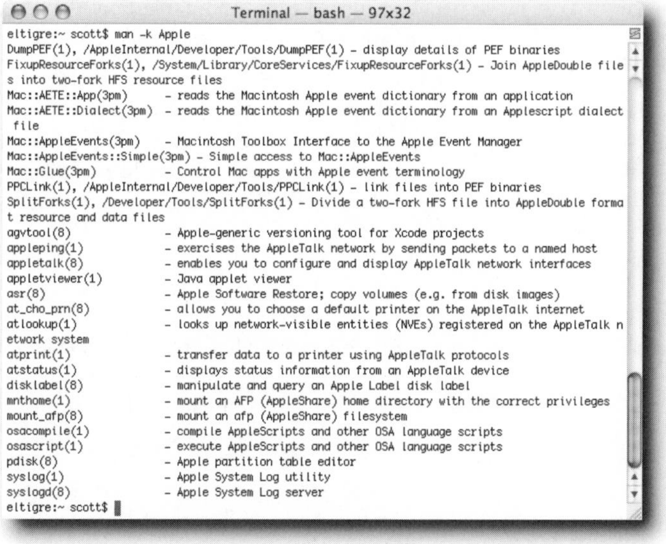

FIGURE 10-3: Results from issuing the man –k Apple command.

If you like extra typing and French words, you can use the apropos command instead of man –k. They're equivalent. Note that man –k (and apropos) only search for a short description for each command—it's fast, but incomplete. If you want to search the entire man text, use man –K (that's an uppercase K). This search takes a long time, and each time it finds a match, it asks if you want to display the matched file. But if you want to search every possible man page, this is the option for you.

More Interesting, Less Practical

Any Unix shell command is practical on the day you need it. For some commands, that day might never come, but the commands are nifty and worth checking out just the same. In this section, you'll take a look at some commands that you'll probably use eventually, and even if you don't, they're good to know.

Find Out about a Command: which

Every young nerd one day looks at his or her shell and asks the fateful question: Where do commands come from? You don't have to be embarrassed by this question. Asking it is a natural part of growing up.

Shell commands are simply little (or not so little) Unix programs that are executed by the shell when you type their names. To find out precisely which program will run when you enter a command, you can use the `which` command. The `which` command? Yes, like this:

```
which apropos
```

and the response you see is this:

```
/usr/bin/apropos
```

So, the `apropos` command is found in the /usr/bin directory. Shell commands are kept in well-known directories. The list of those directories is stored in a variable named $PATH. You can see the names of these directories by using the `echo` command to look at the $PATH variable, like this:

```
echo $PATH
```

You should see a result like this:

```
/bin:/sbin:/usr/bin:/usr/sbin
```

These are four directories—/bin, /sbin, /usr/bin, and /usr/sbin—jammed together with colons between them. By default, the shell search in those places when you type the name of a command.

Open Files

The `open` command lets you open files just as if you had double-clicked them in the Finder. For example, if you type **open ~/Documents/invaders.jpg**, OS X opens the invaders.jpg document in the default application for that file (for JPEG files, it's usually Preview). That's fun, but you don't need the shell to do that. A more powerful feature of `open` is to use it for opening a bunch of files all at once. If you type **open~/Documents/*.jpg**, all the JPEG files in your Documents folder open at once—or more accurately, one after the other.

Remove a File Securely with srm

You probably know that deleting a file on your Mac (and on most computers) just removes its directory entry and marks the disk space used by the file as available for reuse. That's how those magical file-restoring *undelete* utilities work: If you undelete quickly enough, the file's data is usually still around.

But sometimes, you really, really want to make sure that nobody ever sees a file when you're through with it. That's why Apple has the Secure Empty Trash feature in the Finder. Secure Empty Trash not only deletes the files, it scribbles all over the files' data seven times to obliterate what was there before.

You can use the shell command srm (secure removal) to securely delete files without having to pass them through the trash first. Just type srm followed by the name of the soon-to-be-former file. Not only does this zap the file without bothering anything in the trash, it writes over the files data 35 times, like a crayon-wielding toddler, to be even more certain that nothing can be recovered.

Mostly Fun

The commands in this section certainly have real value. Just because I'm putting them in a section called "Mostly Fun" doesn't mean there's anything wrong with them. It's just that for most of us Mac geeks, their entertainment value is likely to outweigh any practical need.

Get File Listings in Color with ls

The ls command lists files for you in the shell. Like many of the most common commands, ls comes with about a zillion options. One of the more curious ones is the -G option, which adds some color to your listings. If you use -G, files and directories will appear color-coded: Directories show up in blue, user-executable programs are red, and drop folders are olive. It's lovely.

Folder or Application?

If you use the -G option to see listings in color, notice that applications like Safari.app and Mail.app appear in blue, the color for directories, rather than in red, which is how executables appear. That's because the .app files are not really executable themselves. They're OS X *packages,* folders that are disguised in the Finder as single icons. The executable itself is buried inside the package in the Contents/MacOS/ directory. It shows up in red.

Make a Banner

Back in the days before graphics were cheap, fast, and built into every computer, people made pictures and giant signs out of text characters. (It's true—ask your parents if you don't believe me.) The banner command is a reminder of how that used to work. If you type **banner "Vote for Pedro"**, you get a spew of number-sign characters (#) that display "Vote for Pedro" in giant letters (see Figure 10-4).

You might want to capture the output into a text file, where you can mess around with it further before you decide if you want to print it out. To get the output into a text file, type **banner "Vote for Pedro" > ~/Documents/banner.txt**. You can then open the file in TextEdit and check it out.

Of course, back in the era when this sort of thing represented advanced graphics, printers put out continuous sheets of paper folded into stacks. Nowadays, if you print the banner, you're going to have to tape the sheets together.

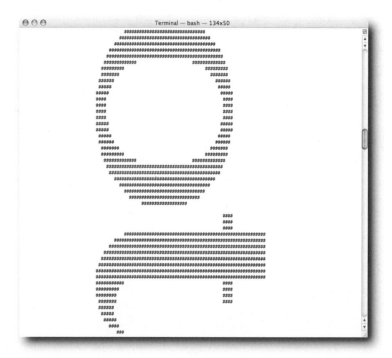

FIGURE 10-4: Part of a banner.

Create a Calendar

Does anybody really know what time it is? Unix does, and it wants to help you out by creating a nice textual calendar for you. Use the `cal` command to get a calendar of any month or year you'd like. Just typing `cal` gets you this month's calendar. To plan ahead for your future wedding or that far-off bar mitzvah, type **cal 2007**. If you want to see when Thanksgiving will fall in a few years, type **cal 11 2010**.

To get the calendar into a file you can read with TextEdit, BBEdit, Word, or Pages, just add a redirect command and a filename, like this: **cal 2007 > calendar.txt** .

Note that `cal` is very literal about the input you give it. If you type **cal 06**, you get a calendar not for 2006, but for the *year 6*. So watch out for that.

Check Your Mac's Uptime

Back in the good old days of Mac OS 9 and earlier, applications were pretty much free to roam around the system and do what they needed to do. But sometimes, they went a little haywire, causing problems that forced us to reboot our Macs. Sometimes, that happened a couple of times a day. That wasn't so good. So Apple brought us Mac OS X, which uses various techniques to help ensure that one bad application won't spoil the whole bunch.

The result is that a frozen or crashed application usually doesn't mean you have to reboot. Hooray! You'll find some Mac users who like to brag about how infrequently they restart their computers. To join in this bragging, you can use the `uptime` command to determine exactly how long it's been since your Mac restarted. When you type **uptime**, it reports the current time, followed by the number of days, hours, and minutes since rebooting. If you're an old Mac user, `uptime` is a great reminder of how far we've come.

Determine Your CPU Model

The brain inside every Mac is a PowerPC microprocessor, also known as a central processing unit (CPU). Apple likes to use cool-sounding names like G4 and G5 for its CPUs. But inside, they have very boring part numbers. To see the part number of your CPU, use the `machine` command. Figure 10-5 shows what happened when I typed the `machine` command into my vintage 2004 iBook G4.

```
eltigre:~ scott$ machine
ppc7450
```

FIGURE 10-5: machine tells you what kind of CPU you have.

Print Text in Reverse

Apple's distribution of Unix includes the `rev` command, which takes text as input and spits it out as backwards text (Figure 10-6). This can be very useful for amusing small children or constructing satanic messages for your next hit record. If you type `rev` followed by the name of a file, the text in the file is reversed line by line and produced in Terminal. If you just type `rev`, you can then enter text, followed by Return. The text is reversed and you can type some more. You can keep going this way until you're tired of it, at which point you just type Command-period to get back to your regular forward-thinking world.

```
eltigre:~ scott$ rev
The quick brown fox jumps over the lazy dog
god yzal eht revo spmuj xof nworb kciuq ehT


Able was I ere I saw Elba
ablE was I ere I saw elbA


You have found the secret message
egassem terces eht dnuof evah uoY
```

FIGURE 10-6: Use rev to reverse text. This is especially handy when you need to reverse some text.

Make Your Family Hear Voices

This one is really cool. With the `say` command, you can actually make a remote Mac talk using the synthesized speech built into Mac OS X. The catch, of course, is that you need a user account on the remote machine, and that computer has to have remote login enabled. Because I'm sure you're the master of your home network, gaining this sort of access to your spouse's (or parents') Mac should be no problem.

Start by logging in to the victim's computer with **ssh** (see "Remote Login with ssh" in this chapter for details). After you're there, you can `say` your piece:

- `say "Let me out of here"` speaks the given text.
- `say -v Fred "It sure is good to get out of that bag"` speaks the text using the specified voice. For a really good time, try Bubbles or Deranged instead of Fred.
- For an ongoing conversation, just type **say**. You can then type a line at a time. Every time you press Return, the remote Mac speaks your text. When you're all done fooling around, type Command-Period to stop.

Another cool way to use this command is `say -o filename "Something"`. This one creates an AIFF file with the spoken text. You can then add the file to your iTunes library if you want to convert it to MP3 or move it to your iPod.

Summary

In this chapter I just barely touched the rich set of shell commands available in Mac OS X. If you're interested in becoming more of a Unix maven, you can devote months or years of your life to the subject. OS X includes about 1000 Unix commands, and that doesn't even include the intricacies of the bash shell, file system, processes, and other deep topics. OS X does a great job of hiding almost all this stuff, but if you're interested, Unix provides an almost unlimited field of study for the curious geek.

Mods

I n the first Part of this book, you learned about cool tips and tricks that you can do without digging inside your Mac too deeply. But if you're still reading, you're not satisfied with just scratching the surface. So here in Part II, I'll show you how to modify the behavior of Mac OS X and its applications. You'll find out how to crack open application bundles, and after you're inside, I'll introduce you to property lists and show you how to use them to make applications do what you want.

After that, I'll give you a tour of Automator, Apple's innovative new feature that lets you perform repetitive, boring tasks without having to get your hands dirty programming or even using AppleScript (unless you really want to). Finally, if you have some programming experience or want to acquire some, I'll show you the tools that Apple has provided for you to create your own programs in Xcode. And even if you're not at all interested in programming, you'll enjoy learning about Quartz Composer, an amazing new graphics tool that's hiding out as a developer tool. That chapter leads nicely into Part III, where you'll see some real down-and-dirty programming.

Inside Application Bundles

Mac OS X uses some slick technology to present its beautiful Aqua face to the world while keeping everything running smoothly behind the scenes. In previous chapters, you've seen a few glimpses of how OS X handles applications and their related bits. In this chapter, you go a lot deeper as you examine what really makes up an OS X application.

What You See Is Not Always What You Get

When you look at the contents of a disk in the Finder, almost every item you see corresponds to a single file. But sometimes, the Finder is lying to you (even though it's for a good cause). Mac OS X provides a way to collect related files into a single entity called a *bundle*, and OS X conspires with the Finder to present bundles as one icon. Applications are the most common examples of bundles. That's right—all those applications on your Mac that look like single files in the Finder. They're really living secret lives as bundles, hiding all sorts of interesting stuff inside.

A bundle is basically a folder that appears in the Finder as a single file. This convenient fiction allows users to easily install and move applications without having to worry about keeping their support files around, and it also prevents casual users from messing up their applications by trashing a necessary file.

Although Mac OS X uses bundles primarily as a way to hide collections of code plus other resources, no rule says that bundles must include pieces of code. A database developer might choose to store databases and indices together in a bundle, for example.

The Mac OS X Installer uses a bundle technology called *packages* to gather all the files needed for installing software into a unit, an installation package. The Installer then extracts the files it needs from the package and puts them where they belong.

Bundle Up

Applications are the most prominent kinds of bundles, but they're far from the only bundles on your Mac. Bundles provide a handy general mechanism for keeping a bunch of stuff behind a single icon. Mac OS X uses bundles in various situations that require code to be kept together with images, property lists, and other flotsam. Screen savers, preference panes, Dashboard widgets, frameworks, and application plug-ins are all bundles, each one with some files that have code and others containing data.

Looking at Bundles

Bundles are folders in disguise, but it's easy for anyone to look behind the mask and see what a bundle contains. To see inside a bundle, you don't have to go any farther than the Finder.

1. In the Finder, choose a bundle to inspect. You can pick any application, screen saver, preference pane, Dashboard widget, or other bundle you like. For this example, use the Spotlight preference pane. You can find it in /System/Library/PreferencePanes/ Spotlight.prefPane.

2. Pull down the Action menu in the Finder window (the one with a picture of a gear) and choose Show Package Contents. This opens a new window with a Contents folder, as shown in Figure 11-1.

3. Look inside the Contents folder to see all the other stuff hidden by the bundle (Figure 11-2).

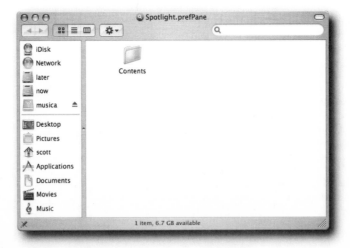

FIGURE 11-1: This folder is hidden inside bundles.

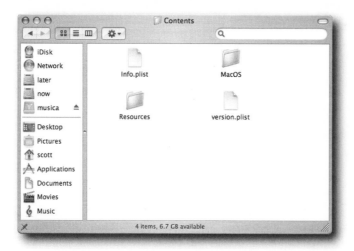

FIGURE 11-2: The bundle's Contents folder contains files and subfolders.

Apple is a little schizophrenic about the terms *bundle* and *package*. Although Apple's developer documentation defines a *bundle* as the fundamental mechanism behind applications, screen savers, and the like, note that the Finder's menu item uses the term *package* instead of *bundle*.

Mac OS X and the Finder collaborate on the bundle illusion to show you a single icon instead of the full bundle contents. But the command line isn't fooled. If you use Terminal, bundles appear like the folders they truly are.

To see how this works, go to a Terminal window and type the following:

```
ls /System/Library/PreferencePanes/Spotlight.prefPane/Contents/
```

That command results in this output:

```
Info.plist   MacOS    Resources    version.plist
```

Those are exactly the same contents you saw in the Finder using the Show Package Contents command. So, you can examine what's inside a bundle using either the Finder or Terminal, whichever you prefer.

Thanks for Showing Up

The Action menu provides a surefire way to tell if an icon is a bundle. If the Show Package Contents item is in the menu, the selected item is a bundle—if the item isn't a bundle, that item simply doesn't appear.

You don't have to use the Action menu to look inside a bundle. The Finder provides a contextual menu shortcut for Show Package Contents. Just Control-click (or right-click) on the bundle you want to explore, and Show Package Contents appears in the contextual menu.

A Tour of Bundle Contents

When you open an application bundle, or most any other kind of bundle, you see a Contents folder at the first level inside. Let's take a look at what's inside the Contents folder.

In this example, you investigate the TextEdit application. You start by seeing (almost) everything there is to see.

1. In the Finder, go to the Applications folder and select TextEdit.

2. Choose Show Package Contents from the Action menu.

3. Click the List View button in the Finder window.

4. Click the triangle next to the Contents folder to see what's inside. The result should look like Figure 11-3. The Contents folder has five items: Info.plist, MacOS folder, PkgInfo, Resources folder, and version.plist. I talk about these in more detail later.

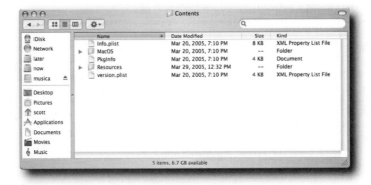

FIGURE 11-3: Finder shows what's in the Contents folder.

5. Click the triangle next to MacOS to see what it contains. There should be a single object, a file named TextEdit. This is a file containing the executable code for TextEdit. When you double-click the TextEdit icon to launch it, Mac OS X runs the code in this file.

6. Click the triangle to open the Resources folder. There's a lot of stuff in there! You see a bunch of folders with the names of various languages (English.lproj, Dutch.lproj, and so on), some files with recognizable file types (Edit.icns contains icons and DocumentWindow.nib comes from the Interface Builder development tool), and a few others (Figure 11-4).

Now that you have an idea of all the files that are hanging around inside application bundles, I discuss what all that stuff is for.

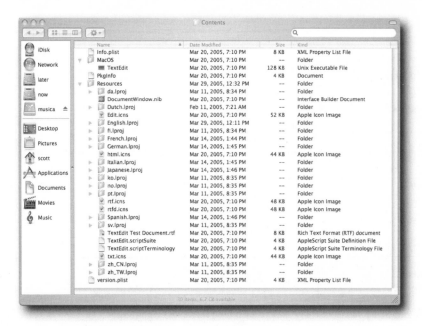

FIGURE 11-4: The Resources folder in TextEdit bundle.

What's What in Application Bundles

In this section, you take a closer look at the files and folders you discovered inside the application bundle. You see what all the pieces are for and how you might play around with them.

MacOS Folder

This folder almost always contains a single file whose name is the same as the application. This file contains the code that Mac OS X executes when you run the application. Although the vast majority of applications have only one executable in the MacOS folder, it's not a requirement. For example, older versions of Calculator (before Tiger) have two executables in the MacOS folder, Calculator and CalcEngine. Calculator is the application; CalcEngine is a helper program that does the math for Calculator.

Resources Folder

The Resources folder in an application bundle has all the miscellaneous stuff the application needs in order to run, besides the code (which you found in the MacOS folder). This includes graphics displayed by the application (including icons, image files, bitmaps, and so on), human-readable text, sounds, and anything else the application developer wants to stash. If the application has any sort of associated files that should always stay with it, even when it's copied or moved, the Resources folder is like a safe deposit box for hiding these.

Seeing Double

What happens if you double-click an executable file inside the MacOS folder? Give it a try and see what happens. First, select the TextEdit file inside the MacOS folder and choose File → Get Info. The Finder lists this file as a Unix Executable File. Now double-click the file. Mac OS X opens the file in Terminal and then executes a command that looks like this:

```
/Applications/TextEdit.app/Contents/MacOS/TextEdit; exit
```

This command runs the TextEdit application, which you can see as it peeks out from behind the Terminal window. Because TextEdit was started from Terminal and not from the Finder, the Terminal window controls its fate: If you close the Terminal window or type Control-period to stop the process, TextEdit immediately goes away. Go ahead and close the Terminal window to make TextEdit go away.

You can use this technique to do something really weird and wonderful: launch multiple instances of the same application. If you repeatedly double-click the executable inside the MacOS folder, you get a new copy of the application running every time. Figure 11-5 shows what your desktop might look like if you try this trick with the Calculator.

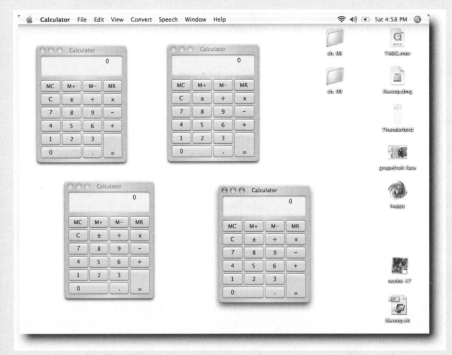

FIGURE 11-5: Have a Calculator! Have another!

This tip is useful if you use the Calculator a lot and you have a big monitor (or even better if you have multiple monitors). You can position multiple Calculators around the screen for easy access.

Now that I've taught you how to do this trick, I need to warn you against using it. Mac OS X applications don't expect to have multiple copies of themselves running under the same account at the same time. It's very easy for the copies to get confused, scrambling their data and preferences. Some applications know the danger and refuse to allow themselves to run multiple copies. Use this tip with great caution, if you use it at all. If you really need multiple calculators, or multiple clocks, or the like, you should use Dashboard widgets, which are explicitly designed to allow multiple copies.

TextEdit and most other application bundles include everything they need to work in various human languages. The process of making an application run in different human languages is called *localization*. The Resources folder usually contains a bunch of folders whose names end in `lproj` (localized project). TextEdit includes localizations for 15 different languages, including English, Japanese, Finnish, and Korean.

Any kinds of files can be buried in a bundle—even documentation. The Xcode application bundle includes a file that describes how to create a data display plug-in for the gdb debugger that comes with Apple's developer tools. You'll find the file conveniently located inside Xcode at /Developer/Applications/Xcode.app/Contents/PlugIns/GDBMIDebugging.xcplugin/Contents /Headers/DataFormatterPlugin.h.

Info.plist

In various chapters earlier in this book, you edited preferences property list files to change the behavior of applications. A second important kind of property list is associated with every application: the information property list file (known to its friends as Info.plist). The Info.plist file tells all about the bundle. This file is mainly used by the Finder and the operating system to learn important information about the application, such as what kinds of files it supports and where to find its icons.

As with preferences property lists, every item in an information property list contains a *key*, which is the name of the item, and a *value* for the item. You can edit information property lists with a text editor or with the Property List Editor application.

Warning

Editing information property list keys is a great way to learn about how applications work with the Finder and the rest of Mac OS X, but it's also an efficient technique for making your application unusable. To be safe, you should make a copy of your application before fooling around with it.

Here's a list of Info.plist keys, what they're for, and their values in the TextEdit bundle, presented in several groups of related keys.

Bundle Identification

The keys in this group identify the bundle to the Finder and to parts of the system that need to know about applications, such as the Launch Services framework.

- **CFBundleDevelopmentRegion.** The default language for the application. For TextEdit and other applications in the U.S. distribution of Mac OS X, this is English.

- **CFBundleDisplayName.** The localized name of the application as displayed in the Finder. TextEdit's name is TextEdit, of course.

- **CFBundleExecutable.** This one is important: It gives the name of the executable file inside the bundle. For TextEdit, this key contains the value TextEdit, because that's the name of the executable.

- **CFBundleIdentifier.** This key contains a string that distinguishes the application from every other application in the world. How is that possible? Mac OS X takes advantage of Internet-style domain name rules to construct unique names for bundles. To make a bundle identifier, an application developer starts with a domain name and then reverses the order of the words, adding the name of the application on the end. So, for example, applications created by Apple have identifiers that start with com.apple. The identifier for TextEdit is com.apple.TextEdit. This weird-looking but clever reverse domain name business ensures that the parts of identifier names go from most general to most specific.

- **CFBundleInfoDictionaryVersion.** This key is created automatically when a developer builds an application. It contains the version number of the information property list structure—the very thing discussed here. By putting a version number in the property list, Apple provides a way to add features in the future while still making sure that old applications don't suddenly blow up when that happens. TextEdit (and all other Tiger applications) have 6.0, the current version number, in this key.

- **CFBundleName.** This key contains the name of the application, as displayed in the menu bar, next to the Apple menu (Figure 11-6). Like other values in the Info.plist, this one can be localized by values in the InfoPlist.strings file inside a localized project (lproj) folder, so if you try to change this value, take a look there as well. TextEdit, of course, has a CFBundleName of TextEdit.

- **CFBundlePackageType.** In another homage to the bygone days of Mac OS 9, this key contains a four-character value that indicates the type of the bundle. For TextEdit and all other applications, this key contains APPL, which by sheer coincidence is similar to (but not exactly the same as) Apple's stock market ticker symbol (AAPL).

- **CFBundleSignature.** In Mac OS 9 days, files were identified by type and creator codes. This key holds the four-character Mac OS 9-style creator code for the bundle, which used to be the way that applications were uniquely identified. For TextEdit, this is set to ttxt, the creator code for the old TeachText application that was TextEdit's great grandapp.

- **CFBundleShortVersionString.** The application displays this string as the version number in its About box. Most applications use a numeric scheme with one or more decimals— TextEdit is version 1.4. But this key is a string, so there's nothing to prevent you from using any characters you want, as demonstrated in Figure 11-7.

- **CFBundleVersion**. This key typically holds the application's build number, which by default is displayed in parentheses following the version number in the About box.

FIGURE 11-6: Change the name the application displays in the menu bar.

FIGURE 11-7: The version string in the About box need not be a number.

Documents

Many property list keys are used to specify the connections between applications and documents.

- **CFBundleDocumentTypes.** This key says which kinds of documents are supported by the application. Each type is represented by a property list data structure called a *dictionary*. TextEdit is prolific in its support: It can handle seven different kinds of documents. Most applications support fewer (Mail has five, iChat two), although some can handle even more types (iTunes supports 23 different kinds of documents). Here you see the kinds of information you can find about each type (not every file type has all these keys).

- **CFBundleTypeExtensions.** The file extensions (such as .txt) supported by this application. TextEdit supports rtf, doc, rtfd, txt, html, htm, and webarchive extensions. Web archiving is a new feature of Safari 2.0 (which comes with Mac OS X Tiger) that provides a way to save all the contents of a Web page.

- **CFBundleTypeIconFile.** This key gives the name of the file containing icons for the given file type. TextEdit's property list includes rtf.icns, txt.icns, and several others.

- **CFBundleTypeMIMETypes.** MIME is an international standard for encoding various types of information as text. (MIME stands for Multipurpose Internet Mail Extensions, which was the original intended use for this standard.) An application can specify a MIME type for the documents it supports instead of or in addition to the other kinds of identifying information in its property list. TextEdit supports MIME types text/plain and text/rtf.

- **CFBundleTypeName.** This key contains a name for the document type. This is either a nice human-friendly name like Apple HTML Document or a Cocoa type like NSStringPboardType. TextEdit handles these type names: Microsoft Word Document, Apple SimpleText Document, Apple HTML Document, Apple Web archive, NSRTFPboardType, NSTRFDPboardType, and NSStringPboardType.

- **CFBundleTypeOSTypes.** This key is a blast from the past. Back in the Mac OS 9 days, each file's type was specified by a four-character string. This key specifies the four-character strings for the file types the application supports. TextEdit names RTF (that's RTF followed by a blank, to make four characters), W8BN, W6BN (not weird radio stations but actually files created by older versions of Microsoft Word), TEXT, sEXT, and ttro.

- **CFBundleTypeRole.** This one is pretty cool: It specifies what this application knows how to do with documents of this type. There are four possible values: Editor, Viewer, Shell, and None. (Specifying None means the bundle is declaring information about a type, such as an icon, but doesn't know how to handle the documents.) TextEdit is a viewer for some documents, an editor for others.

- **LSTypeIsPackage.** This rarely used key specifies if the specified document type is to appear as a package. Few applications have this key, but TextEdit is one of them, because it bundles up RTF documents with images, so this key is set to `true` for rtfd files.

- **NSDocumentClass.** Cocoa apps can use this key to give the name of the NSDocument subclass that should be instantiated to create documents of this type. TextEdit doesn't use this one.

- **LSIsAppleDefaultForType.** This key declares that the application is the default for opening documents of a particular type. TextEdit names itself the default for txt, rtf, rtfd, and ttro documents.

Associated Files

An application's property list includes a few entries that tie the application to various kinds of files.

- **CFBundleHelpBookFolder.** This key points at the location of the application's Help files. This name is assumed to be a folder inside the lproj folders that contains the localized versions of the application. TextEdit's help folder is called TextEditHelp, naturally.

- **CFBundleHelpBookName.** This key contains the name of the Help book as it will appear in the Help viewer (see Figure 11-8). TextEdit's is called TextEdit Help. Most applications name their help books after themselves.

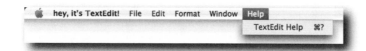

FIGURE 11-8: CFBundleHelpBookName shows up in the Help viewer.

- **CFBundleIconFile.** Here's where the developer gets to specify a custom icon for the bundle. This key contains the name of a file in the bundle's Resources folder that holds the icons. TextEdit keeps its icon in a file called Edit.icns file, but there's no rule about what the name of the file must be.

Charles Finley? Cold Fusion? Cruel Fish?

No doubt you noticed that most of the keys in Info.plist start with CF. So what's CF? It stands for *CoreFoundation*, which sounds like an Isaac Asimov novel but is actually the basic framework of code that OS X applications use. Anything that starts with CF is a constant, class, or other element defined by CoreFoundation. And by the way, the LS prefix is for the *LaunchServices* framework, which launches applications and associates documents with applications. You might already know that the NS prefix stands for NeXTStep, the system from NeXT, Inc. that was the original source of much of the foundation of Mac OS X.

Miscellaneous

This section lists a few other property list keys that don't fit neatly into any of the preceding categories.

- **NSAppleScriptEnabled.** This value indicates whether users can control the application via AppleScript. TextEdit supports AppleScript, as all good applications should, so this key is set to YES.

- **NSHumanReadableCopyright.** This key, beloved by lawyers everywhere, provides a textual copyright for the application. TextEdit sets this value to Copyright (©) 1995-2005, Apple Computer, Inc.

- **NSMainNibFile.** This key contains the name of the application's main nib file. Nib files are created by Interface Builder and furnish the blueprint for the application's user interface features, such as windows, menus, and controls. The main nib file is usually localized and kept in the lproj folder. TextEdit sets this key to Edit, because its main nib file is named Edit.nib.

- **NSPrincipalClass.** The application's main class, usually a subclass of NSApplication or NSApplication itself, it kept in this key. TextEdit has NSApplication in this key.

- **NSServices.** Applications use this key to tell Mac OS X about services they provide to other programs. These services are listed in the Application → Services menu of other applications. TextEdit contributes two services: New Window Containing Selection and Open Selected File.

Apple provides the Property List Editor application for examining and changing Info.plist files and other property lists. For a more structured look at some of the keys described in this section, check out the freeware application AppHack, written by Sveinbjorn Thordarson. You can download AppHack at http://sveinbjorn.vefsyn.is/apphack.

version.plist

The last item inside the application bundle is the version.plist file. This file contains version strings and other information for use by the Mac OS X Installer.

Localized Strings

As you saw in the previous section, applications can be customized for various countries and languages by including localized project (lproj) folders inside the application bundle. Files that are outside any of the lproj folders are considered nonlocalized: They can be used no matter what language the application is running in.

The much-discussed Info.plist file is in the main Contents folder of the bundle, outside the localized projects, but developers can still localize the contents of Info.plist by including a file named InfoPlist.strings in an lproj folder. Any strings defined in an InfoPlist.strings file take precedence over the values from the application's Info.plist file. That's how TextEdit can have TextEdit Help in English, AideTextEdit in French, and Ajuda Editor de Texto in Portuguese.

The Do-it-Yourself Bundle

You can play around with bundles by creating your own bundle in the Finder. There's no practical reason to do this—it's just for fun and experimentation. In practice, bundles are created by development systems like XCode as a part of the process of building software. You can create your own bundle using only the Finder. Here's how:

1. In the Finder, choose File → New Folder to get an ordinary, everyday folder.

2. Click the new folder to make sure it's selected (it might already be selected).

3. Now that the folder is selected, click its name to select the text for editing.

4. Type a new name for the folder. Use any name you want, as long as you put **.wdgt** at the end (Figure 11-9). Press Return when you're done editing.

5. The Finder will warn you that you're about to do something really interesting by adding .wdgt to the name. Click Add to let the Finder know you really want to do this.

FIGURE 11-9: You can create your own bundle in the Finder just by renaming a folder.

Instantly, your innocent folder takes on a new appearance: It now has the generic Dashboard widget icon. You've convinced the Finder that you have a widget bundle, just by renaming the file to add .wdgt to the end. Kind of shocking, isn't it? You can get the same effect (with a different icon) by using a different suffix, such as .app, instead of .wdgt. You can now do all the normal bundle things with your fake widget, including choosing Show Package Contents from the Action menu (Figure 11-10). Of course, when you do, you'll see that the bundle-ized folder is still empty.

FIGURE 11-10: It's not really a Dashboard widget, but it really is a package.

Now you can rename the bundle again, this time removing the magical .wdgt suffix. After another confirmation dialog from the Finder, your folder is once again a folder.

To make the widget back into a folder:

1. In the Finder, select the folder-that-thinks-it's-a-widget.

2. Choose File ➜ Get Info.

3. Make sure the disclosure triangle in the Name & Extension section is open (Figure 11-11).

4. Remove the .wdgt extension from the name and close the Info window.

5. When you get the Are You Sure? warning, click OK.

The widget is now a folder again.

FIGURE 11-11: Finder Info window.

Summary

Applications and other Mac OS X bundles are intricate, complex creatures. When you find out what lives inside an application, it creates a new appreciation for how well all this stuff works. With the knowledge and tools provided in this chapter, you can peek and poke around your applications all you want. Just be sure to back up before trying anything really crazy.

Preferences and Property Lists

Almost every Mac OS X application has a Preferences item in its
application menu. You've been there a thousand times, making sure
your wishes are obeyed as you change settings to get the application
to work the way you want.

Have you ever wondered where those settings go after you change them? Of
course you have, because you're the curious type. In this chapter, I'll discuss
the intricate system Mac OS X uses to keep track of your preferences. You'll
also find out how preferences are stored in domains, and I'll look at various
tools for viewing and changing preferences.

Property Lists for Preferences

Applications must remember preferences even after you quit and restart them,
so obviously, preferences have to be stored in files. Specifically, OS X apps use
property list files to keep track of their settings. You might remember property lists from the discussion way back in the previous chapter on information
property lists, or Info.plist files, that hold important details about applications
and other bundles. What do those files have to do with preferences? Very little, except that both take advantage of the general property list mechanism. A
property list is simply a well-structured file that uses XML to store its information. Preference files and information property lists are two different kinds
of property lists that perform two different functions.

Like all official XML files, property lists are defined by a formal *document
type definition* (DTD) that describes its features. Every property list includes
a link to its DTD. At the top of property list files, you see the following line:

```
<!DOCTYPE plist PUBLIC "-//Apple Computer//
DTD PLIST 1.0//EN"
"http://www.apple.com/DTDs/PropertyList-1.
0.dtd">
```

The last part of this declaration is a link to the actual DTD at www.apple.
com/DTDs/PropertyList-1.0.dtd. You can check it out if you're keen
to see exactly how a property list is structured.

Mac OS X provides a strict scheme for naming preferences files (although the scheme is a suggestion, rather than a requirement). Preferences filenames are constructed using the application's bundle identifier, which is stored in the Info.plist file. The bundle identifier uses a reverse domain name format (as discussed in Chapter 11) in which the filename starts with a unique domain name with the words reversed, such as *com.apple*, and then adds the application name and the suffix .plist at the end. So, for example, preferences are found in *com.apple.iChat.plist*, *com.ranchero.NetNewsWire.plist*, and *com.microsoft.Word.plist*. Other applications are naughty and fail to obey the reverse-domain naming system, but virtually all preferences files end with .plist.

Preferences property lists show up in two places: in a global folder at /Library/Preferences, and in a user-specific folder at ~/Library/Preferences. Preferences from files stored in the global folder are applied to all users of the application. The user-specific files keep track of specific settings for each user, naturally.

Applications can store preferences files in both places. The file in /Library/Preferences holds system-wide settings that are imposed on all users. The local version in the user's home directory has preferences that apply to that user only. If an application has preferences files in both folders, the user's settings override the global values, just as it should be. For example, Keynote stores preferences in both folders. In practice, most preferences files are in the user's home directory at ~/Library/Preferences rather than in the global folder.

Looking at Preferences Files

Now take a look at some real preferences files that have been running around in the wild. Don't worry—they don't bite.

Using TextEdit

Property list files such as preferences and Info.plist files are vital to your Mac's function. But deep down, they're basically just humble text files. That means you can see and edit them with text editors, such as TextEdit. I'll prove this by using TextEdit to take a look at the preferences file for the Preview application.

In the previous chapter, you opened Info.plist files directly with TextEdit, and everything was fine. But preferences property lists are a little bit different. Rather than storing their data as text in XML format, Mac OS X Tiger applications save preference files in a binary format. This is a new feature in Tiger—previous versions of OS X stored preferences as plain text.

Binary preferences files behave exactly the same as XML text files, except in three ways—two of them good, the third not as good:

- Mac OS X can read and write binary files more quickly than text files. I'm talking about small fractions of a second here, but faster is faster.

- Binary files take up less disk space than text files. Once again, the difference isn't enormous, but the more applications you have, the more space you save.

- You can read and edit text files directly with any text editor. Binary files must be converted to text format before you can read them (and mess around with them).

Obviously, the third point presents a small roadblock for folks like us who want access to preferences files. If you try to open a preferences file that's stored in binary format, you get something like what you see in Figure 12-1.

FIGURE 12-1: You can open binary preferences files in TextEdit, but you won't enjoy it.

Luckily, this isn't as bad as it might seem, because a command-line tool named `plutil` (property list utility) is there to save the day. You can use `plutil` to convert a binary-format preferences file to text format, making it suitable for a text editor. Here are all the steps for opening the Preview preferences as a text file:

1. Open Terminal and type the following two commands, pressing Return at the end of each line:

   cd ~/Library/Preferences/
   plutil –convert xml1 com.apple.Preview.plist

   If you get no response other than the command-line prompt again, that's a good thing; it means the command completed without any errors. If you got an error message, check your typing and try again. When this step is successfully completed, `plutil` has converted the preferences file to handy text.

2. Type the following command into Terminal:

   open –e ~/Library/Preferences/com.apple.Preview.plist

   Using the `open` command with the `–e` option opens the given file in TextEdit. It's the same as double-clicking TextEdit and opening the file there; but as long as we're already in Terminal, this is probably easier.

After you type the `open` command, you should see the preferences file in TextEdit, looking much more presentable, as shown in Figure 12-2.

FIGURE 12-2: Preview's preferences file is displayed in TextEdit.

You can run the `plutil` command whenever you want to use a text editor to see what's going on inside a preferences file. You don't even have to convert the files back to binary format when you're done: Applications have no trouble dealing with text-based preferences files. However, if you change anything in the application that causes it to modify the preferences file, it is converted back to binary format when it's written back to disk. If you ever open a preferences file and it looks like the gibberish shown in Figure 12-1, just use `plutil` to convert it to text.

Looking back again at Figure 12-2 and scanning down the slightly nerdy text, you can see various keys, all of which start with PV (Preview) including:

- PVGeneralSelectedTab, PVGeneralThumbnailSize and PVGeneralWindowBackgroundColor, which correspond to the settings of the same names in Preview's preferences dialog.

- A bunch of keys for Preview's Images preferences, such as PVImageOpeningMode, PVImageDefaultImageSizing, and PVImagePrintingCenterImage.

Not every preference key is connected to a control for changing it in the user interface. That's the fun of finding and hacking hidden preferences. Later in this chapter, you get into changing things that live inside property lists.

Using Property List Editor

When you take a look at a property list in TextEdit, you might say to yourself, "There must be a better way." And as you probably know, there is: the Property List Editor application that ships as part of Apple's free Xcode Tools.

Note If you don't have a copy of Apple's Xcode Tools, drop whatever you're doing (even if what you're doing is reading this book) and go to `developer.apple.com`, where you can register as an Apple developer for free and download the tools (also for free). Or, just find your Tiger DVD—the Xcode Tools are right there on the disk.

Property List Editor provides a more structured way of looking at preferences and other property list files. Property List Editor is the default application for property lists: When you double-click one, it opens in Property List Editor whether the file is XML or binary format.

File Conversion Details

If a file is already in text format, and you inadvertently ask `plutil` to convert it to text, nothing happens (which is good). The `plutil` command just humors you and runs without a problem, and the file stays in text format, just as you want it.

If you want to look at a whole bunch of preferences files, you don't have to bother converting them one at a time. With a magical single line typed into Terminal, you can change all your preferences files (and other property lists) to text format. Here's the command:

```
find ~ -name "*.plist" -exec plutil –convert xml1 {} \; -print
```

This command finds all property list files in your home directory and converts them to text format, listing the names of the files as it goes along. (If you don't want to see the list of files as they're processed, leave off the "`; -print`" at the end of the line.) After you run this command, you can use your favorite text editor to examine and modify the files. For best results, it's a good idea to quit other applications before you use this script, so as not to disrupt any preferences-communing that applications might be doing. And remember that an application's preferences file turns back into binary format the next time it's written out to disk, so you might have to run this script multiple times. If you're going to be doing that a lot, you could consider turning the command it into an AppleScript application. To do that, enter a one-line AppleScript command that reads like this:

```
do shell script "find ~ -name \"*.plist\" -exec plutil –convert xml1 {}
\\; -print"
```

Then save the script as an application. Whenever you want to reconvert all property lists to text, just run the application.

One Size Fits All

You used TextEdit to examine the property list, but you don't have to. It's just a text file, and you can use any text editor you want, as long as it creates plain text files. You're not limited to Aqua editors like TextEdit, BBEdit, and TextWrangler. Of course, if you prefer, fire up your favorite command-line editor, such as vi, pico, or emacs, and edit away.

Now take a look at the Preview preferences file, this time in Property List Editor (Figure 12-3).

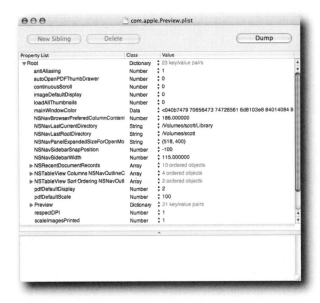

FIGURE 12-3: Preview's preferences file in Property List Editor.
You don't have to convert the file to text before opening it.

Property List Editor provides pretty much the same information as TextEdit, but it's a lot easier to look at. You don't have to scan all those keys inside angle brackets—instead, the keys, classes, and values are arranged neatly in columns. You can use the disclosure triangles to show and hide details of particular nodes.

To edit the name or value of a key in Property List Editor, double-click to select it, then type the new value. For Boolean values, you choose Yes or No from a pop-up menu. You can't specify the values of Dictionary and Array keys directly. Their values are the keys they contain. Class names are listed in a pop-up menu. To change a class, just click its name and pick the new one from the list.

If you need to see the raw text of a property list instead of the pretty structure provided by Property List Editor, click the Dump button at the upper right. Property List Editor displays a text version of the file in the lower pane of the window, as demonstrated in Figure 12-4. The dumped text doesn't update as you edit the file. If you make changes, you have to click Dump again to update the text.

FIGURE 12-4: Use the Dump button to get a textual representation of the file.

You can't edit the text in the Dump pane, but you can select and copy it. So that's better than nothing.

TextEdit versus Property List Editor

It's the battle of the century! Bigger than Alien vs. Predator! Which tool should you use for editing preferences files: TextEdit or Property List Editor? Take a look at some of the distinctions between these tools. Here are the advantages of using Property List Editor:

- Property List Editor is a specialized tool made for this job. It knows the particular structure of property lists and presents the information in a format that's more readable and better organized.

- It helps you avoid errors because you don't have to type (or even know) the syntax of keys, although you can still screw up by misspelling a key or giving it the wrong value.

- You can use disclosure triangles to hide and show parts of the property list structure, focusing on just the areas you want to see. Or, if you want to see everything at once, you can Option-click a triangle to see all the keys in its hierarchy. Option-click again to completely close the hierarchy.

- The keys are presented in alphabetical order, no matter how they're listed in the file itself. This can sometimes make it easier to find keys, but it can also destroy any logical grouping of keys in the file.

- It reads and understands both text and binary format files. You don't have to bother converting files to XML before you can edit them.

- It's easier to open files in Property List Editor. Because it's the default application for property lists, all you have to do is double-click a file to see it in Property List Editor.

TextEdit has some advantages over Property List Editor:

- TextEdit has a Find command that helps you quickly locate a value. Property List Editor doesn't have one.

- TextEdit shows you the raw truth of what's in the file. If the file's creator meticulously laid out its contents in a logical order, you'll see that order. By comparison, Property List Editor presents a structured, alphabetized version of the file's contents, rather than the actual contents. Even the Dump button provides a re-creation of what's in the file rather than the actual text.

- TextEdit is available on every computer running Mac OS X. Property List Editor is only there if you (or the person whose computer you're using) has installed Developer Tools.

From this comparison, it's clear why most people prefer Property List Editor most of the time for editing property lists. Use TextEdit if you need to search the file, you want to see and touch the file's actual contents, or you like living on the edge.

Defaults and Domains

To change preferences settings in Mac OS X, you don't have to edit preferences files directly. The `defaults` command gives you access to preferences settings from Terminal. You can use the `defaults` command to perform all sorts of fun tasks with preferences, including reading and changing keys, adding keys, and searching for values.

When you use the defaults command, you specify a *domain*, which lets you choose to see the preferences of a particular application or the system. An application's domain is the name of its bundle identifier, such as *com.apple.iTunes* or *com.omnigroup.OmniOutliner*. These correspond to the application's plist file. There's also a global preferences domain, which lists preferences stored in /Library/Preferences/.GlobalPreferences.plist and ~/Library/Preferences/.GlobalPreferences.plist.

You can do a bunch of cool stuff with the `defaults` command. Here's a summary of its options:

```
defaults read
```

This command, which you'll probably want to try once and never again (because of the copious output) lists all the defaults (preferences) defined by all domains. It's an impressive list.

```
defaults read <domain>
```

Example: `defaults read com.apple.iCal`

Use this one to see all the defaults for a given application. You can also see all the system defaults by using `defaults read –globalDomain` or `defaults read –g`, as shown in Figure 12-5.

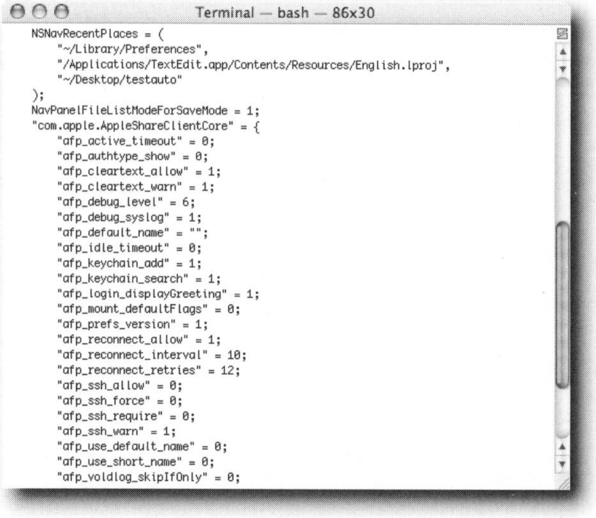

FIGURE 12-5: Global settings displayed by the defaults command.

```
defaults read <domain> <key>
```

Example: `defaults read com.ranchero.NetNewsWire notepadOpenAtStartup`

This command lets you choose a single setting to see what its value is.

```
defaults read-type <domain> <key>
```

Example: `defaults read-type com.apple.iChat VCDefaultCamera`

Every property list entry has a data type, such as string or integer. You can use the `read-type` command on the rare occasion when you know a setting's key, but not its type.

```
defaults write <domain> <plist>
```

Example: `defaults write com.nobody.someapp '{hockeyPuckSize = (12, 12); locations = (45, 34, 87, 56); };'`

This command grants you the immense power to replace an entire `defaults` domain—remember, that's usually a property list file—with new values. Here's a Special Usage Tip: Never use this command, ever. It's a super-simple way to completely destroy a preferences file without any recourse. If you really want to play around with this command, make sure you back up your preferences file first. Even then, please remember the Special Usage Tip.

```
defaults write <domain> <key> <value>
```

Example: `defaults write com.apple.terminal Columns 60`

This is the primary command to use for setting a single key in an application. Be sure you type the name of the key carefully. If you misspell the name of the key, the `defaults` command dutifully saves the new key just as you typed it, and you'll have two separate keys: the original one, unchanged, and a new one, with a typo, that doesn't do anything.

Note

Instead of the domain name, you can use –app followed by the name of the application. So, in the previous example, you could also type **defaults write –app terminal Columns 60**.

Value Types

When you put a value in a `defaults write` command, you can optionally specify the value's type, like this:

```
defaults write com.papercar.diskdoctor NewUsers -integer 3
```

The valid basic types you can specify are the following:

```
-string <stringValue>    // Text value
-data <hexDigits>        // Raw hexadecimal digits
-integer <integerValue>  // Whole number
-float <floatValue>      // Real number
-bool <true | false | yes | no>  // Boolean value (true/false)
-date <dateValue>        // Calendar date
```

In addition to these, there are two structured types: `array` and `dictionary`.

```
-array <value1> <value2> ...
    // A collection of values whose order is unimportant
-dict <key1> <value1> <key2> <value2> ...
    // A collection of values, each with an identifying key
```

When you write these types, the type specifier is required. Otherwise, `defaults` isn't quite sure what you're trying to do. Here is an example of what these data types look like:

```
defaults write com.mysoft.myapp testpref -array 10 18 85
```

This creates this preference in the domain: `testpref = (10, 18, 85);`

Here's another example:

```
defaults write com.mysoft.myapp somepref -dict name Fred city Boston hair brown
```

This creates this preference: `somepref = {city = Boston; hair = brown; name = Fred; };`

If you use `defaults write` with a setting that already exists, you wipe out the previous setting and replace it with the new value. That might not be what you want to do, especially with arrays and dictionaries. To allow you to modify an existing array or dictionary, defaults provides the `-array-add` and `-dict-add` values. Use these to add new values to arrays and dictionaries without disturbing the old ones. With `-dict-add`, you can replace a single value in the dictionary and leave the other ones alone. For example, to change the dictionary you just specified, use this command:

```
defaults write com.mysoft.myapp somepref -dict-add city Denver
```

This command changes the setting to:

```
somepref = {city = Denver; hair = brown; name = Fred; };  .
```

And just like that, we've moved Fred to Denver. Note that even though the option is named `-dict-add`, you can use it to replace a value, not just add one.

```
defaults rename <domain> <old_key> <new_key>
```

Example: `defaults rename com.tmbg.minkcar fineSong greatSong`

Use this command to rename a key in the domain, should you ever want to do that.

```
defaults delete <domain>
```

Example: `defaults delete com.apple.TextEdit`

As you might guess, this command removes all they keys in the given domain. This one is not as unlikely as it might seem. If you have a damaged preferences file, this is the equivalent to throwing it out and starting again.

```
defaults delete <domain> <key>
```

Example: `defaults delete com.mycompany.myapp MisspelledKey`

Use this command to remove an unwanted key from the defaults database. This is especially useful if you accidentally typed the wrong name for a key and you want to get rid of it neatly.

```
defaults domains
```

If you're interested in exploring `defaults`, but you're not sure which domains exist for you to play with, use this command to get a list of all the available domains. Figure 12-6 shows a typical list of domains on a relatively fresh installation of Mac OS X Tiger.

```
defaults find <word>
```

Example: `defaults find 'layer'`

FIGURE 12-6: Result of the defaults domains command.

This powerful option is handy for finding a key or value by name, even if you don't know which domain it's in or anything else about it. Use this command to track down an elusive key that you know you saw late one night, but you can't remember exactly where. Figure 12-7 gives an example of how this works.

```
defaults help
```

As with most other commands, you can type `man defaults` to get a relatively thorough description of how defaults works. If you want a quick summary of how to use the `defaults` command, instead of a thorough description, use `defaults help`.

When Changes Take Effect

When you use `defaults` to change a setting, you probably won't see the changed behavior right away. Generally, you have to quit the application and restart it to make the change appear. For system applications like the Dock, the easiest way to make this happen is with the command line, like this:

```
killall Dock
```

(Be sure to spell Dock with an uppercase D. The killall command is very picky about case.) The Dock process also controls Exposé and Dashboard, so you can use killall Dock to make your changes to those features appear.

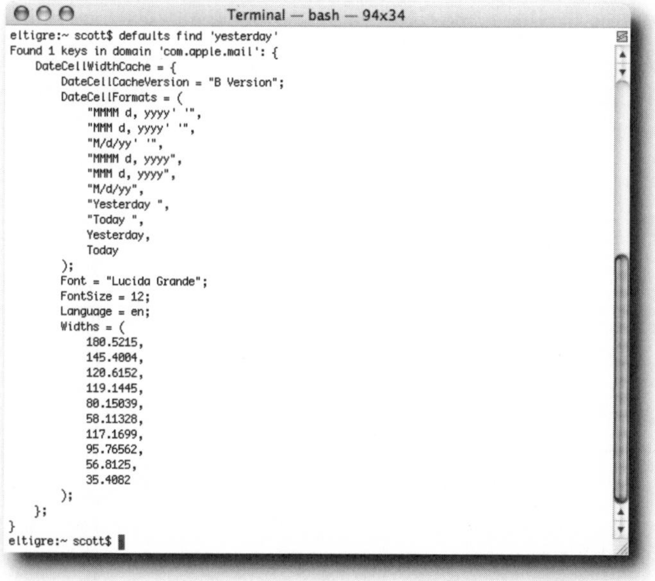

```
eltigre:~ scott$ defaults find 'yesterday'
Found 1 keys in domain 'com.apple.mail': {
    DateCellWidthCache = {
        DateCellCacheVersion = "B Version";
        DateCellFormats = (
            "MMMM d, yyyy' '",
            "MMM d, yyyy' '",
            "M/d/yy' '",
            "MMMM d, yyyy",
            "MMM d, yyyy",
            "M/d/yy",
            "Yesterday ",
            "Today ",
            Yesterday,
            Today
        );
        Font = "Lucida Grande";
        FontSize = 12;
        Language = en;
        Widths = (
            180.5215,
            145.4004,
            120.6152,
            119.1445,
            80.15039,
            58.11328,
            117.1699,
            95.76562,
            56.8125,
            35.4082
        );
    };
}
eltigre:~ scott$
```

FIGURE 12-7: Finding the word "yesterday" with the defaults find command.

In some cases, you might have to log out or even restart your Mac to see the change.

If you use a text editor or Property List Editor to modify the preferences file directly, make sure you quit the application first, to avoid confusing it. When you're done messing around, run the application and you should see the results of your handiwork.

Changing Preferences Three Different Ways

Congratulations! You now know three distinct techniques for viewing and changing preferences: a text editor, the specialized tool Property List Editor, and the defaults command-line tool. So which one should you use?

If you're comfortable with Terminal and the command line, the defaults command is probably the quickest and easiest way to change a setting. But you have to remember the syntax or defaults will yell at you, and nothing good will happen. Also, defaults has its limits: You can't use it to easily change a nested structured value, such as an array of dictionaries.

Going beyond Property List Editor

If you find yourself spending a lot of time with property lists, and you want to step it up to the next level, take a look at Brian Webster's PlistEdit Pro utility (`http://homepage.mac.com/bwebster/plisteditpro.html`, $25 license, free trial). See Figure 12-8 for a sample screen.

PlistEdit Pro goes beyond Apple's free tool with a bunch of handy additions, including a Find and Replace command, the capability to edit in both the structured view and the text view, full AppleScript support, and many other terrific features.

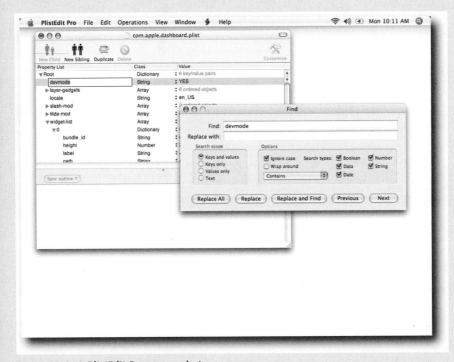

FIGURE 12-8: A PlistEdit Pro screen shot.

Property List Editor is a safer, more comfortable environment for seeing and editing preferences. It's hard to make a mistake that will wreck your preferences file, and you get easy access to every value, even those that are nested deep inside complex webs of arrays and dictionaries.

TextEdit provides even more direct access to your preferences file, without the safety net of Property List Editor. Use TextEdit or another editor if you want to see what's actually stored in the file.

When you use an editor to perform surgery on a preferences file, you might find that you don't have the necessary file system permissions to change the file. In that case, you have to use an editor that temporarily changes permissions for you, such as TextWrangler or BBEdit, or you have to deal with the permissions problem manually. The `defaults` command is more convenient: It avoids the file permissions problem because you're not editing a file directly.

Summary

Hacking application and system preferences is a great way to find out things about your Mac that you didn't know before and to get it to perform new tricks. As long as you're careful about what you do with your preferences files (always back them up before you start stabbing at them), you can have endless fun adventures with your settings.

Automator

Mac OS X Tiger is one of the most highly programmable operating systems in the world. Although most of OS X is proprietary, Apple defines a vast set of application programming interfaces and a superb set of developer tools for writing your own programs.

But Macintosh computers are used by all sorts of people, not just programmers. Only a relatively small percentage of Apple's users are prepared to write software in Cocoa or Carbon, using programming languages like Objective-C and C++.

Apple believes that savvy users should be able to automate their Macs, even if they're not interested in learning to program in C. So Apple created Automator, new in Mac OS X Tiger, to help users lash together automated ways to repeat common tasks. Automator joins AppleScript, an Apple technology that has been around since the 1980s and is a popular method for making your Mac life easier.

This chapter introduces Automator and whets your appetite about how you might use it to streamline and customize your Mac.

AppleScript and Automator: Something Old, Something New

Before you are introduced to Automator, let's talk a bit about AppleScript, Apple's venerable tool for user programming. Apple-Script is a scripting language that's used to control applications and other parts of Mac OS X. AppleScript looks a lot like English. For example, here's a bit of script that works with Apple's Mail application:

```
on getMessageCountsForMailboxes(theMailboxes)
    tell application "Mail"
        repeat with eachMailbox in theMailboxes
            set mailboxName to name of eachMailbox
            try
                set messageCount to (count of
                (messages of eachMailbox))as string
                set unreadCount to unread count of ¬
                eachMailbox as string
                on error errText number errNum
                    if errNum is equal to -1712 then
                        set messageCount to "Too many"
                        set unreadCount to "Too many"
                    end if
            end try
            my addToOutput(mailboxName,messageCount ¬
            & "(" & unreadCount & " unread)")
        end repeat
    end tell
end getMessageCountsForMailboxes
```

Although AppleScript programs look easy to read and are nicely formatted by the Script Editor (as shown in the preceding code), don't allow yourself to be seduced: AppleScript is a real programming language, with real syntax rules that can be unforgiving if you don't follow them exactly. AppleScript unquestionably is more inviting than conventional languages like C and Objective-C, but it still presents a barrier to many users, who can run AppleScripts but not write or modify them.

But wait—there's something new! Automator, a new feature freshly unwrapped for Mac OS X Tiger, is designed to fill the gap for those clever folks who can't or don't want to script but still want to make repeated tasks easier to perform. Automator lets users streamline jobs by stringing together individual actions, then saving and reusing the set of actions. Using Automator involves no scripting or programming. Figure 13-1 shows what you see when you run the Automator application and start putting steps together.

Automator creates a high level of automation that didn't exist before Tiger. I'll spend the rest of this chapter discussing Automator and its machinations.

Automator Is Not AppleScript

When Apple introduced Automator in 2004, there was speculation and confusion that Automator was nothing but a higher-level interface on AppleScript. It's easy to see how that false assumption could arise, because both technologies are used to automate work. But it's not true. Automator provides a scripting-free way to perform repetitive tasks. Those tasks can be defined in AppleScript, Cocoa, or bits of both; but in any case, Automator is not just a pretty non-programming face on AppleScript.

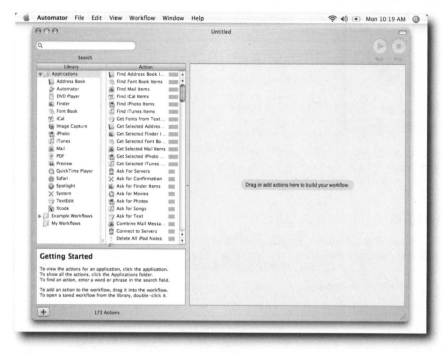

FIGURE **13-1:** Automator requires no programming.

Mixed Automation

Mac OS X Tiger provides many tools for automating tasks: AppleScript, Automator, and conventional applications are just the most popular. There are also platform-independent scripting languages, such as JavaScript, Perl, Python, and Ruby, all of which are standard parts of Mac OS X Tiger. One of the coolest things in OS X is the way you can mix and match scripting and programming tools as necessary. Bits of code from different languages and technologies can be combined in various ways to create the final result, with each tool specializing in what it does best.

Automator

Apple describes Automator as acting "like a robot inside your computer." The Automator icon shows that robot (see Figure 13-2), who somewhat resembles Marvin the paranoid android from *The Hitchhiker's Guide to the Galaxy*. Note also that the robot is carrying a tube that looks alarmingly like a rocket launcher. But don't worry: The tube is meant to simulate the way information flows through Automator, not to direct any weapons.

FIGURE 13-2: Automator
icon in Tiger.

Actions

When you run the Automator application, what you see looks a lot like Figure 13-3. On the
left are two columns, Library and Action. The Library column is mostly a list of applications
you have installed on your Mac. The Action column is a list of individual activities you can
string together in Automator.

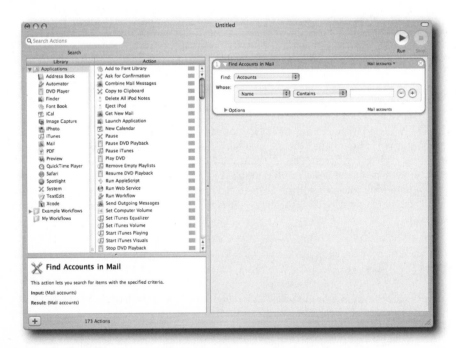

FIGURE 13-3: Automator lists applications and actions you can use.

When you start Automator, the Applications folder is selected in the Library column, which means that all actions from all applications are displayed in the Action column. To get an idea of what an Action can do, click one of them. When you click Find iCal Items, the description area in the Automator window provides some information about the action, as shown in Figure 13-4.

FIGURE 13-4: Description for Find iCal Items action.

The description includes a note saying that the action's result is a value of type iCal items. Every action defines one output (the result), and (optionally) one input. Take a look at another: If you want to play along at home, click Combine Mail Messages and check out its description (Figure 13-5).

This time, the action's description includes both an input and a result. You make things happen in Automator by combining actions together into sequences called *workflows*. You add an action to a workflow by dragging it to the workflow area on the right side of the screen. When you add an action, it displays a user interface panel in which you can specify exactly what you want the action to do. For an example, take a look at Figure 13-6, which shows what happens when you add an Ask For Finder Items action to the workflow.

FIGURE 13-5: Description for Combine Mail Messages action.

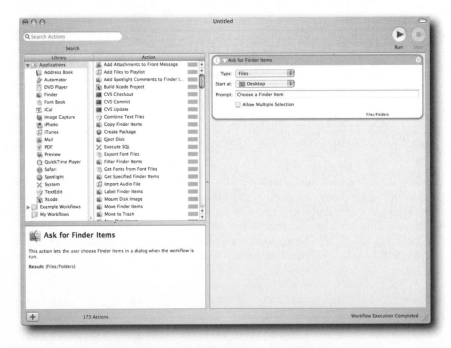

FIGURE 13-6: Ask For Finder Items action displayed in workflow area.

Ask for Finder Items puts up a dialog and lets the user pick one or more files that are then passed on to the next action. When you create the workflow, Ask For Finder Items lets you decide the type of items to ask for (files, folders, or either), which folder the dialog should display when it first appears (any folder you want), what text you want to use for a prompt, and whether to allow the user to pick more than one item.

Tiger includes more than 150 actions. They're provided by the applications that come with Tiger and by the system itself. To see only the actions that are associated with a particular application—maybe you're such a music fiend that you care only about iTunes and nothing else—click that application in the Library column. If you're interested in a particular kind of action, you can search for it by typing in the Search field in the toolbar.

Here are a few more examples of interesting and wacky Automator actions you might want to try:

- **Run Web Service.** This action lets the user interact with a Web service using a technology called XML-RPC SOAP, which despite all the scary big letters is simply a way to exchange information with a remote computer via the Web. You can use this action to access all sorts of cool information on the Web, including weather, stock quotes, and traffic information.

- **Pause.** Use this action when you're building a workflow to give your user a chance to rest a bit. You can specify how many seconds the pause should last.

- **Run AppleScript.** This handy action provides a bridge between any workflow and any AppleScript program. Use it to type in and run any AppleScript.

- **Run Shell Script.** As if Run AppleScript isn't powerful enough, you can also call Run Shell Script to execute any shell command. This command gives you access to the vast set of Unix commands in Mac OS X. The result of the action is the standard output of the command.

- **View Results.** When you're piecing together your workflow, you inevitably have times when you can't figure out why something isn't working as you expected. When that happens, you can use the View Results action as a debugging tool. By inserting a View Results action between two other actions, you can see what's being passed along in the workflow. View Results doesn't change anything it handles, but it shows you the value in order to help you figure out exactly what's going wrong and where.

- **Find Finder Items.** This action searches your disk for files that match your specifications. This is one of a whole set of Find actions that use Tiger's Spotlight technology to search for stuff quickly. Several other applications provide similar actions, including Find iTunes Items, Find iCal Items, and Find Mail Items. A generic Spotlight action also lets you specify an actual Spotlight search and do something with the result.

- **Ask for Songs.** This iTunes action shows the power Automator has to reach inside applications and let you use key parts of them in your workflow. The Ask for Songs action shows the user a dialog (Figure 13-7) that lists all iTunes songs and playlists and lets the user pick one or more songs. There's even a search field to help find specific tracks and a Play button to preview a selection. With this action, you can build a workflow that asks the user for songs, builds a playlist, and then plays the playlist in iTunes. These are all pretty good tricks to pull off without any programming.

FIGURE 13-7: When a workflow runs the Ask for Songs action, the user gets to choose iTunes playlists and songs from a dialog.

These are just a few of the more interesting actions that come with Mac OS X Tiger. You can find a bunch more when you explore Automator.

Note   Actions themselves are bundles stored in the /System/Library/Automator folder.

Workflows

You use Automator to build workflows by dragging actions from the Action column on the left side of the screen to the workflow area on the right. When you build a workflow, data flows from one action to the next. Apple says that Automator was inspired by Unix tools and their capability to use the output of one tool as the input to the next, like this:

```
% ls Documents/ | grep ".doc"
```

This command lists the files in the Documents/folder and then passes the output to another command that searches and lists files whose names contain ".doc". In this example, the output of the `ls` command is sent as input to the `grep` command via a *pipe*, represented in shell script by the vertical bar symbol. (Now you know that the object the robot in Automator's icon is holding is a pipe. In fact, an early version of the program was called Pipeline.)

In an Automator workflow, you can think of the result (or output) of one action being piped to the next action as its input.

To demonstrate how workflows are built and some of the handy features of Automator, you can put together a simple workflow that lets the user create a new iTunes playlist without directly using iTunes. Here are the steps:

1. Click that funky robot icon to start Automator.

2. In the Library column, click iTunes to see the iTunes actions.

3. Drag the Ask for Songs action and drop it in the workflow area on the right. Your Automator window should look like Figure 13-8.

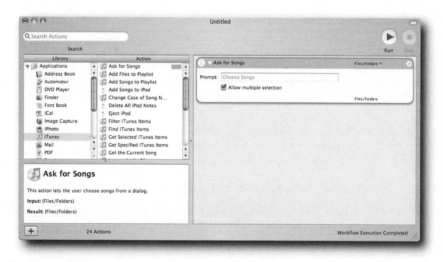

FIGURE 13-8: New workflow with the Ask for Songs action.

Notice a few interesting things here including the following:

- On its right side, the action shows the type of its input (Files/Folders) and result (Files/Folders).

- The Ask for Songs action has a field for you to fill in a parameter, a prompt string that the Workflow will use when it runs.

- There's a check box to allow or prevent the user from picking more than one song.

Notice also that as soon as you drop the Ask for Songs action, the items in the Action column rearranged themselves. As you add actions to the workflow, Automator notes the result type of the last action you added and puts actions with compatible input types at the top of the list.

4. Back in the Action column, drag Add Files to Playlist to the workflow area and drop it under the previous action. As an alternative to dragging, you can add an action to the end of a workflow by double-clicking it.

5. Click the New playlist Named: radio button and type in a name for your practice playlist. For best results, don't use the name of a playlist you already have in iTunes. If you can't think of a name to use, try typing **Can't think of a name**.

6. Now try running the workflow to see what happens. Click the big arrow above the Run button in the upper-right corner.

You should see a dialog appear that lets you choose songs. Go ahead and pick several, using the Shift key to add to your selection. When you're done, click OK. The workflow continues on and creates your playlist as specified. To check the results, switch to iTunes and look in the Source list. You should see your newly created playlist there among the others. It worked!

Let's put together another workflow and check out a few more Automator features. This time, you make a workflow that takes any files that are selected in the Finder, copies them into a particular folder, and then opens the files in TextEdit.

1. In Automator, choose File ➔ New to create a new workflow to play with.

2. In the Library column, choose Finder. Check out the many groovy Finder-directed actions, such as Filter Finder Items and New Folder. You're not going to use those specific items now, but they're groovy anyway.

3. Grab the Get Selected Finder Items action and drag it over to the workflow area. This action gets the files and folders that are selected in the Finder at the time the workflow runs and returns a result that lists those items.

4. Add a Copy Finder Items action to the workflow, but instead of dragging and dropping, double-click the item in the Action column. This shortcut adds the action to the end of the workflow.

5. Click the To: pop-up in the Copy Finder Items panel to set the destination for the copied files. You can use the Other menu item at the bottom to create a new folder to hold the copies.

6. Finish the workflow by opening the freshly copied items in TextEdit. For this, you need an Open Finder Items action, so grab one from the Action column and drop it into the workflow area (or just double-click it).

7. Click the Open With: pop-up and choose TextEdit. This forces the files to be opened with TextEdit, which works as long as they're among the many types that TextEdit understands. The workflow should now look like Figure 13-9.

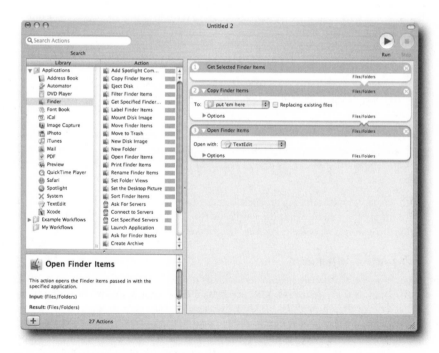

FIGURE 13-9: The three-step workflow is now complete.

Your workflow is all done, so try it out. Go to the Finder and select three or four files of various kinds. (Don't worry right now whether TextEdit can open them all—trust me.) Go back to Automator and click the Run button. Then sit back and watch the robot do its thing. As each action runs in turn, it sports a spinning progress indicator, which is replaced by a stylish green checkmark when it finishes. When the last action runs, TextEdit becomes active and opens the files you selected in the Finder. If you selected any file types that TextEdit chokes on, such as applications or folders, TextEdit puts up an alert saying the file type isn't supported. TextEdit opens all files it groks and displays them for you. The robot is rolling now.

View Results

Because everything is working perfectly, let's risk its stability by changing it. In the Library column, click Automator. This reveals several interesting actions that don't fit with any other application, including Run Shell Script, Run AppleScript, and Wait For User Action. You're going to use the View Results action. Drag the View Results action to the workflow area. As you drag it, the steps under it slide away to make room. Drop it right after Step 1, so that it becomes the new Step 2. Now you have a four-step workflow: Get Selected Finder Items, View Results, Copy Finder Items, and Open Finder Items.

View Results simply displays the result from the previous action—it doesn't serve any other purpose. View Results is used as a debugging step, a sanity check that allows you to see a value at the time the workflow runs. If you're a programmer, it's a lot like `printf` or `NSLog`. To see how it works, select some Finder items and then run the workflow again. Figure 13-10 shows what happened when I did that on my computer.

The text in the View Results panel describes the items that were selected in the folder when you ran the workflow. If you're familiar with AppleScript, you probably recognize the View Results text as an AppleScript object. Automator workflows use this syntax for passing results from one action to the next.

Adding the View Results action doesn't change anything functional—it just gives us humans more information about what the workflow is doing. You can add any number of View Results actions to a workflow to help you understand and debug it.

Show Action When Run

Because you're a curious person, you probably noticed that some actions, such as Copy Finder Items and Open Finder Items, have an item labeled Options at the bottom of their panels. What's the deal with that? To find out, go to the Open Finder Items panel (the last step in the workflow) and click the disclosure triangle next to Options. This reveals the semisecret, super-useful Show Action When Run check box. Show Action When Run is kind of inscrutable—a better name for this check box might be Ask User At Runtime. When the user runs the workflow, if this box is checked, it will stop at this step and ask the user for input.

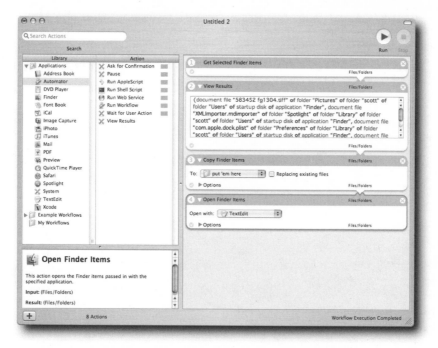

FIGURE 13-10: View Results shows which Finder items were selected.

The best way to explain this feature is by demonstration. In the Open Finder Items panel, click Show Action When Run to turn on the check box. Then click Run to run the workflow. This time, instead of going fully automatic, the workflow stops when it gets to the last step and presents a dialog to the user (Figure 13-11).

When you turn on Show Action When Run, the selection you make when creating the workflow (in this case, choosing TextEdit as the application for opening the files) is just a default. Every time the workflow runs, the user can pick the application to use for opening the files. Clearly, this Show Action When Run thing is pretty powerful. Let's try it again, this time on the Copy Finder Items action.

Reveal the options for Copy Finder Items and you see a slightly more complicated set of controls. Copy Finder Items lets you specify two different values: whether to replace existing files and where to put the copies. The Show Action When Run setting lets you specify whether the user should get to change one or both of those values. For example, you can allow the user to choose whether to replace existing files, but not where the copies go.

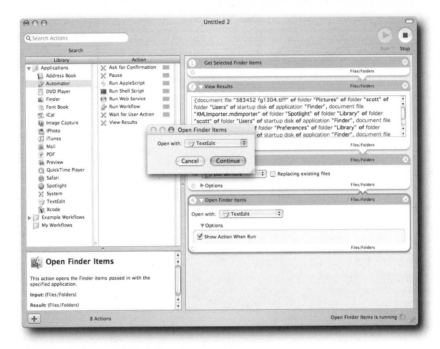

FIGURE 13-11: Show Action When Run option stops the action and waits for user input.

The Show Action When Run option greatly amplifies the usefulness of many actions, espe-cially the set of *Get Specified* actions: Get Specified Mail Items, Get Specified Address Book Items, Get Specified iCal Items, and so on. By turning on Show Action When Run for these actions, you can effectively allow the user to pick from most of the data types defined by Mac OS X applications.

Saving Workflows

Building and running workflows in Automator is a fun geeky pastime, but workflows wouldn't be much good if they couldn't escape from Automator after they're debugged, polished, and finished. You can save a workflow in three formats: as an application, plug-in, or workflow file.

- Save as an application if you want to let other people run the workflow just by double-clicking it.

Note

When you save a workflow as an application, you (or anybody else) can still open the application in Automator and see or change any details. Looking at workflows created by other people is a great way to learn more about Automator.

- Use the workflow file format to provide a series of steps that can be easily customized or used from within other workflows (with the Run Workflow action), but can't be double-clicked to run (double-clicking a workflow file opens the file in Automator).

- Mac OS X defines several places that host workflows in special ways. You can get your workflow into these exclusive locations by using Save As Plug-In. When you save as a plug-in, you can make your workflow show up in various strange and wonderful ways:

    - In the Finder, your workflow can appear as a contextual menu item that shows up whenever you click a file or folder.

    - Your workflow can be a Folder Action, which runs whenever an interesting event happens to a given folder.

    - In iCal, your workflow can do its work when an event's alarm is triggered.

    - Your workflow can be triggered in the Image Capture application when a camera is connected.

    - You can add your workflow to the PDF menu that appears in every application's Print dialog.

    - Your workflow can show up in the bottom section of the system-wide Scripts menu, which is primarily used for listing AppleScripts.

Note

Workflow plug-ins are simply standard workflow files that are saved in specific, well-defined folders. For the Finder, iCal, Image Capture, and Folder Actions, the workflows are saved in the user's Library/Workflows/Applications/ folder. For the PDF menu, the magic directory is the user's Library/PDF Services/ folder. The Scripts menu keeps its workflows in the same places as its AppleScripts, which are the user's Library/Scripts/ folder and the global /Library/Scripts/ directory.

Whenever you run an application or plug-in that started life as a workflow, the right side of the menu bar displays the name of the current action, a progress spinner, and a teeny tiny stop sign you can click if you want to make the workflow stop running (see Figure 13-12).

FIGURE **13-12: The menu bar displays workflow progress and a Stop button.**

Type Matching and Conversion

When you add an action to a workflow, the action panel displays its input and result types. The result-type information is designed to help you figure out which actions you can use next in the workflow. Because the result of one action is fed to the next, the type of data has to be compatible in order for it to flow along.

Types of data passed from one action to the next are often the same, but they don't have to be identical in order for the data to flow to the next step. If a result type doesn't match the input type of the next action, Automator looks for a special action called a *conversion action* to change the value from one type to another. If there's a conversion action available, Automator happily and invisibly converts the data from one type to the other at runtime. Most of these conversions are relatively esoteric and occur between types that are already quite similar, such as from an iTunes object to an alias of that object.

Note

Conversion actions don't appear in the Action column in Automator windows. They're invoked automatically as needed when workflows run. Although conversion actions are shy, here's how you can get a list of them: Go to the Finder, open the folder /System/Library/Automator, switch to list view, click the Kind column, and scroll until you see Conversion Action in the Kind column.

If you have two actions with incompatible types next to each other in your workflow, and no conversion action is available, the type names turn red to show you that the data won't flow from one to the next.

Automator Tips and Tricks

Automator provides a bunch of handy tweaks you can use to fine-tune the way your workflows look and behave. Here are some tips on what they are and how they work:

- After you add actions to the workflow area, you can mess around with their order just by dragging them around. As you drag, the other actions move aside to make room.

- If your dragging skills are subpar, you can rearrange actions by clicking the step number that appears at the start of every action. That click summons a pop-up menu that lets you choose a new location for the step.

- That same pop-up menu contains a Disable item that effectively turns the action off without removing it from the workflow. There's a corresponding Enable item to get the action working again.

- To get rid of an action step completely, use the Delete item that appears in the step's pop-up menu. If you're more of a keyboard person, you can select the step and press Delete.

- This one is kind of cool: You don't have to stick with the standard names of actions when you incorporate them into your workflow. Just choose Rename from the step's pop-up menu, and you can call it anything you like. This is especially important (and impressive) for steps that show windows or dialogs to the user. Automator uses the name of the step as the title for the window. You can see an example in Figure 13-13 (note the window name).

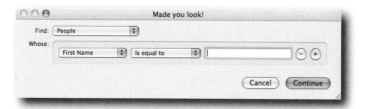

FIGURE 13-13: Custom step names appear as window titles.

- Life does not always flow smoothly. Sometimes you might find it convenient to have an action that doesn't bother using the result from the action before it. To disconnect one action's result from the following action's input, look at the input type (such as Files/ Folders or URLs) that appears at the top-right of the step panel, where two adjacent steps usually point at each other to show their solidarity. If the input type has a triangle on it, you can click to show a pop-up menu. Choose Ignore Results From Previous Action to make the two steps independent and stop the result from flowing through. For example, you might activate this option if you have an Ask For Confirmation step, which is typically used to present a dialog box to the user but also passes its input through to its output. When you use this, you usually won't be interested in the output. To ignore its result, when you add the following step, you choose Ignore Results From Previous Action.

- To see an action's description in the lower-left corner of an Automator document, you can select the action either in the Action column or in the workflow area, if you've already put that action in the workflow.

Automator includes a log that lists each action as it happens. To see the log, choose Show Log from the View menu. The log rises out of the top of the Automator window like a bubbling lava dome (see Figure 13-14); or if you move the Automator window so that there's space below it, the log appears at the bottom. If you watch the log as you run the workflow, you see each step start running, do its job, and then change its status to Completed in the log. You also get to see when those elusive conversion actions are called in (see "Type Matching and Conversion" in this chapter).

FIGURE 13-14: You can display an event log for Automator windows.

Creating Your Own Actions

You can use Mac OS X Tiger and the Xcode Tools to create your own Automator actions. Most actions are associated with an application, but that's not strictly necessary.

You create an action in Xcode by starting a new project. Xcode lets you design an action using Cocoa or AppleScript, or a combination of both. To start playing around with creating your own action, just start Xcode, make a new AppleScript Automator Action project, and then click Build and Go. You'll have a perfect Automator action that does nothing at all, but from there you can start to experiment and learn about how actions work.

Note Find out everything you ever wanted to know about how to create your own Automator actions by reading Apple's Automator Programming Guide, located in the Developer Reference Library installed on your disk with Xcode tools or online at `http://developer.apple.com/documentation/AppleApplications/Conceptual/AutomatorConcepts/index.html`.

Summary

Automator presents something entirely new: a remarkably powerful level of automation that requires no programming or scripting. If Automator becomes as popular as AppleScript, there will likely be thousands of workflows available for download, as user groups and developers start to create for this new technology. If you're interested in what Automator can do, this is your chance to get in on the ground floor of a very cool tool.

Xcode and Other Tools

A pple produces a stellar collection of software for programmers
called Xcode Tools. The Xcode Tools are based on open source
software, including compilers and command shells, but lots of
Apple technology has been added. Two wonderful secrets about Xcode
Tools: They're not really just for programmers, and they're free to anybody
who wants them. Xcode Tools come in the package with Mac OS X Tiger,
right on the DVD. If you can't find your OS X install disc, all you have to
do is go to http://developer.apple.com, get a free membership to
the Apple Developer Connection, and download the Xcode Tools. (If you
would rather not sit through a 500MB download, you can order the tools
on CD for $20.)

In this chapter, you'll look at some cool things you can do with just a hand-
ful of the Xcode Tools. In general, I'll skip over the standard uses for stuff,
focusing instead on whatever is fun, edgy, unusual, and wacky—because
that's what we do.

Xcode Tools

The Xcode Tools are Apple's construction kit for making software. The
Xcode Tools include a zillion different applications, compilers, debuggers,
command-line tools, libraries, utilities, and other handy bits and pieces to
help developers create software.

Two programs lie at the heart of the tools: the Xcode application and
Interface Builder. The Xcode application is an integrated development environment (IDE) for editing code and building applications. Figure 14-1
shows you what the Xcode IDE looks like.

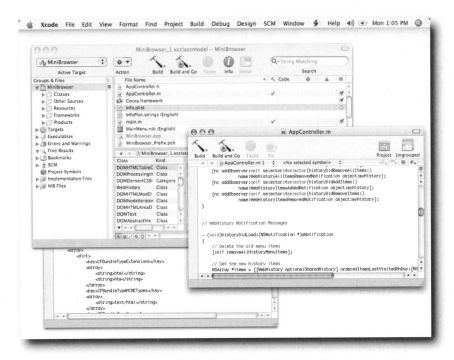

FIGURE 14-1: The Xcode application provides an integrated development environment for creating software.

Xcode is mainly for professionals and serious hobbyists, but even if you're not in one of those categories, you can still get familiar with Xcode and fool around with it.

Xcode Projects

Xcode speaks lots of different languages and knows many tricks. Xcode is the place to go for all kinds of Tiger development, whether it's in C, Objective-C, C++, or Java. Starting a new project in Xcode is as easy as choosing New Project from the File menu. Xcode has templates for a vast set of project types, so you pick the kind you want and Xcode starts you off with the skeleton of a finished product. Figure 14-2 shows the dialog that appears when you choose New Project.

FIGURE 14-2: The New Project dialog in Xcode lets you choose from dozens of different project types.

The standard project types, such as Cocoa and Carbon applications, are on the list, of course. Here are some of the more obscure and intriguing project types you can create in Xcode:

- Five different flavors of command-line tools, including simple C-based programs as well as tools that link against various OS X frameworks.

- Automator actions, written primarily either in Cocoa or AppleScript.

- Lots of different kinds of plug-ins, including Address Book actions, Interface Builder palettes, screen savers, and Spotlight metadata importers.

- Many different types of Java projects, such as applications and applets based on AWT, Swing, or JNI.

- And the most perverse, wacky choice of all: an empty project.

Project Central

When you select File➔New Project, Xcode looks for Xcode projects in the folder /Library/ Application Support/Apple/Developer Tools/Project Templates and lists them as project types in the New Project dialog. The highest-level Folders in Project Templates correspond to the categories shown in Xcode's New Project dialog. Here's the complete list of Xcode project categories and templates that ship with Xcode 2.0:

- Action: AppleScript Automator Action, Cocoa Automator Action.

- Application: AppleScript, AppleScript Document-based, AppleScript Droplet, Carbon, Cocoa, Cocoa Document-based, Cocoa-Java, Cocoa-Java Document-based, Core Data, Core Data Document-based.

- Bundle: Carbon, CFPlugIn, Cocoa.

- Command Line Utility: C++ Tool, CoreFoundation Tool, CoreServices Tool, Foundation Tool, Standard Tool.

- Dynamic Library: BSD Dynamic Library, Carbon Dynamic Library, Cocoa Dynamic Library

- External Build System.

- Framework: Carbon, Cocoa.

- Java: Ant-based Application Jar, Ant-based Empty Project, Ant-based Java Library, Ant-based Signed Applet, Ant-based Web Start Application, Java AWT Applet, Java AWT Application, Java JNI Application, Java Swing Applet, Java Swing Application, Java Tool.

- Kernel Extension: Generic Kernel Extension, IOKit Driver.

- Standard Apple Plug-ins: Address Book Action Plug-in for C, Address Book Action Plug-in for Objective-C, AppleScript Xcode Plug-in, IBPalette, Image Unit Plug-in for Objective-C, Installer Plug-in, Metadata Importer, Preference Pane, Screen Saver, Sherlock Channel, Sync Schema.

- Static Library: BSD Static Library, Carbon Static Library, Cocoa Static Library.

In case you're not counting, that's 53 different project templates. Collect them all!

Interface Builder

The revolution in graphical user interfaces really picked up momentum when the Macintosh shipped in 1984. But it wasn't until 1988 that developer tools really began to join the party, as Steve Jobs and the gang at NeXT, Inc. released Interface Builder. This tool was designed around an obvious fact: It's silly to use textual tools to design applications that have graphical interfaces. Plenty of graphical layout tools came before, but Interface Builder innovated by allowing programmers to specify relationships and connections between objects (and between functions in the code) just by drawing lines from one object to another.

Interface Builder survives today as a crucial member of Apple's suite of Xcode tools. You can see the latest version in Figure 14-3.

FIGURE 14-3: A typical Interface Builder screen.

Developers use Interface Builder when they create Cocoa applications, and it's also used for various other kinds of projects, such as Automator actions, that include graphical user interface elements. Interface Builder includes a handy Test Interface mode that lets you try out the user interface without having to build and run the application. Test Interface mode is represented by a Frankenstein-style switch that appears in the menu bar: Throw the switch to return to Interface Builder from test mode.

When you design interface elements and their connections, Interface Builder saves your work in one or more nib files, a vestigial acronym for *NeXT Interface Builder*. When you run an OS X application, it opens and reads its associated nib file to figure out what the windows and menus look like and how they behave. Those nib files provide your hook for changing the way things work. In this section, you learn how to tinker with stuff in a nib file to modify how applications look and act.

Warning

Although applications expose some of their internals through nib files, they aren't designed to support all the changes that random geeks like us inflict with Interface Builder. The changes you make with Interface Builder won't always work the way you would like them to—sometimes, they won't have any effect at all. Other times the effect is bad. The only way to know for sure is to try. And please, before you alter any of your applications, take a brief moment to make a backup copy of the program, just in case your surgery mangles the original beyond repair.

When you use Interface Builder to modify an application's nib files, you have access to a great deal of the application's user interface and a lot of its features. You can perform two broad classes of hacks with Interface Builder:

- Cosmetic changes involve moving, resizing, and renaming items in the user interface. These kinds of changes are easy to perform and often have the effect you intend.

- Functional changes add new features or modify the way existing features work. These kinds of changes are trickier to pull off and less likely to be successful because they involve more of the application's code, which is the part of the program that's governed least by the nib file.

In this section, you work through a couple of application mods that are mostly cosmetic. The point of these examples is not so much to teach you how to make these specific changes, but to introduce the general idea of customizing user interface bits with Interface Builder.

Customizing TextEdit

For the first instructive demonstration, you modify the Preferences window that lives inside TextEdit. Figure 14-4 shows this window in its standard, uncorrupted state.

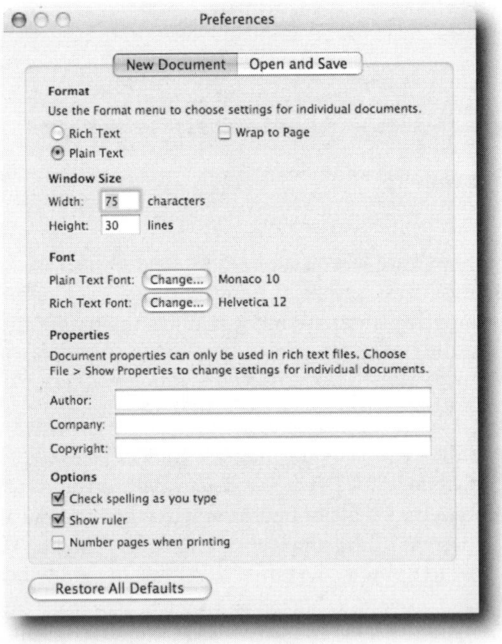

FIGURE 14-4: The pristine TextEdit Preferences window.

Here are the steps for editing the window:

1. Before starting, make sure that TextEdit isn't running and that you've created a backup copy of TextEdit.

2. Go to the Finder and navigate to /Developer/Applications/Interface Builder. Double-click Interface Builder to open it.

Note If you don't have Interface Builder or even a Developer folder, you probably haven't installed the Xcode Tools. Go to developer.apple.com for information on how to join the Apple Developer Connection and get the Xcode tools for free.

3. When Interface Builder opens, you see the Starting Point dialog. Click the Open button.

4. The `nib` file you want to open is buried inside the TextEdit bundle. Unfortunately, the Open panel in Interface Builder doesn't let you dig inside bundles. But you can use a trick: With the Open panel visible, press the slash key. A Go To The Folder sheet appears, into which you can type a pathname. Type **/Applications/TextEdit.app/ Contents/Resources/English.lproj/** (Figure 14-5) and click Go.

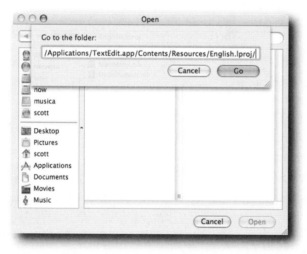

FIGURE 14-5: You can get inside a bundle from an Open panel by typing a slash and then a pathname.

5. Now the Open panel lists the files inside TextEdit's English.lproj folder. Click the Preferences.nib file and click Open to see the file in Interface Builder.

6. TextEdit's Preferences window is now open and you can get your grubby hands on it. Start by changing the layout of items to something funkier. You can move elements around—buttons, text fields, check boxes—just by dragging them to their new locations.

7. Next, resize the Author, Company, and Copyright fields to make them a bit shorter, just because you can.

8. Now click the Check Spelling As You Type check box and choose Tools → Show Inspector. You see a very cool window called labeled NSButton Inspector (Figure 14-6).

FIGURE 14-6: Interface Builder's Inspector examines the Check Spelling As You Type check box.

9. The Inspector provides several interesting settings for the check box:

   ▪ Edit the Title field to change the name that appears on the check box.

   ▪ Use the Key Equiv popup and Key Mod check boxes to add a keyboard shortcut to the item.

   ▪ Type the name of a system sound (such as Frog or Submarine) into the Sound box to make a sound play every time the box is checked.

Note You can test your changes immediately, right there in Interface Builder, by choosing File → Test Interface or pressing Command-R. The Preferences dialog comes alive, and you can click and type to check out your handiwork. When you're done testing and you want to return to Interface Builder, choose the Quit Interface Builder item (which, in this case, actually quits Test Interface mode) in the Interface Builder menu. Next, press Command-Q or click the tiny switch icon to the right of the Help menu.

10. Next, use the Inspector to monkey around with text fields. You have several to choose from: Width, Height, Author, Company, and Copyright. Click whichever one you like. The Inspector window should now read NSTextField Inspector.

11. Click the black rectangle next to Text Color and choose a fine, tasteful color to be used for the field's text. Then do the same thing for Background Color. Red on blue looks particularly nice.

12. In the Alignment options, click the second one from the left, the one with two arrows pointing at a vertical line between them. This setting centers the text in the field.

13. When you're done making changes, use File → Test Interface (Command-R) to test your changes. When you're satisfied press Command-Q to quit the test mode, Command-S to save your changes, and Command-Q again to quit Interface Builder.

14. Back in the Finder, start TextEdit, open Preferences and have fun with your changes. Figure 14-7 shows an example of the havoc you can cause with this technique.

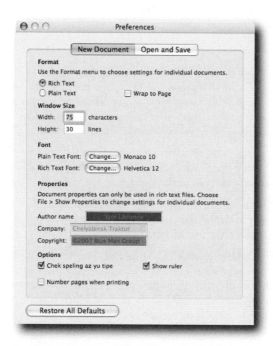

FIGURE 14-7: The new and improved TextEdit Preferences window.

Customizing iChat

In this next example, you're going to do some practical work to make iChat a little friendlier.

1. Be sure you have a backup copy of the iChat application, and quit iChat if it's running.

2. If Interface Builder isn't running, start it up. You'll find it in /Developer/Applications.

3. When Interface Builder opens, click Open in the Starting Point dialog.

4. Type a slash to get the secret Go To The Folder sheet, then type **/Applications/ iChat.app/Contents/Resources/English.lproj/** and click Go.

5. Double-click the MainMenu.nib file. You should see iChat's menu bar, as shown in Figure 14-8.

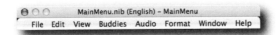

FIGURE 14-8: iChat MainMenu.nib.

6. Click the Buddies menu to see its items. That's a long menu! I don't know about you, but I don't use an awful lot of items in that menu: Some of their functions are usually available by double-clicking a name or clicking a button, and others are rarely needed. You're going to take all those unused menu items—everything from Invite To Chat on down the end of the menu—and hide them away in a single unused submenu.

7. Go to the Cocoa-Menus palette and grab a separator line. You find it right under the Font menu. Drag the separator to the Buddies menu until it's under Request Authorization and then release it. The separator should now be the last item in the menu, for the moment.

8. Go back to the Cocoa-Menus palette and get a Submenu object. Drag it to the Buddies menu and drop it all the way at the bottom, under the separator. Note that the Submenu comes with a single item, generically named Item.

9. Now you relocate all the items from Invite To Chat through Request Authorization into the new submenu. It would be great to select them all and just drag and drop, but unfortunately, Interface Builder doesn't support drag and drop for multiple menu items. So instead, you can use Copy and Paste. Selecting all the items is a little tedious, too. You should be able to select the first one and then Shift-click the last to select them all, but Interface Builder is a little behind the times and doesn't support that feature (for you terminology buffs, that's called *continuous selection*). To select all the items, click Invite To Chat and then Shift-click each of the other items, one at a time, to add them to the selection. Be sure to click the separator below Send File. When you're done, your Buddies menu should look like Figure 14-9.

FIGURE 14-9: Use Shift-Click to select all these menu
items one at a time.

10. With all those menu items selected, cut them with Edit ➜ Cut or Command-X. Ah, the
    menu is looking better already.

11. Click the Submenu at the bottom and choose Edit ➜ Paste (Command-V). The itinerant
    items reappear in the submenu.

12. The placeholder Submenu item named Item is now at the bottom of the submenu. To
    get rid of it, click to select it and then press Delete.

13. Now you have to give the submenu a real name. Double-click the word Submenu to
    select it for editing and then type the new name. You can use **Other Stuff**.

14. At this point, you still have an extraneous separator line left over from the menu's old
    layout: Note that there are two separators in a row above Other Stuff. Click one of them
    to select it and then press Delete to vaporize it.

15. Use the File ➜ Test Interface feature to check your work. The windows go away and the
    iChat menus (from File to Help) appear in the menu bar. Pull down the Buddies menu
    to see the deprecated items in the Other Stuff submenu.

16. If everything looks right, quit the Test Interface mode, save the `nib` file, quit Interface
    Builder, and run your customized iChat (Figure 14-10).

FIGURE 14-10: The finished, customized version of iChat.

Warning You should be careful when fooling around with forces of nature like tornados, blizzards, and Apple software. When a new version of Mac OS X or a system update comes along, there's a chance that your customized versions of TextEdit, iChat, or other applications will be silently blown away by the new software. When you customize an application, make sure you keep a backup copy of your version to prevent the next update from ruining your day.

Quartz Composer

Quartz Composer is a new application included with Xcode Tools 2.0. Quartz Composer lets you play with and learn about the amazing Quartz graphics features built into Mac OS X Tiger without having to learn APIs or write programs. Documents you create with Quartz Composer, called *compositions*, can be turned into QuickTime movies or OS X screen savers. In this section, you use Quartz Composer to create a nifty screen saver without very much effort. It will take you a while to follow all the steps, but I promise the results will be worthwhile.

Warning Quartz Composer is supercool and highly addictive. Before you start using it, be sure you have several hours (or perhaps an entire night) to dive in and try things out, because you might find it hard to walk away.

1. Go to /Developer/Applications/Graphic Tools and run Quartz Composer. You might get an alert complaining that your Mac's hardware won't support all the program's greatest features, but that's OK. If you get the alert, read what it says and click Continue.

2. Next, you see the New Composition Assistant offering several types of templates to start our composition. For this example, you start from scratch; so just click Cancel to make the Assistant go away.

3. Use File ➔ New to create a new, empty composition. You see two windows: The one that looks like a checkerboard is called the viewer; and the other is the editor.

4. On the left side of the editor window, make sure Patch Library is selected. In Quartz Composer, a *patch* is an individual graphical element or process. Patches are the building blocks you use to make compositions. You start this one with a cube. Look down the Name column in the Patch Library until you find the patch named Cube—it's in the Renderer category. Double-click Cube to add a cube patch to the composition. Instantly, if not sooner, a box labeled Cube shows up in the editor. There's also a cube showing in the viewer—you can't see it, because it has no color or texture yet, but you can tell it's there because it's blotting out the grid background (Figure 14-11).

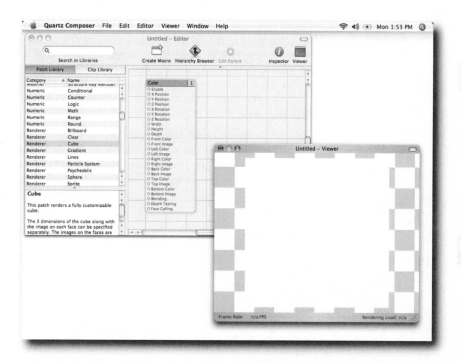

FIGURE 14-11: Your composition starts with a cube. You only know it's there because part of the background is obscured.

5. Your cube is pretty boring right now. But if you take a look at the cube patch in the editor, you see that it has a bunch of values you can use to fill it that should make it more interesting. Let's start by putting something on the front of the cube. In the Patch Library, find Image Importer (it's in the Generator category) and double-click to add one to the composition.

Note There are various ways to find the patch you're looking for. By default, the Patch Library is sorted by category. You might find it more useful to alphabetize the patch names—click the Name column to do that. If you know any part of the name of the patch or category, you can type text in the Search In Libraries field to get instant results. Note that some patches have a bullet in front of their names. The bullet indicates that these patches work best with graphics hardware that's not present on the computer running Quartz Composer, so they will run slowly if used on this computer. (These patches are what that the alert in Step 1 was warning about.)

6. Click the new Image Importer patch to select it. Click the Inspector button in the toolbar (you can also choose Editor → Show Inspector or press Command-I).

7. In the Inspector, click the pop-up menu and choose Settings.

8. Now you need to find a nice picture to put on a cube face. Click Import From File and navigate to any image you want in almost any format, including JPEG, TIFF, PNG, TIFF, or PDF. For best results, pick an image that's square or nearly so. If you can't find any images you like, look in the current user's Pictures folder. When you locate the image you want to use, double-click it. If you prefer, there's a cool shortcut: Drag an image file and drop it into the Image Data area in the Inspector. The image you picked should appear in the Image Data area.

9. Now you tell the cube to display the image you selected. In the editor, click the little circle next to the word Image in the Image Importer and drag to the circle next to Front Image in the Cube patch. You should see a yellow wire strung between the two circles or *ports* (Figure 14-12). Take a look in the viewer window—the cube now has the selected image on its face.

FIGURE 14-12: Quartz Composer connects ports with yellow wires.

10. One of the most powerful features of Quartz Composer is its ability to create compositions that don't just sit there—they live, breathe, and move. To move your cube, you must change some of its settings repeatedly over time. In particular, if you change the rotation settings, the cube changes its orientation, and you see different parts of it. By changing the rotation values over and over, the cube spins. Quartz Composer includes a patch called an *Interpolation* that supplies an ever-changing stream of values. Find Interpolation in the patch library and double-click to add one to the composition.

11. Click the interpolation patch to select it, and then click Inspector to see its values. You want the cube to rotate by varying its orientation between 0 and 360 degrees, so ask the interpolation to supply values that go from 0 to 360. In the Inspector, click the pop-up menu and choose Input Parameters. Leave Start Value at 0 and change End Value to 360. The Duration value determines how many seconds it takes to complete the interpolation. Set that value to 20. Leave the other values as they are.

12. Now that you have a source of values from 0 to 360, you need to supply those values to the cube for its rotation. Drag from the Result port of the Interpolation to the X Rotation port of the cube. Take a look at the viewer window. The cube is in motion! You should see the cube tumbling endlessly forward, all faces white except for the front, which still has an image on it. That's pretty neat, but you're just getting started.

13. Because the cube is only changing its x-rotation, you never see its left and right sides. To fix that, you can spin the cube on its y-axis at the same time, and offset the z-rotation a bit (but not change it continuously). In the editor, drag another connection from the Results port, this time hooking it to the cube's Y Rotation. Click the Cube patch, and then click the Inspector button. Go to the Input Parameters panel. In the Z Rotation field, type **90**, and then close the Inspector. Now the cube is tumbling, and all six faces eventually come into view.

14. Quartz Composer is drawing the cube over and over again, but something is missing: You see only one frame of the cube animation at a time. What's happening to the previous frames? As a development and debugging aid, Quartz Composer automatically erases the viewer before every redraw. This automatic erasing won't happen when you use the composition outside Quartz Composer. To see what that will look like, choose Viewer → Disable Background Erasing and take a look at the viewer. You soon get a big smear of cubes everywhere it's been drawn (Figure 14-13). That's not what you want. To prevent this from happening, you need a patch that erases each old frame of the cube before drawing a new one. Find the Clear patch in the Patch Library and double-click to create one.

15. You've added the Clear patch, and now the viewer window is . . . completely black! Nice job, Picasso! What's gone wrong? Take a look at the yellow numbers in the upper-right corner of the Cube and Clear patches. The number for Cube is 1, and Clear is 2. These numbers represent the *rendering layer* for each patch. Because the Clear patch was just added, it got rendering layer 2, the last layer in this composition. Compositions are processed in order of their rendering layers. So each time through the composition, the cube is drawn, and then cleared to black! That's why you're seeing only a black screen in the viewer. To fix this problem, you need to reverse the order. Clear the screen first, and then draw the cube. Control-click the title of the Clear patch and choose Rendering Layer. Now pick Layer 1. Note that the Rotating Cube's layer automatically changes to 2; and in the viewer window, your cube is back with the background now cleared to black.

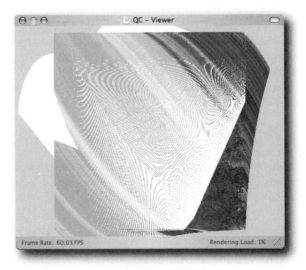

FIGURE 14-13: The cube draws over itself repeatedly and eventually creates a big blur.

16. Sure, you've got a rotating cube, but five of the faces are blank. That's some boring cube! You can make it better by putting things on the other faces, using various patches to show how cool Quartz Composer is. Start by adding an image from a Web page. Find the Image Downloader patch and double-click to add one. Open the Inspector, go to the Input Parameters panel, and type **http://images.apple.com/home/2005/images/ ipodfamilyphoto20050223.jpg** into the Image URL field.

17. Connect the Image port of the Image Downloader patch to the cube's Left Image port. The Web image should instantly appear on the right face of the tumbling cube. (If it doesn't, double-check to make sure you typed the URL correctly.)

18. The next face is practical: It's going to show the time of day. You add three patches: System Time, Date Formatter, and Image With String. Run a wire from System Time to Date Formatter via their Time ports. Make a connection from Date Formatter to Image With String using their String ports. Finally, connect the Image output from Image With String to the Right Image port on the cube. Now you have the time of day on the right face of the cube.

19. The time display is kind of messy: It's scaled and hard to read. Let's fix that. Click Image With String, then click Inspector, and go to the Settings panel. Change both the Horizontal and Vertical Alignment to Center. (Change the font to something else if you like.) Click Fixed Dimensions (in pixels). Fill in an Image Size of 1024 by 1024, and a font size of 200. The time now looks a lot better.

20. Wouldn't it be cool if one of the cube faces continuously showed a QuickTime movie clip? Let's do it. Add an Image With Movie patch to the composition and open the Inspector. Go to the Input Parameters panel and type the path to a QuickTime movie (for example, **/Users/scott/Documents/myMovie.mov**, or download a movie trailer

from **www.apple.com/quicktime**). Connect the Image With Movie patch's Image output to the Cube's Top Image input. Take a look at the viewer—you should see the movie playing on the cube's top face as it rotates into and out of view. Awesome! Figure 14-14 shows the composition at this point.

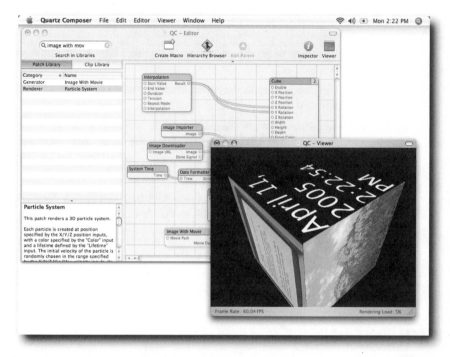

FIGURE 14-14: The composition with images on four faces.

Two blank faces still remain on the cube, but I'll leave those to you and your creativity now that you have a feel for how it works. Here are some ideas you can use to dress up those faces:

- Use a Host Info patch to display various bits of interesting and obscure information, such as the current user name, computer name, OS version, or CPU load.

- Set the background color of the cube faces by using the Inspector to change the Front Color, Left Color, and so on.

- Hook an Interpolation patch to an RGB Color patch to continually change the colors you put on the faces.

When you're all done with the cube, it's easy to make it into a screen saver. Just use File → Save As and navigate to the current user's Library/Screen Savers folder. Save the composition into that folder. When you go to System Preferences and click Desktop & Screen Saver, you see your composition at the bottom of the list, available as an official screen saver. Click, select, and enjoy.

Note When you install Tiger, it doesn't create the user's Library/Screen Savers folder by default. If you navigate there and find no such folder, you can click the New Folder button in the Save dialog to create it.

Like Disneyland, a Quartz Composer document is never truly finished as long as there is imagination left in the world. If you want to play more with Quartz Composer, here are a just a few of the many interesting features you might want to investigate:

- Use a Lighting patch to get the nifty effect of shining a light on objects in your composition.

- Check out the Clip Library in the editor window to add a pulsating Apple logo or shimmering background.

- Add a Mouse controller to use the mouse to slide your objects around on the screen. This won't work in a screen saver because moving the mouse deactivates the screen saver.

- Grab a Random patch to feed random inputs to an object, such as the location values for a cube, to make it warp around the screen.

- Believe it or not, Quartz Composer can read RSS feeds and display them in a composition. For a stunning example of how this works, check out the RSS Visualizer screen saver that comes with Mac OS X Tiger.

For more ideas about what you can do with Quartz Composer, check out the folder at /Developer/Examples/Quartz Composer. Quartz Composer is an amazing tool for creating beautiful images without any programming. Enjoy exploring everything it can do.

The Ultimate Hack

For the last part of this chapter, I present a different kind of hack. This one is a technical-social hack that was perpetrated by Ron Avitzur, proprietor of Pacific Tech (www.pacifict.com) and legendary creator of the Graphing Calculator application that began shipping with Apple's first Power Macintosh computers in the early 1990s. When Apple was developing the Power Macintosh line, Ron's Graphing Calculator project was cancelled. But Ron didn't let that stop him. For months, he snuck into Apple, and with a combination of determination, help from others, and luck, Ron managed to complete and ship Graphing Calculator to more than 25 million customers.

In 2004, Ron wrote down his story and published it on his company's Web site. There was an immediate and powerful response. Several hundred comments were posted on Slashdot, the hugely trafficked developer Web site. Soon, *Newsweek* picked up the story of the Graphing Calculator, and *This American Life*, a program on National Public Radio, ran a segment on the tale.

Ron's story explains the unusual circumstances and dedication that led to the creation of Graphing Calculator, and I highly recommend you read it. You can find the story at www.pacifict.com/story. Ron still works on improving Graphing Calculator, and you can download the Mac OS X version, which is no longer shipped by Apple, at www.pacifict.com/FreeStuff.html.

Summary

Whether or not you're a programmer, the Xcode Tools are very handy to have around. Add the fact that they're free, and Xcode becomes an unbeatable value. Use the Xcode Tools, both those described in this chapter as well as all the others, and read the Graphing Calculator Story to inspire yourself to create something great.

Hacks

P art III consists of eight OS X programs, including source code and descriptions. If you're a programmer, you want to be one, or you're just interested in finding out what makes programs tick, you'll be very interested in Part III. Everything you've done so far has been done without programming. Sure, Part II gets into some funky shell commands and powerful utilities, but Part III is pure hardcore coding.

To create Part III, I asked some veteran Mac programmers to write various bits of code. You'll find examples of applications, Dashboard widgets, a Spotlight metadata importer, a system service, and a command line tool. Seven of the eight hacks are original works, and the other is an amazing project that plumbs the lowest levels of the Mac runtime.

Some of the code in Part III shows how to perform useful techniques, such as Badger, which demonstrates what you can do with an application tile in the Dock. Other projects, like Commando, create tools and let you peek behind the scenes at the source to learn how they work.

Part III is a great opportunity to sample a variety of actual Mac code, no matter what you're interested in.

Badger

I'll start off Part III with a fairly simple but fun hack: fooling around with the application's Dock icon. Every running application has the capability to modify its Dock icon at will by changing the icon's appearance and making it bounce to get the user's attention. You explore those features in this chapter, and also take a look at how to implement a contextual menu for your Dock icon.

A Review of Dock Features

One of the most prominent user interface changes in Mac OS X is the Dock, that ubiquitous strip of icons lining the bottom (or the side, if you're one of the cool kids) of your screen. The rectangular space that includes each icon is called a *tile*. The Dock manages to show lots of different kinds of information in one place, as shown in Figure 15-1, including the following:

- All the currently running applications. Each one is indicated by an icon with a small black triangle under it.

- Other favorite applications that aren't running, which you can add simply by dragging them to the Dock from the Finder.

- Minimized windows, which go to the Dock when you click a window's yellow minimize button.

- Any other Finder items you use frequently, such as documents and folders, which you can add just by dragging them to the Dock on the right side of the vertical divider line.

FIGURE 15-1: The famous Mac OS X Dock.

Every new Mac OS X user notices when icons in the Dock start hopping up and down (side to side, if your Dock is on the right or left). And that's exactly the point: Icons bounce in the Dock to get your attention, for either of two reasons:

- A running, inactive (that is, not frontmost) application is asking for attention.

- An application is launching.

Cross-Reference

If you think bouncing Dock icons on launch are just too cute or annoying, see Chapter 2 in the section titled "The Bouncing! The Bouncing!" to learn how to make them stop doing that.

Some icons in the Dock are even more dynamic: They change their appearance to convey additional information to users. For example, the iCal icon in the Dock shows the current day of the month, whereas Apple's Mail application adds a number in a circle, called a *badge*, to tell you how many unread messages are waiting in your Inbox.

Every icon in the Dock has a contextual menu. You can see a Dock icon's contextual menu by using any of several standard actions:

- Control-click the icon's tile.

- If you have a mouse with more than one button, right-click the tile.

- Point at the tile and then press and hold the mouse button.

Every application icon in the Dock has five standard menu items: Keep In Dock (or Remove From Dock if the application is usually kept there), Open at Login, Show In Finder, Hide, and Quit. The Dock menu also lists the application's open windows, with a check mark next to the one that's frontmost (see Figure 15-2).

FIGURE 15-2: The Dock menu for an application lists its windows and several commands.

Every application can add its own commands to the standard items that are in the Dock menu. For example, iTunes adds a whole bunch of handy commands, such as transport controls (Play, Pause, Next Song, Previous Song) and even the name of the current song and artist, which aren't commands at all, just useful information.

About the Badger Hack

This hack is called Badger because it messes around with Dock icons by applying a dynamic badge and performing other tasks. Specifically, here's what Badger does:

- Creates a dynamic badge in the Dock that changes every second.
- Removes the badge for 1 second every 7 seconds.
- Bounces the Dock icon every 10 seconds.
- Implements a Dock menu with a couple of handy menu items, including one that stops the icon from bouncing.

Figure 15-3 shows Badger in action.

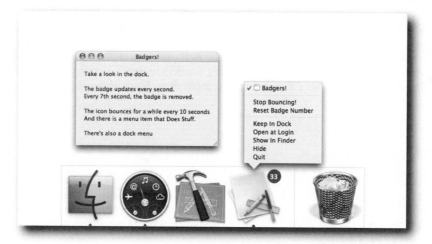

FIGURE 15-3: Badger in the Dock.

The Cocoa framework and Quartz drawing calls provide most of what you need for this hack. Your main jobs are to write code to draw the Dock icon and bounce it periodically.

Badger was created by **Mark Dalrymple**. Mark is a man of many talents and interests. He has been programming Macs since 1985 and Unix since 1990, so for Mark, Mac OS X is a perfect match. Working feverishly from his secret lair somewhere in western Pennsylvania, Mark finds time to write books (*Core Mac OS X and Unix Programming*, *Learn Objective-C on the Macintosh*), create balloon animals, perform music, and curate one of the world's leading collections of stuffed (plush) badgers. Mark occasionally journeys to rural Georgia to teach programming at the legendary Big Nerd Ranch. Find out more about Mark, including how to hire him, at `borkware.com`.

Interface Builder

Badger uses a simple, fairly standard nib file. To create one, start by opening Xcode and making a new Cocoa Application project. In your new project, double-click MainMenu.nib to start Interface Builder. In Interface Builder, subclass NSObject to create an AppController class. Then add an outlet (name it menu) and two actions (resetNumber and stopBouncing). Instantiate a new AppController.

Still in Interface Builder, drag a menu from the objects palette, rename it Dock Menu, and add two menu items: Stop Bouncing and Reset Badge Number. Connect the menu items to their actions in AppController, and connect AppController's menu outlet to the new menu. Finally, connect the File's Owner outlet named delegate to the AppController instance.

Source Code

The source consists of a header file (AppController.h) and its implementation (AppController.m). As with all other code in this part of the book, you can type it, or you can download it from the book's Web site at www.wiley.com/compbooks/extremetech. If you have the time and you really want to get a feel for what's in the code, I recommend you type it in, but if you just want to get it working, I understand.

Here are the source files and a description of what they contain.

AppController.h

The header file, AppController.h, is created by Interface Builder. It supplies information that defines the interface of AppController—that is, the names and parameters of methods, but not the code itself (that's in the next file).

```
// AppController.h starts here
```

You always import the Cocoa framework goodness first.

```
#import <Cocoa/Cocoa.h>
```

Next, create an AppController instance in Interface Builder and connect its outlet and actions there.

```
@interface AppController : NSObject

{
```

The application has a Dock menu: a contextual menu that appears when the user control-clicks, right-clicks, or mouses down and holds on the Dock icon. Here's the outlet for the Dock menu, created by Interface Builder.

```
    IBOutlet NSMenu *menu;
```

You're going to draw a badge on the Dock icon, then change it every second and remove it every seven seconds. Therefore, you need a timer to tell you when to mess with the badge.

```
NSTimer *timer;
```

Because you're going to deface the Dock icon, you must keep a copy of the original around so you can restore it later.

```
NSImage *originalApplicationIcon;
```

The badge consists of a number and some graphics. For the number part, you want an object to hold the text attributes when you draw it.

```
NSDictionary *textAttributes;
```

You'll be incrementing the badge number every second, so you need a variable to keep track of the current value.

```
int badgeNumber;
```

You'll also bounce the Dock icon every 10 seconds, just for fun. You create a menu item to temporarily stop the bouncing. Here are a couple of variables you can use to handle the bouncing.

```
    int userAttentionRequest;
    int startedBouncingAt;
}
```

Interface Builder has defined a couple of the methods that correspond to the commands in the Dock menu.

Call `stopBouncing:` to make the Dock icon cease its occasional bouncing spree.

```
- (IBAction) stopBouncing: (id) sender;
```

Call `resetNumber:` to start the badge value at one again.

```
- (IBAction) resetNumber: (id) sender;
@end // AppController
```

AppController.m

AppController.m contains the implementation for AppController and the logic for Badger's features. I discuss each of AppController's methods, what they do, and how they work. The first bits of AppController.m are the usual start for an implementation file.

```
// AppController.m starts here
#import "AppController.h"

@implementation AppController
```

init

Begin by initializing the AppController object and performing some one-time setup. You need a timer object so that you know when to change the badge: once every second. When the timer fires, you want to call the `timerFired:` method, which then decides what to do.

```
// Start by initializing the controller object.
- (id) init
{
    if (self = [super init]) {
```

Next, you need to create the timer that tells the code when to change the badge. Make the timer fire every second and call `timerFired:` when it does. See the description of `timerFired:` for more info.

```
        timer = [NSTimer scheduledTimerWithTimeInterval: 1.0
                    target: self
                    selector: @selector(timerFired:)
                    userInfo: nil
                    repeats: YES];
            [timer retain];
```

Next, you grab a copy of the application's icon. This is useful because you're going to manipulate—that is, draw on top of—the icon in the Dock, but every seven seconds you want to put the original icon back. You call `applicationIconImage` to get it.

```
        originalApplicationIcon =
            [[NSApp applicationIconImage] copy];
```

For your last act of initialization, set up the `textAttributes` object to use for drawing the number badge on the Dock icon. Later, you call `drawAtPoint:withAttributes:` using the `textAttributes` object you create here. The dictionary consists of object/key pairs. This dictionary contains two pairs: one to set the color to white, the other to specify the font as bold system font, size 14. Text attributes are defined by the class `NSAttributedString`.

```
        textAttributes =
            [NSDictionary dictionaryWithObjectsAndKeys:
            [NSColor whiteColor],
            NSForegroundColorAttributeName,
            [NSFont boldSystemFontOfSize: 14],
            NSFontAttributeName,
            nil];
        [textAttributes retain];
        return (self);
} // init
```

badgeImageWithCount:

The main job of this hack is adding a badge to the Dock icon. Most of the drawing work for that is done here in the `badgeImageWithCount:` method. Given a number (the incrementing badge count), `badgeImageWithCount:` draws a red circle with a purple diamond on it and then puts the current count on top of that lovely background.

First, you create a rectangle to contain the badge and then allocate an image object that you can draw in.

```
// Draw a badge with the given number on it.
- (NSImage *) badgeImageWithCount: (int) number
{
```

You need a rectangle in order to draw the badge. You call `NSMakeRect` and make the rectangle 32 by 32 pixels.

```
    float badgeSize = 32;
    NSRect rect = NSMakeRect (0, 0, badgeSize, badgeSize);
```

Now you need an image object to hold the stuff you're going to draw. Call `NSImage` to allocate the image.

```
    NSImage *badge;
    badge = [[NSImage alloc] initWithSize: rect.size];
```

Get ready to draw into the image by calling `lockFocus`.

```
    [badge lockFocus];
```

Now it's time for the actual drawing fun. You're going to use Cocoa's graphic features to create the badge image. The primary tool is a bezier path, a Quartz object that defines the circle and diamond of the badge. You set the color appropriately as you draw and fill the path. Finally, you draw the number to complete the badge.

First, you have to clear out the image so that only the parts that are drawn change when you apply the badge to the Dock icon. You do this by creating a *clear* NSColor object, making it the current color and then painting the badge's rectangle with it.

```
    [[NSColor clearColor] set];
    [NSBezierPath fillRect: rect];
```

Now draw the first part of the badge: a red circle. You need a new bezier path for this. Allocate a new bezier path that's an oval inscribed in the badge's rectangle. Because the rectangle is a square, the oval will be a circle. Next, set the current color to red and paint the oval with it.

```
    NSBezierPath *bezierPath;
    bezierPath = [NSBezierPath bezierPathWithOvalInRect: rect];

    [[NSColor redColor] set];
    [bezierPath fill];
```

Now you need to draw the diamond on top of the circle. To do this, you need to restart the path by throwing away the points that define the circle. Now, add the diamond and fill it with the color (purple).

```
[bezierPath removeAllPoints];
```

Starting at a point halfway across the badge, create the path by drawing four diagonal lines. Note that you actually only draw three of the diagonals, calling `lineToPoint:` for each. The final diagonal segment comes automatically when you call `closePath`, which adds a line from the current point to the path's starting point.

```
[bezierPath moveToPoint: NSMakePoint (0, badgeSize / 2.0)];
[bezierPath lineToPoint: NSMakePoint (badgeSize / 2.0,
    badgeSize)];
[bezierPath lineToPoint: NSMakePoint (badgeSize, badgeSize /
    2.0)];
[bezierPath lineToPoint: NSMakePoint (badgeSize / 2, 0)];
[bezierPath closePath];

[[NSColor purpleColor] set];
[bezierPath fill];
```

Now draw the badge number in white on the text, using an NSString object.

```
[[NSColor whiteColor] set];
NSString *numberString;
```

Set the string to the value of the number (which was passed into this method, remember) using the `stringWithFormat:` method. You can pass `printf()` formatting codes to `stringWithFormat:`. Here you use the code `%d` to indicate a signed integer.

```
numberString = [NSString stringWithFormat: @"%d", number];
```

The string is now ready—draw it centered in the badge `rect` using the utility routine `drawString:centeredInRect:` (described in the next section).

```
[self drawString: numberString
    centeredInRect: rect];
```

You're done drawing the badge, so finish up.

```
[badge unlockFocus];

return ([badge autorelease]);
```

```
} // badgeImageWithCount:
```

Note that although you have now drawn the badge, you haven't actually applied it to the Dock icon yet. That comes later, in `updateBadge`, which calls `badgeImageWithCount:` before putting the badge on the Dock icon.

drawString:centeredInRect:

When you created the badge with the `badgeImageWithCount:` method, you called a utility function named `drawString:centeredInRect:` to actually draw the image into the badge rectangle. Here's the code for this handy utility.

```
// Given a string and a rectangle, draw the string centered in
// the rectangle.

- (void) drawString: (NSString *) string
    centeredInRect: (NSRect) rect
{
```

Declare an `NSSize` and set it to the size of the text you're drawing.

```
    NSSize size = [string sizeWithAttributes: textAttributes];
```

Declare an `NSPoint` and set it to the center of the rectangle.

```
    NSPoint startPoint;
    startPoint.x = rect.origin.x + rect.size.width / 2 -
        size.width / 2;
    startPoint.y = rect.origin.y + rect.size.height / 2 -
        size.height / 2;
```

Draw the string at the center point you've computed.

```
    [string drawAtPoint: startPoint
        withAttributes: textAttributes];

} // drawString: centeredInRect:
```

updateBadge

The `updateBadge` method contains the code that actually replaces the icon in the Dock. If the current badge number (which increments every second) is an even multiple of seven, you remove the badge and draw the original application icon, just to show how it's done. Otherwise, you take the badge, draw it on a copy of the icon and then tell the application to use the newly badged icon in the Dock.

This method has the code that actually changes the icon in the Dock. You start by tearing off a copy of the original icon, because it's the basis for the badged version you're about to draw.

```
- (void) updateBadge
{
    NSImage *icon = [originalApplicationIcon copy];
```

To demonstrate that you can restore the original icon, you do so every seventh second. Check to see if this is one those times. If so, skip the part where you draw on the icon.

```
if (badgeNumber % 7 != 0) {
```

If you reach this point, you're going to put the badge on the icon. Start by calling `badgeImageWithCount:` to create the image object.

```
NSImage *badgeImage =
    [self badgeImageWithCount: badgeNumber];
```

Get ready to draw the badge on the icon.

```
[icon lockFocus];
```

Draw the badge in the icon's upper-right quadrant—in other words, one-fourth of the way down and left of the upper-right corner. To figure out where that is, get the size of the icon and multiply each coordinate by three-fourths (.75).

```
NSSize size = [icon size];
NSPoint badgePoint;
badgePoint = NSMakePoint (size.width * 0.75,
    size.height * 0.75);
```

Draw the badge on the icon.

```
[badgeImage dissolveToPoint: badgePoint
    fraction: 1.0];
[icon unlockFocus];
}
```

Finally, tell the application to set its Dock icon to the one you built here.

```
[NSApp setApplicationIconImage: icon];
```

Release the icon, lest you leak an icon object every time through this method.

```
[icon release]
```

```
} // updateBadge
```

The `updateBadge` method is called by `timerFired` once every second. Next up, stroll through the code for `timerFired`.

timerFired:

Way back in the `init` method, you created a timer that fires every second. You can use this timer event to perform various periodic tasks:

■ Increment the number that's used for the badge.

■ If the badge number is an even multiple of 10, start the Dock icon bouncing.

■ If it's been five seconds since the icon started bouncing, stop that nonsense.

Note Icons in the Dock can only bounce when their applications are not frontmost. If Badger is front-most, its icon will not bounce.

The `timerFired:` method is called once every second, as you requested in the application's `init` method. When it's called, increment the badge number. Check to see whether it's time to start or stop bouncing.

```
- (void) timerFired: (NSTimer *) timer
{
```

`badgeNumber` is the variable you use to keep track of what should be drawn on the icon's badge.

```
    badgeNumber++;
```

Now you draw the new badge and change the icon in the Dock. The `updateBadge` method does all that.

```
    [self updateBadge];
```

Now you need to handle the bouncing cases. If you're at a multiple of 10, call `requestUser Attention` to start bouncing the icon. You use `NSCriticalRequest` to do that, which keeps the icon bouncing until the request is cancelled or the application comes to the front. You can also use `NSInformationalRequest` to bounce the icon one time only.

Note that `requestUserAttention` returns a value for the request.

```
    if (badgeNumber % 10 == 0) {
        userAttentionRequest =
        [NSApp requestUserAttention: NSCriticalRequest];
```

Also, remember when the icon started bouncing, so you know when five seconds have elapsed and it's time to stop.

```
        startedBouncingAt = badgeNumber;
    }
```

Check to see if the started bouncing five seconds ago. If so, knock it off! Call `cancelUser AttentionRequest` using the value you saved when you made the request.

```
    if (badgeNumber == startedBouncingAt + 5) {
        [NSApp cancelUserAttentionRequest:
            userAttentionRequest];
    }

} // timerFired:
```

stopBouncing:

The stopBouncing: method gets called by the Dock menu's Stop Bouncing! item. It simply asks the application to cancel the user attention request that started the bouncing. To cancel the request, you need the value that requestUserAttention: returned. That's why you created a global variable, userAttentionRequest, to hold the return value.

This method was created in Interface Builder as an action method of the AppController object. To make this method work with the Dock menu, you wire them together in Interface Builder.

```
- (IBAction) stopBouncing: (id) sender
{
    [NSApp cancelUserAttentionRequest: userAttentionRequest];

} // stopBouncing
```

resetNumber:

The resetNumber: method was created in Interface Builder as an action of AppController and then connected to the Reset Badge Number item in the Dock menu. It simply sets the badgeNumber global back to 1, and then it calls updateBadge to draw the new value on the icon.

```
- (IBAction) resetNumber: (id) sender
{
    badgeNumber = 1;
    [self updateBadge];
} // resetNumber
```

applicationDockMenu:

You can specify your own Dock menu by implementing the applicationDockMenu: delegate method. All you do is return the menu you loaded from the nib. You can also use this technique to build or modify a Dock menu as the application is running, rather than loaded from the nib file, which is pretty cool.

```
- (NSMenu *) applicationDockMenu: (NSApplication *) sender
{
    return (menu);
} // applicationDockMenu:
```

dealloc

The `dealloc` method cleans up anything left lying around. It deletes the timer object and various other objects you created along the way. It's good Cocoa style to use your `dealloc` method to release objects you created.

```
- (void) dealloc
{
```

Invalidate the timer to make sure it won't fire any more and it is removed from the run loop. Then release it.

```
    [timer invalidate];
    [timer release];

    [textAttributes release];
    [originalApplicationIcon release];

    [super dealloc];

} // dealloc
```

Extra Credit

If you want to explore more about Dock icons, badging, and bouncing, here are some tweaks you might like to pursue:

- Change the style of the badge (colors and shapes), or simply make it bigger so it's easier to read. See NetNewsWire for an example of a large badge. You can get NetNewsWire at `ranchero.com/netnewswire/`.

- There's no rule that says you have to use the original icon as the basis for the badged version. You can do anything you want when you change your icon. For example, the icon for the instant messaging client Adium is a duck, and when a message comes in, the duck flaps its wings. See if you can think of something even more clever. (You can get Adium at `www.adiumx.com`.)

- The Stop Bouncing item only turns off bouncing temporarily, until the next multiple of 10 comes around. Change this to make Stop Bouncing a toggle instead.

- If you put Badger in the Dock permanently and then quit the application, the badged icon is the one that stays in the Dock. Add code to reset the icon to the original before quitting.

- Badger's Dock menu never changes. What fun is that? Add a dynamic Dock menu that you build on-the-fly in the `applicationDockMenu` method. Or, if you want to keep the static Dock menu, you can rip out the `applicationDockMenu` code and implement the Dock menu entirely in Interface Builder by connecting the File's Owner `dockMenu` outlet to the Dock menu object.

Summary

Mac OS X gives you the power to change your application's Dock icon and to give it a static or dynamic menu. Most of the work is done for you in Cocoa, so you can concentrate on cooking up cool uses for these features.

Word of the Day

One of the niftiest and most-publicized new features in Mac OS X Tiger is Dashboard, an environment for running mini-applications called widgets (see Figure 16-1). Dashboard is cool because it provides quick access to lots of useful functions, but it's even better than that, because creating Dashboard widgets is relatively simple compared to many other programming projects. In this chapter, you learn how widgets are built, and then you create the useful Word of the Day widget that you can use on your very own Mac.

About Dashboard

Dashboard, the environment where widgets live, has a distinctive look. When you're doing your usual work, you don't see Dashboard or its widgets. To make Dashboard appear, you can perform any one of several actions:

- Press a function key. You set this up in System Preferences, Dashboard & Exposé panel.

- Move the mouse to a particular screen corner. This is also set in System Preferences.

- Click the Dashboard application icon in the Dock.

When you activate Dashboard, all active widgets come swooping into view at once, collected together in their own layer that appears on top of your regular windows and desktop. When you're done with Dashboard, you click on anything that's not in the widget layer, and Dashboard flies away with an Apple-style visual flourish.

chapter 6

in this chapter

- ☑ Learn how to build a widget

- ☑ Check out HTML, CSS, and JavaScript in widgets

- ☑ See what's inside the Word of the Day widget

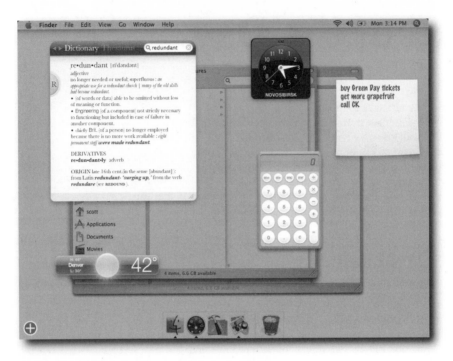

FIGURE 16-1: Dashboard and an assortment of widgets.

Dashboard includes the *widget bar*, a gallery of available widgets that appears under the Dock (Figure 16-2). You activate a widget by clicking it in the widget bar.

FIGURE 16-2: The Widget bar.

About Word of the Day

Word of the Day (see Figure 16-3) is a tidy widget, created by Josh Carter, that retrieves a vocabulary word every day via the Web.

FIGURE 16-3: Word of the Day
widget doing its thing.

Word of the Day taps into the Yahoo service of the same name. Yahoo's Word of the Day provides a word and its definition every day via an RSS feed. Josh's Word of the Day widget uses the XMLHttpRequest method to get this RSS feed and then displays what it learns.

Josh Carter is a talented software engineer, avid motorcyclist, and all-around nice guy. Josh has been a Mac fan for a long time and has the programming chops (and collection of Macs) to prove it. Josh admits to having participated in some curious endeavors in his past, including the legendary General Magic and Geek Radio efforts, which helped prepare him for his fine contributions to this book. Josh lives in Colorado with his wife and parrot.

Building a Widget

One of the best facts about widgets is that you can create them without a lot of programming. Widgets are basically Web pages—they're composed of HTML markup, CSS (Cascading Style Sheets, a standard for defining the look of Web pages) style information, and JavaScript code, all bundled together with an information property list and sprinkled with magic Apple dust. In this section, I'll cover the details you need to know in order to build your own widgets.

Because widgets use HTML and related technologies, there's no concept of *compiling* a widget. Every shipping widget exposes most or all of its inner workings, which provides you with a great opportunity for learning how widgets work and even reusing code that you find in other widgets (with the author's permission, of course).

Starting to build a widget is different from beginning most other kinds of Macintosh programming projects. Apple doesn't supply an Xcode template you can use for creating a widget. Instead, the easiest way to create your own widget is to start with an existing widget. You can build on one of the widgets that ships with Mac OS X Tiger, or you can start with a developer sample, such as GoodbyeWorld or BlankWidget.

Note   You can find the sample widgets in /Developer/Examples/Dashboard/.

Anatomy of a Widget

Like applications and other collections of code and resources, Dashboard widgets are bundles. Widget bundles have the .wdgt extension.

Most widgets consist of five files:

- A file with extension .html describes the basic appearance of the widget.
- A .css file contains the style sheet information for the widget, in CSS format.
- The .js file holds the JavaScript code for the widget.
- The Default.png file contains an image that's displayed in Dashboard when the widget is starting up.
- The Info.plist file holds various properties and settings that describe the widget.

Note   Although most widgets have at least these five files, they're not all required. The minimally functional widget consists of the .html, Default.png., and Info.plist files.

Widgets can have more than these five files in their bundles. In particular, most widgets have an Icon.png file that holds the widget's icon for display in the widget bar. Figure 16-4 shows Icon.png files for several standard widgets. Note that both of the standard images for a widget, the Default.png and Icon.png files, must use the Portable Network Graphics (PNG) format.

FIGURE 16-4: Icon.png files hold the icons for widgets.

Some widgets have several more images that they display as needed. Widgets with many images sometimes collect all their image files into a single Images subfolder inside the widget bundle. The bundle can contain any support files needed by the widget.

The HTML File

The widget's HTML file uses standard HTML markup to describe the visual layout of the widget. This file's name is usually has the name of the widget plus the .html extension, but it can actually have any name—the name is specified in the Info.plist file.

Most widgets include separate CSS and JavaScript files. The HTML file must explicitly reference these separate files in order to use them. The syntax for including a CSS file is the following:

```
<style type="text/css">
   @import "Widget.css";
</style>
```

To include a JavaScript file, use this syntax:

```
<script type='text/javascript' src='Widget.js' charset='utf-8'/>
```

Many widgets have user-changeable settings, such as the time zone in the Clock widget, the city in the Weather widget, or the stock symbols to track in the Stocks widget. Users manipulate these settings through a Preferences interface, as shown in Figure 16-5. To get to the Preferences screen, users click the info button, a small *i* that appears when the mouse hovers over the widget. After the user clicks the info button, the widget appears to flip around smartly and expose its reverse side where there are controls for setting preferences.

FIGURE 16-5: Widgets can have a preferences view.

When you create a widget, you specify the layout for both the standard and preferences views in the HTML file. To separate the views, each is enclosed in its own `<div>` layer. When the widget first appears, the `<div>` for the preferences side is hidden by assigning it a CSS class whose `display` attribute is none. When the user clicks the info button, the widget calls the `widget.prepareForTransition` function, hides the front layer, shows the back layer by changing the CSS styles of the layers, and calls `widget.performTransition`.

When the user changes a preference value, the widget calls `widget.setPreferenceForKey` to store the new setting. To read a preference value, the widget calls `widget.preference ForKey`.

Apple supplies standard code for supporting the info button and preferences transitions. You can see this code in any of the examples in the /Developer/Examples/Dashboard folder.

The CSS File

Most widgets use a CSS (cascading style sheet) file to provide style information for the widget's visual elements. The CSS file lets you assign styles to user interface elements that are defined in the HTML file. Although most widgets have a CSS file, it's not required.

When the user clicks anywhere on a widget and drags it, the widget moves around on the screen. You might want to define parts of your widget that don't allow the user to drag by grabbing there. These areas are called *control regions*. For example, you can't drag the Calculator widget by its buttons. If you try, the Calculator stays right where it is.

Scattered Scripts

Remember that although virtually every widget has a separate file for JavaScript, it is not expressly required. And most widgets, even those with a JavaScript file, place a few lines of JavaScript in the HTML file because it's more convenient. The JavaScript code in HTML files usually consists of one or two lines of code for handling occurrences such as click and mouse events.

You can specify rectangular and circular areas that will not be used for dragging the widget if the user mouses down and drags there. You can specify control regions using the `-apple-dashboard-region` property in the style associated with those areas. In the property, you specify the shape (circle or rectangle) and offsets from the top, right, bottom, and left edges of the area. For example, all the round buttons in the Calculator widget include this property in their style:

```
-apple-dashboard-region: dashboard-region(control circle 0 0 0 0);
```

Every button that uses this property has its entire area specified as a control region—the four zeroes indicate no offset from the edges of the element, which means the whole button is a control region. This style prevents the user from dragging the Calculator by its buttons. The Equals button is more complex: It's actually composed of a circle, a rectangle, and another circle, stacked vertically. This is how the control region for the Equals button is specified in Calculator.css:

```
-apple-dashboard-region:
    dashboard-region(control circle 0 0 43px 0)
    dashboard-region(control rectangle 13px 0 13px 0)
    dashboard-region(control circle 43px 0 0 0);
);
```

The JavaScript File

The logical heart of a widget is its JavaScript file. This file, which typically has the extension .js, contains most of the JavaScript code that makes the widget work. If you create a widget, you can use any JavaScript code you want, but particular properties and methods are especially useful.

Most of the JavaScript properties, methods, and events you work with in your widget belong to either the window object or the widget object. This section lists some useful window and widget properties, methods, and events.

Live Resizing

Some widgets, such as the Dictionary widget that comes with Mac OS X Tiger, allow the user to change their sizes by dragging a resize control (also known as a grow box) in the window. You can enable live resizing by adding a resize control and some code to your widget.

In your HTML file, define the resize box:

```
<img id='resizeControl'

src='/System/Library/WidgetResources/resize.png'

onmousedown='mouseDown(event);'/>
```

Create style information for the resize box in your CSS file:

```
#resizeControl {

    position:absolute;

    right: 2px;

    bottom: 2px;

    -apple-dashboard-region: dashboard-region(control rectangle);

}
```

Finally, put the JavaScript code for the actual resizing in your .js file:

```
function mouseDown(event)

{

    var x = event.x + window.screenX;

    var y = event.y + window.screenY;

    document.addEventListener("mousemove", mouseMove, true);

    document.addEventListener("mouseup", mouseUp, true);


    lastPos = {x:x, y:y};

}
```

```
function mouseMove(event)
{
    var screenX = event.x + window.screenX;
    var screenY = event.y + window.screenY;
    window.resizeBy(screenX - lastPos.x, screenY - lastPos.y);
    lastPos = {x:screenX, y:screenY};
}


function mouseUp(event)
{
    document.removeEventListener("mousemove",  mouseMove, true);
    document.removeEventListener("mouseup", mouseUp, true);
}
```
And there you go: live resizing for your widget.

Window Properties

You might be especially interested in a couple of window properties:

- `window.document`: This contains the document object for the widget.
- `window.widget`: This property is the widget object itself.

Window Methods

Here are the window methods you might want to use:

- `window.alert (value)`: Use this method to write the given value to the system's console.log file, which you can view with the Console application.
- `window.resizeBy (width, height)`: Use this method to change to size of the widget by the amounts shown.
- `window.resizeTo (width, height)`: Use this method to resize the widget to the given absolute dimensions.

Window Events

The following are window events for widgets:

- window.onfocus: The system sends the onfocus event to your widget when it becomes frontmost. You can use this event to perform some action when your widget is activated. For example, the Calculator widget shows a blue *backlight* behind its display when it becomes frontmost.

Note

> Unlike windows in the standard Aqua user interface, OS X makes no visible changes to widgets when they become frontmost. So, if you want your widget to look different when it's in front, you have to implement the difference yourself in the window.onfocus method.

- window.onblur: The active widget gets an onblur event when it ceases to be frontmost.

Although I discuss the the window properties, methods, and events you're most likely to use in widgets, JavaScript defines many others for window objects. For more information on JavaScript windows, see any reference on JavaScript, such as www.croczilla.com/~alex/reference/javascript_ref/ or get a good JavaScript book, such as *JavaScript Bible* by Danny Goodman (John Wiley & Sons) or *JavaScript for the World Wide Web: Visual QuickStart Guide* by Tom Negrino and Dori Smith (Peachpit Press).

The Widget Property

Every widget is represented in JavaScript by a widget object. The widget object includes the following property:

- widget.identifier: This property is an integer that's unique to each running instance of your widget. You can use it in code to distinguish one copy of your widget from another. Some widgets, such as the World Clock and Weather widgets, can be useful in multiples.

Widget Methods

The widget object defines several interesting methods you can use to make your widget perform interesting tasks:

- widget.openURL(URL): This method dismisses the Dashboard layer and opens the given URL in the user's default browser.
- widget.openApplication(bundleID): You can use this method to open an application from your widget. The parameter is in the form of the application's CFBundleIdentifier: for example, com.apple.Preview or com.spiny.logorrhea. The Dashboard layer goes away before the application opens.

- `widget.system(command, listener)`: This powerful method gives you a way to execute shell commands from your widget. You can call shell commands *synchronously*, which means that the widget does not continue running until the call is done, or *asynchronously*, which means the widget immediately resumes execution even while the shell command is running. To perform the shell command synchronously, set the `listener` parameter to NULL. To call the shell command asynchronously, pass the name of a method in the `listener` parameter. The system calls that method when the shell command is done. If you're not sure what to do, just call the command synchronously.

  You can see the shell command's output after it's finished. When you call the command synchronously, the shell output is in `widget.system.outputString`. When you call it asynchronously, the `widget.system` call returns an object with the shell output in its `outputString` field.

Widget Events

Widgets can receive the following events:

- `widget.onshow`: When the user activates Dashboard, every open widget receives an `onshow` event. You can use this event to perform some action when your widget reappears with the rest of Dashboard.

- `widget.onhide`: Dashboard sends an `onhide` event to every widget right before the Dashboard layer goes away.

- `widget.onremove`: When the user closes your widget, Dashboard sends it an `onremove` event. You can use this event to be sure your widget is ready to vanish, saving preferences and any other persistent values.

Info.plist

Every widget must include an information property list in a file named Info.plist. Several property list keys are required:

- `MainHTML`: This key is a string containing a path to the widget's main HTML file. The path is relative within the widget's bundle. Most widgets simply set this key to the name of the widget plus the extension .html.

- `CFBundleIdentifier`: This required string is the standard bundle identifier, as included in other code bundles. The `CFBundleIdentifier` value is in the reverse domain form, as in com.apple.TextEdit.

Fun with Debugging

A new runtime environment like Dashboard requires new debugging tricks. Here are a few tips and techniques you can use as you're creating your own cool widgets:

- You can examine your widget's appearance and do some of your testing in Safari. This works because widgets are fundamentally Web pages, and Dashboard and Safari both use Apple's Web Kit to display content. To try this technique, just open your widget's main HTML file in Safari.

- You can use the `alert()` method to put debugging messages into the console.log file.

- If you suspect your widget is having a problem that requires you to reload its HTML file, click the widget and press Command-R to reload it. As a bonus, you get to see a cool Dashboard visual effect.

- You can run a widget by double-clicking it, no matter which directory it's in. Double-clicking a widget brings up the Dashboard layer and opens the widget.

In addition to these required identifiers, you can declare some optional properties in the information property list:

- `CloseBoxInsetX` and `CloseBoxInsetY`: Use these keys to move the Close box down and to the right from its standard position in the upper-left corner. If you don't specify these values, the Close box appears in the standard location.

- `AllowNetworkAccess`: Set this Boolean property to `True` if your widget gets any information from the Internet.

- `AllowSystem`: If your widget includes any shell command calls with the `widget.system` object, set this property to `True`.

- `AllowFileAccessOutsideOfWidget`: If you want your widget to have access to files that aren't in its bundle, include this property and set it to `True`.

- `AllowJava`: Set this property to `True` if your widget requires access to any Java applets.

- `AllowFullAccess`: Use this property if you want to allow access to all external resources without the finer granularity of permitting some and forbidding others.

Note When you include any of the Allow keys in your property list, the first run of the widget produces an alert warning the user that the widget hasn't been used before. This is a security feature designed to prevent malicious code from running a potentially destructive or intrusive widget without the user's knowledge.

The Default Image

The Default.png file, which was described earlier in this chapter, is a required component of every widget. If you create a widget that has no Default.png file, the widget appears in the widget bar. But when the user clicks the widget, Dashboard simply sounds an alert.

If your widget doesn't specify its height and width in its Info.plist, the widget uses the height and width of the Default.png file.

The Icon File

You can create a custom icon that can be used to represent your widget in the widget bar. To make a custom icon, create your icon and store it in a file named icon.png. If you don't supply a custom icon, Dashboard displays the default widget icon in the widget bar (Figure 16-6).

FIGURE 16-6: The Default widget icon.

Creating Word of the Day

This section lists the files that make up Word of the Day and describes how they go together to create a widget. Like most widgets, Word of the Day includes HTML, CSS, and JavaScript files that define its appearance and behavior. To change the way the widget looks, you usually edit its CSS files. The usual way to modify how the widget works is to change its JavaScript file.

The HTML File

Every widget must include an HTML file. This section contains the listing for the WordOfTheDay.html file.

The first part of the file imports the style sheet and JavaScript file.

```
<html>
<head>
   <!-- Import widget style sheet -->
   <style type="text/css">
      @import "WordOfTheDay.css";
   </style>

   <!-- Import JavaScript code for widget logic -->
   <script type='text/javascript' src='WordOfTheDay.js'
      charset='utf-8'/>
</head>
```

The rest of the HTML file, which is remarkably short, displays the background and defines a few objects that will be styled by the CSS file.

```
<body onload="onLoad();">
```

The default image background is usually the same as the image in the widget's Info.plist. This must be a PNG file.

```
<img src="Default.png">
```

Use span tags for each separately positioned element because these tags are designed for inline content and don't imply any formatting change as div tags can. The CSS file shows where these are positioned. Also, use id attributes instead of class attributes because id implies that only one element will have that identifier.

The next section of the file defines span tags for various elements in the display. To see which part of the widget is controlled by each tag, see the description of the CSS file later in this chapter.

```
   -->
<span id="wotdTerm">(loading)</span>
<span id="wotdDesc">

   <!--- Part of speech, e.g. noun, adjective, etc. -->
   <span id="wotdWordType"></span>

   <!-- Definition of word, follows immediately after -->
   <span id="wotdWordDef"></span>
</span>

<!-- Date goes in lower right corner -->
<span id="wotdDate"></span>

</body>
</html>
```

The JavaScript File

Like most widgets, Word of the Day includes a separate JavaScript file, which is presented in this section. This file defines the JavaScript methods that are called when various events are sent to the widget, such as `onLoad`, as well as methods defined by the widget to do its own work, such as `updateWordOfDay`.

Global Variables

The first part of the file defines a small number of global variables.

```
/**
 * Global request, set up in updateWordOfDay() and used in
 * handleStateChange().
 */
var request = null;

/** Timer, runs every hour while visible to update word of the
day. */
var timer = null;
var nextUpdate = null;
```

onLoad

Dashboard sends the `onload` event when the widget is first loaded, and the widget handles the message with the `onLoad` method.

```
/** Called when the page is loaded. */
function onLoad()
{
   /* Set up show/hide handles which we'll use to start and
    * stop the update timer.
    */
   if (window.widget)
   {
      widget.onshow = onShowHandler;
      widget.onhide = onHideHandler;
   }

   /* Need to call the Show handler manually first time. */
   onShowHandler();

   return 0;
}
```

onShowHandler

The `onShowHandler` function is called when the widget gets the `onshow` event, which happens every time the widget becomes visible (along with the rest of Dashboard).

```
/** Called when widget is shown. */
function onShowHandler()
{
```

Because the timer is only running when the widget is visible, you need to check manually if the current time has gone past the interval you set.

```
if (nextUpdate == null)
    {
        /* No last time; update now and set next update
         * threshold.
         */
        updateWordOfDay();
        nextUpdate = new Date();
        nextUpdate.setHours(nextUpdate.getHours() + 1);
    }
    else
    {
        var now = new Date();

        if (now.getTime() > nextUpdate.getTime())
        {
            /* We haven't been shown in over an hour, so update
             * now.
             */
            updateWordOfDay();
            nextUpdate = now;
            nextUpdate.setHours(nextUpdate.getHours() + 1);
        }
    }
```

Set the timer for further updates, firing once per hour. Although you might not have Dashboard open for hours, you have ways to put widgets on the desktop and keep them around all the time. Also, this timer technique is useful for widgets with shorter timer intervals.

```
if (timer == null)
    {
        timer = setInterval('updateWordOfDay();', 60 * 60 *
1000);
    }
}
```

onHideHandler

When the Dashboard layer goes away, all widgets receive the onhide message. In Word of the Day, that event triggers a call to onHideHandler.

```
/** Called when widget is hidden. */
function onHideHandler()
{
    /* Clear the update timer; we don't want it running while
     * the widget is hidden.
     */
    if (timer != null)
    {
        clearInterval(timer);
        timer = null;
    }
}
```

updateWordOfDay

The `updateWordOfDay` method calls the Web service to get a new word. This method uses the handy `XMLHttpRequest` function to get data from the Word of the Day service. When this method is called, the reply is handled by the `handleStateChange` method.

```
function updateWordOfDay()
{
    request = new XMLHttpRequest();

    /* Set our callback for when the request changes state (e.g.
     * when the content is loaded.
     */
    request.onreadystatechange = handleStateChange;

    /* Using your own web server is a handy and fast way to test
     * before pointing your widget at the real server.
     */
    // request.open("GET", "http://localhost/~Josh/wotd.xml");

    /* Send off the request. */
    request.open("GET", "http://education.yahoo.com/rss/wotd");
    request.send(null);
}
```

handleStateChange

The `handleStateChange` workhorse routine is called after the widget gets updated XML data from the service. This method parses the result from the service and sets the appropriate properties of the document object to the right values.

```
/**
 * Called from the XMLHttpRequest any time the request state
 * changes. We'll only do interesting stuff when it's done.
 */
function handleStateChange()
{
    /* Update only if XML request completed with good status */
    if (!(request.readyState == 4 && request.status == 200))
    {
        return;
    }

    /* Get the first (and in this case only) "item" element */
    var item =
        request.responseXML.getElementsByTagName("item")[0];

    /* Extract the title and description from the item */
    var title =
        item.getElementsByTagName("title")[0].firstChild.data;
    var desc =
        item.getElementsByTagName("description")[0].
firstChild.data;
```

The term (the word itself) and the date are combined in the `title` element, with a dash between them. I'll split those into two parts.

```
var a = title.split(" - ");
var term = a[0];
var date = a[1];
```

Next, extract the part of speech and definition so we can style them separately. Part of speech is in parentheses, and the definition follows.

```
a = desc.match(/(\(\S+\)) (.*)/);
var type = a[1];
var definition = a[2];
```

Finally, update the widget by setting the content of each element identifier to the new content obtained from the Web service.

```
document.getElementById("wotdTerm").innerText = term;
document.getElementById("wotdWordType").innerText = type;
document.getElementById
    ("wotdWordDef").innerText = definition;
document.getElementById("wotdDate").innerText = date;

request = null;
}
```

The CSS File

This section describes the CSS file for Word of the Day. This file contains CSS style information for elements defined in the HTML file. This is the file to change if you want to alter the font, color, or position of elements in the widget.

body

The `body` element simply defines a style for the body of the widget.

```
body {
    margin: 0;
}
```

wotdTerm

The `wotdTerm` style is applied to the Word of the Day itself when it's displayed by the widget. The style defines the font, text color, alignment, and other settings.

```
#wotdTerm {
    font: 20px "Lucida Grande";
    font-weight: bold;
    text-align: left;
    color: black;
    position: absolute;
    top: 9px;
    left: 12px;
}
```

wotdDate

The `wotdDate` style is used to format today's date, which appears in the lower-right corner of the widget.

```
#wotdDate {
    font: 10px "Lucida Grande";
    font-weight: normal;
    text-align: left;
    color: black;
    position: absolute;
    top: 104px;
    left: 90px;
}
```

wotdDesc

The word description, which is the line that gives the word's part of speech and definition, is described in a style named `wotdDesc`. Within `wotdDesc`, additional styles refine the definition for the two separate pieces of the description.

```
#wotdDesc {
    font: 14px "Cochin";
    font-weight: normal;
    text-align: left;
    color: black;
    position: absolute;
    top: 36px;
    left: 12px;
    width: 172px;
}
```

wotdWordType

The word's part of speech is formatted using the `wotdWordType` style. The only difference from the style defined by `wordDesc` is that text is italicized.

```
#wotdWordType {
    font-style: italic;
}
```

wotdDef

The `wotdDef` style specifies `normal` style to ensure that the word's definition is not italicized.

```
#wotdWordDef {
    font-style: normal;
}
```

Info.plist

This section describes the all-important Info.plist file in the Word of the Day bundle. The Info.plist file starts with the standard header.

```
<?xml version="1.0" encoding="UTF-8"?>
<!DOCTYPE plist PUBLIC "-//Apple Computer//DTD PLIST 1.0//EN"
"http://www.apple.com/DTDs/PropertyList-1.0.dtd">
<plist version="1.0">
<dict>
```

To permit your widget to reach across the Internet for its daily word, you have to set AllowNetworkAccess to True. When you set this value, the first time the widget is run, Dashboard puts up a warning asking the user to confirm that it's okay to run the widget. You also set the AllowMultipleInstances key to let the user run any number of copies of your widget.

```
<key>AllowMultipleInstances</key>
<true/>
<key>AllowNetworkAccess</key>
<true/>
```

Next are various properties that identify the bundle: CFBundleIdentifier, CFBundleName, CFBundleShortVersionString, and CFBundleVersion.

```
<key>CFBundleIdentifier</key>
<string>com.multipart-mixed.widget.wordoftheday</string>
<key>CFBundleName</key>
<string>Word Of The Day</string>
<key>CFBundleShortVersionString</key>
<string>1.0</string>
<key>CFBundleVersion</key>
<string>1.0</string>
```

Finally, you define the vital MainHTML and DefaultImage properties, along with the optional (but handy) Height and Width properties. (If you leave out Height and Width, the widget simply uses the values from the default image.)

```
<key>MainHTML</key>
<string>WordOfTheDay.html</string>
<key>DefaultImage</key>
<string>Default</string>
<key>Height</key>
<integer>130</integer>
<key>Width</key>
<integer>200</integer>
</dict>
</plist>
```

Extra Credit

Looking for more things to do to make Word of the Day even cooler? Try these:

- Give Word of the Day a custom icon. Just create an icon, save it as icon.png, and then add the file to the bundle.

- Hook Word of the Day to Mac OS X's Dictionary application so you can compare the definitions provided in each place.

- Use your knowledge of control regions to make the Calculator widget draggable by its buttons.

- Add a button to speak the Word of the Day using OS X's speech synthesizer.

Summary

Dashboard and its widgets are among the greatest of all the new features introduced by Tiger. With a little imagination and work, you can create widgets that make users' computing lives easier and more fun. Word of the Day provides a great introductory lesson into how widgets work—and just using it makes you smarter.

Top Tunes

In this chapter, I present Top Tunes, another widget for Apple's cool Dashboard feature that was added to Mac OS X Tiger. This time, you'll get a little more advanced than you did with Word of the Day in the previous chapter, as you plumb the depths of the iTunes Music Store to extract information about the songs and albums that are selling best or have just been added.

About Top Tunes

Top Tunes (pictured in Figure 17-1) is a widget that talks to the iTunes Music Store about music. When you run Top Tunes, it shows you the top album on iTunes, with arrow buttons you can use to see the next four best-selling albums.

FIGURE 17-1: Top Tunes widget.

Top Tunes knows how to display various kinds of information from the store. You can choose from several categories, and you can show up to 100 top items from any category, as demonstrated in Figure 17-2.

FIGURE 17-2: You can see up to 100 items in any category.

Top Tunes gets this vital information from public RSS feeds kindly provided by Apple via the iTunes Music Store. For details on how to construct URLs for these feeds, see phobos.apple.com/WebObjects/MZSearch.woa/wa/MRSS/rssGenerator.

Like most widgets, Top Tunes comes with a preferences view that appears on the *back* of the widget (Figure 17-3). This is where the user determines how many and what kind of items to show.

FIGURE 17-3: Top Tunes preferences view.

This widget was created by **John A. Vink** (JAV). JAV has worked as a software engineer in Silicon Valley for more than a decade. He is a proud native of Canada. JAV's favorite band is INXS, which should be obvious if you take a close look at Top Tunes' startup screen. He is the co-creator of beloved cartoon character Flirburt, who will possibly appear soon in his own feature-length film. Find out more about JAV by visiting www.javworld.com.

Origins of Top Tunes

Like most programming projects, Top Tunes did not start out as a bunch of empty files. John based Top Tunes on the XML-requesting code in the Stocks widget, and he used code from the Goodbye World example widget to support preferences and the info button.

The HTML File

This section dissects the TopTunes.html file, which defines the appearance of the widget and the preferences view on the back of the widget.

head

TopTunes.html starts with the head section. Because TopTunes (like most widgets) is split into separate files for HMTL, JavaScript, and CSS, you must reference the other files here: the CSS file with a `<style type>` tag, and the JavaScript file with a `<script type>` tag.

```
<html>
<head>

<style type="text/css">
  @import "TopTunes.css";
</style>
<script type='text/javascript' src='TopTunes.js'
  charset='utf-8'/>

</head>
```

div (Main View)

The body section contains the definition of the widget's appearance. First, we call `setupWidget` when the widget is first loaded. After that is a `div` section for the main view (with id `"front"`) of the widget, laid out as a table. The table elements reference classes in the CSS file, such as `albumArt` and `artist`. There's also a definition for the Refresh button.

```
<body onload="setupWidget();">

<div id='front' onmousemove='mousemove(event);'
  onmouseout='mouseexit(event);'>
  <img src="Images/Background.png">
  <table class='maintable'>
    <tr><td colspan=2>
      <div id='header'></div>
    </td></tr>
    <tr>
      <td width=100px>
        <div id='art' class='albumArt'></div>
      </td>
      <td width=225px>
        <div id='rank'></div>
        <div id='artist' class='artist'></div>
        <div id='albumTitle' class='album'></div>
        <div id='navigate'>
          <table>
            <tr align='center'>
              <td onclick=
              'navigate(-1);'>
              <div class='navigate'>
              <img src="Images/prev.png"></div>
              </td>
              <td onclick=
```

```
              'navigate(1);'>
              <div class='navigate'>
              <img src="Images/next.png"></div>
              </td>
          </tr>
        </table>
      </div>
    </td>
  </tr>
</table>
<span id='refresh' onclick='refresh(event);'>refresh</span>
```

The rest of the div section defines the info button that opens preferences (the tiny *i* and the circle behind it that appears on mouseover). This code is boilerplate, taken directly from /System/WidgetResources.

```
<div class='flip' id='fliprollie'></div>
  <div class='flip' id='flip' onclick='showPrefs(event);'
    onmouseover='enterflip(event);'
    onmouseout='exitflip(event)';></div>
</div>
```

div (Preferences View)

TopTunes.html also defines the preferences view on the "back" of the widget. This view is in a separate div section. This view includes the input field for the number of results, a pop-up menu to choose what to display, and the Done button to flip the widget back around. The input field calls resultsChanged when the user edits it. The Done button and its code are taken directly from /System/WidgetResources.

```
<div id='back'>
  <img src="Images/BackBackground.png">
  <table class='maintable'>
    <tr><td>
    <span class="prefsLabel">Number Results:</span>
    </td><td>
    <input id='numresults'
      onchange='resultsChanged(event);'></input>
    </td></tr>
    <tr><td>
    <span class="prefsLabel">List:</span>
    </td><td>
    <select id='listPopup' onchange='changeList(this);'>
      <!-- Popup menu for the choice of text -->
      <option value=1>Songs</option>
      <option value=2>Albums</option>
      <option value=3>New Releases</option>
      <option value=4>Just Added</option>
      <option value=5>Featured and
       Exclusives</option>
```

```
    </select>
    </td></tr>
    <tr><td>
    <img class="doneButton" src="Images/done.png"
      onclick='hidePrefs()' />
      <!-- Done button; dismisses preferences -->
    </td></tr>
  </table>
</div>

</body>
</html>
```

The JavaScript File

The TopTunes.js file contains most of the JavaScript code for the widget. The first part of the file defines some local variables.

```
var numAlbums = 0;      // number of items to display
var currentAlbum = 0;   // rank of currently displayed item
var list = 0;           // which list is being displayed
var result;             // array of items from music store
var needRefresh = false; // set when contents are new
```

setupWidget

The setupWidget function is called when the widget first appears. This function ensures the widget has a valid number for the list preference.

```
function setupWidget()
{
  list = window.widget.preferenceForKey("list");
  if (list == null)
    list = 1;
  fetchNewMusic(xml_callback);
}
```

fetchNewMusic

The fetchNewMusic function is called to get information from the RSS feed supplied by the iTunes Music Store. It reads data using the XMLHttpRequest function (which is also used by the Stocks widget that comes with Tiger).

The URL used in XMLHttpRequest includes a genre parameter that lets the caller specify which genres should be considered for the results. In Top Tunes, this parameter was designed by the programmer to include only genres that met his particular tastes. You might want to change that—see phobos.apple.com/WebObjects/MZSearch.woa/wa/MRSS/rssGenerator to create your own URL.

Note   For more information on XMLHttpRequest, see `http://developer.apple.com/internet/webcontent/xmlhttpreq.html` .

```
function fetchNewMusic(callback)
{
  if (window.widget)
  {
    var xml_request = new XMLHttpRequest();
    xml_request.onload = function(e)
      {xml_loaded(e, xml_request, callback);}
    xml_request.overrideMimeType("text/xml");
    var limit = window.widget.preferenceForKey("numResults");
    if (limit == null)
      limit = 5;
    var urlList = urlForCurrentList();
    xml_request.open("GET",
      'http://ax.phobos.apple.com.edgesuite.net/WebObjects/
      MZStore.woa/wpa/MRSS/' + urlList +
      '/sf=143441/genre=000c100/limit=' +
      limit + '/rss.xml');
    xml_request.setRequestHeader("Cache-Control",
      "no-cache");
    xml_request.send(null);
  }
}
```

refresh

The widget calls the `refresh` method when the user clicks the Refresh button. This method reloads the items by calling `fetchNewMusic`.

```
function refresh (event)
{
  fetchNewMusic(xml_callback);
}
```

urlForCurrentList

The `urlForCurrentList` function is called by `fetchNewMusic` to convert the user's list selection to text that becomes part of the URL for `XMLHttpRequest`.

```
function urlForCurrentList()
{
  switch( list )  // find out which option was chosen
  {
    case 1:
      return "topsongs";
      break;
    case 2:
      return "topalbums";
      break;
    case 3:
      return "newreleases";
      break;
    case 4:
      return "justadded";
      break;
    case 5:
      return "featuredalbums";
      break;
  }
}
```

xml_loaded

The `xml_loaded` function is called after RSS information is read from the iTunes Music Store. This function then parses the RSS to retrieve information that's displayed by the widget. First, it calls `getElementTextNS` to pull each element type from the Music Store results. It then combines all the retrieved elements into the result.

```
function xml_loaded (event, request, callback)
{
  try
  {
    if (request.responseXML)
    {
      result = new Array;
      var items =
        request.responseXML.getElementsByTagName("item");

      for (var i = 0; i < items.length; i++)
      {
```

```
        var title =
            getElementTextNS("itms", "album", items[i], 0);
        var artist =
            getElementTextNS("itms", "artist", items[i], 0);
        var song =
            getElementTextNS("itms", "song", items[i], 0);
        var songLink =
            getElementTextNS("itms", "songLink", items[i], 0);
        var albumLink =
            getElementTextNS("itms", "albumLink", items[i], 0);
        var artistLink =
            getElementTextNS("itms", "artistLink", items[i], 0);
        var songLink =
            getElementTextNS("itms", "songLink", items[i], 0);

        var images = items[i].getElementsByTagName("coverArt");
        var image;
        if (images.length > 0)
          image = images[images.length-1].firstChild.data;
        else
          image =
            getElementTextNS("itms", "coverArt", items[i], 0);

        result[result.length] = {title:title, artist:artist,
                albumLink:albumLink, artistLink:artistLink,
                image:image, song:song, songLink:songLink};
      }

  }
  else
    alert("xml_loaded no request.responseXML");

  try
  {
    callback(result);
  }
  catch (ex)
  {
  }

}
catch (ex)
{
  alert("xml_loaded Exception " + ex);
}
}
```

getElementTextNS

This method retrieves the text of an element in the XML document, using the name of the element as a key. Most of the work in this method is done by calling getElementsByTagName.

```
function getElementTextNS(prefix, local, parentElem, index) {
    var result = parentElem.getElementsByTagName(local)[index];
    if (result) {
        if (result.childNodes.length > 1) {
            return result.childNodes[1].nodeValue;
        } else {
            return result.firstChild.nodeValue;
        }
    } else {
        return null;
    }
}
```

xml_callback

The xml_callback function is called after fetchNewMusic gets information from the Store. It calls drawNewInfo to make sure the widget is displaying the new data.

```
function xml_callback(result)
{
    currentAlbum = 0;
    numAlbums = result.length;
    drawNewInfo();
}
```

drawNewInfo

The drawNewInfo function uses the document's getElementById call to extract information for the widget and draw it. This function inserts href tags into the artist and album names to build hyperlinks to the iTunes Music Store.

```
function drawNewInfo()
{
    document.getElementById('artist').innerHTML = "<a href="
        + result[currentAlbum].artistLink + ">"
        + result[currentAlbum].artist + "</a>";
    if (result[currentAlbum].song != null)
        document.getElementById('albumTitle').innerHTML =
            "<a href=" + result[currentAlbum].songLink + ">"
            + result[currentAlbum].song + "</a>";
    else
        document.getElementById('albumTitle').innerHTML =
            "<a href=" + result[currentAlbum].albumLink + ">"
            + result[currentAlbum].title + "</a>";
    document.getElementById('art').innerHTML = "<img src="
        + result[currentAlbum].image + ">";
```

```
document.getElementById('rank').innerText = currentAlbum
  + 1;
document.getElementById('header').innerText = "Top "
  + numAlbums + " " + currentList();
}
```

currentList

The currentList function converts the user's selection index in the list (1 through 5) into the name of a category. Note that this is similar to, but not the same as, the lookup performed by urlForCurrentList.

```
function currentList()
{
  switch( list )  // find out which option was chosen
  {
    case 1:
      return "Songs";
      break;
    case 2:
      return "Albums";
      break;
    case 3:
      return "New Releases";
      break;
    case 4:
      return "Just Added";
      break;
    case 5:
      return "Featured Albums & Exclusives";
      break;
  }
}
```

navigate

The navigate function is called when the user clicks one of the arrows on the widget. After the current album is changed, navigate calls drawNewInfo to redisplay the widget's information.

```
function navigate(direction)
{
  currentAlbum = currentAlbum + direction;
  if (currentAlbum < 0)
    currentAlbum = numAlbums - 1;
  else if (currentAlbum > (numAlbums - 1))
    currentAlbum = 0;
  drawNewInfo();
}
```

showPrefs

The showPrefs function flips the widget around and displays the preferences view on the back. First, showPrefs calls widget.prepareForTransition to prevent anything in the user interface from changing. Then, showPrefs uses CSS styles to hide the front of the widget and show the back. The call to widget.performTransition displays the preferences. All this code is standard and used in every widget that includes preferences, although you can add code for your widget if you'd like. The rest of the function gets values from stored preferences and hides the circle (fliprollie) that appears behind the Preferences button on mouseover.

```
function showPrefs()
{
  try
  {
    needRefresh = false;

    var front = document.getElementById("front");
    var back = document.getElementById("back");

    if (window.widget)
      widget.prepareForTransition("ToBack");

    front.style.display="none";   // hide the front
    back.style.display="block";   // show the back

    if (window.widget)
    {
      setTimeout ('widget.performTransition();', 0)
      var numResults =
        widget.preferenceForKey("numResults");
      if (numResults != null)
      {
        document.getElementById("numresults").value =
numResults;
      }
      document.getElementById("listPopup").selectedIndex =
list - 1;
    }

    document.getElementById('fliprollie').style.display
      = 'none';
  }
  catch (ex)
  {
    alert("Exception " + ex);
  }

}
```

hidePrefs

When the user clicks the Done button on the back of the widget, the button calls `hidePrefs`. This function performs actions that are the reverse of `showPrefs`. The preferences view is hidden and the main view is shown. The `widget.performTransition` call flips the widget so that the front is showing. Like `showPrefs`, the `hidePrefs` function code is standard in all widgets that have preferences, although it's okay if you want to add code to perform additional work.

```
function hidePrefs()
{
  try
  {
    if (needRefresh)
      fetchNewMusic(xml_callback);

    var front = document.getElementById("front");
    var back = document.getElementById("back");

    if (window.widget)
      widget.prepareForTransition("ToFront");

    back.style.display="none";
    front.style.display="block";

    if (window.widget)
      setTimeout ('widget.performTransition();', 0);
  }
  catch (ex)
  {
    alert("Exception " + ex);
  }
}
```

resultsChanged

The preferences view includes a field in which users can specify how many albums to display. When the user modifies the value in the field, it calls `resultsChanged`, which changes the associated preference value and flags the widget for redrawing.

```
function resultsChanged (event)
{
  var results = document.getElementById('numresults').value;
  if (results != null)
  {
    if (window.widget)
      widget.setPreferenceForKey (results, "numResults");
  }

  needRefresh = true;
}
```

changeList

The preferences view includes a pop-up menu that lets users specify the type of information to get from the iTunes Music Store—songs, albums, new releases, and so on. When the user changes the value in this menu, the menu calls `changeList`, which modifies the associated preference value and flags the widget for redrawing.

```
function changeList(elem)
{
  list = parseInt(elem.options[elem.selectedIndex].value);
  if (list != null)
  {
    if (window.widget)
      widget.setPreferenceForKey (list, "list");
  }
  needRefresh = true;
}
```

Info Button Animation

Every widget with preferences has an Info button, which appears on the widget as a tiny *i* when the user mouses over the widget. As a further visual flourish, the Info button gains a translucent circle around it when the mouse pointer is hovering directly over the button. The remaining code in the JavaScript file is a standard set of functions used to animate the Info button in the standard way.

The functions used for the Info button animation are:

- `mousemove`
- `mouseexit`
- `animate`
- `limit_3`
- `computeNextFloat`
- `enterflip`
- `exitflip`

Here's the code for these functions:

```
var flipShown = false

var animation = {duration:0, starttime:0, to:1.0, now:0.0,
from:0.0, firstElement:null, timer:null};
```

```
function mousemove (event)
{
  if (!flipShown)
  {
    if (animation.timer != null)
    {
      clearInterval (animation.timer);
      animation.timer  = null;
    }

    var starttime = (new Date).getTime() - 13;

    animation.duration = 500;
    animation.starttime = starttime;
    animation.firstElement =
      document.getElementById ('flip');
    animation.timer = setInterval ("animate();", 13);
    animation.from = animation.now;
    animation.to = 1.0;
    animate();

    flipShown = true;
  }
}

function mouseexit (event)
{
  if (flipShown)
  {
    // fade in the flip widget
    if (animation.timer != null)
    {
      clearInterval (animation.timer);
      animation.timer  = null;
    }

    var starttime = (new Date).getTime() - 13;

    animation.duration = 500;
    animation.starttime = starttime;
    animation.firstElement =
      document.getElementById ('flip');
    animation.timer = setInterval ("animate();", 13);
    animation.from = animation.now;
    animation.to = 0.0;
    animate();
    flipShown = false;
  }
}
```

```
function animate()
{
  var T;
  var ease;
  var time = (new Date).getTime();


  T = limit_3(time-animation.starttime, 0,
    animation.duration);

  if (T >= animation.duration)
  {
    clearInterval (animation.timer);
    animation.timer = null;
    animation.now = animation.to;
  }
  else
  {
    ease = 0.5 - (0.5 * Math.cos(Math.PI *
      T / animation.duration));
    animation.now = computeNextFloat
      (animation.from, animation.to, ease);
  }

  animation.firstElement.style.opacity = animation.now;
}

function limit_3 (a, b, c)
{
    return a < b ? b : (a > c ? c : a);
}

function computeNextFloat (from, to, ease)
{
    return from + (to - from) * ease;
}

function enterflip(event)
{
  document.getElementById('fliprollie').style.display =
    'block';
}

function exitflip(event)
{
  document.getElementById('fliprollie').style.display = 'none';
}
```

The CSS File

The TopTunes.css file holds the style sheet information for the main and preferences views. This section lists the CSS style objects defined by TopTunes.css. Figure 17-4 shows the Top Tunes screen with labels representing CSS styles for each part of the widget.

FIGURE 17-4: The appearance of each part of the widget is determined by a CSS style.

albumArt

The `albumArt` class provides the CSS information for the album cover displayed in the widget.

```
.albumArt {
  width:100px;
  height:100px;
}
```

album

Top Tunes uses the `album` class to define the text that displays the album title.

```
.album {
  left:16px;
  top:2px;
  font: 12px "Helvetica Neue";
    font-weight: bold;
    color: rgb(166,179,202);
    text-shadow: rgba(0,0,0,0.5) 0px -1px 1px;
  text-align:center;
}
```

artist

The `artist` class is applied to the name of the artist on the widget.

```
.artist {
  left:16px;
  top:2px;
  font: 12px "Helvetica Neue";
    font-weight: bold;
    color: rgb(166,179,202);
    text-shadow: rgba(0,0,0,0.5) 0px -1px 1px;
  text-align:center;
}
```

navigate

The arrows for moving to the next and previous items use the `navigate` class.

```
.navigate {
  text-align:center;
  top:2px;
  width: 112px;
}
```

header

The `header` object provides the style for the large text at the top of the widget.

```
#header {
  font: 24px "Helvetica Neue";
    font-weight: bold;
  text-align:center;
}
```

back

The `back` style is assigned to the preferences view on the back of the widget. Initially, this value is set to `display:none`, which hides the preferences. When preferences are switched in, the value changes to `display:block`, which makes the back view appear, while the front view is set to `display:none`.

```
#back {
  display:none;
}
```

numresults

Top Tunes uses the `numresults` object to define the appearance of the input field on the preferences screen. Users type the desired number of albums from the iTunes Music Store into this field.

```
#numresults {
  width:120px;
  font-size:11px;
}
```

prefsLabel

The `prefsLabel` class defines the style for text labels on the preferences screen.

```
.prefsLabel {
  font: 12px "Lucida Grande";
  font-weight: bold;
  color: white;
}
```

maintable

The `maintable` class describes the appearance of the main part of the Top Tunes widget, which is defined as a table.

```
.maintable {
  position:absolute;
  top:10px;
  left:10px;
  width:325px;
}
```

rank

Top Tunes uses the `rank` style to display the item rank of the current item at the iTunes Music Store.

```
#rank {
  text-align:center;
    color: rgb(255,255,255);
  font: 18px "Helvetica Neue";
    font-weight: bold;
    line-height: 200%;
  background: url(Images/rank.png) no-repeat center;
  height: 40px;
  width: 225px;
}
```

refresh

The Refresh button in the Top Tunes widget uses the refresh style listed here.

```
#refresh {
  opacity:0;
  position:absolute;
  bottom: 12px;
  left: 18px;
  font: 12px "Helvetica Neue";
    font-weight: bold;
    color: rgb(255,255,255);
}
```

Preferences Support

The remaining classes and objects are standard and are used to support the Info button (flip, fliprollie) and the preferences view (doneButton).

```
.flip {
  position:absolute;
  bottom: 12px;
  right: 12px;
  width:13px;
  height:13px;
}

#flip {
  opacity:0;
  background: url(file:///System/Library/WidgetResources
          /ibutton/white_i.png) no-repeat top left;
  z-index:8000;
}

#fliprollie {
  display:none;
  opacity:0.25;
  background: url(file:///System/Library/WidgetResources
          /ibutton/white_rollie.png) no-repeat top left;
  z-index:7999;
}

#doneButton {
  position:absolute;
  top:100px;
  text-align:center;
}
```

Info.plist

This section describes the information property list (Info.plist) that's part of the TopTunes.wdgt bundle.

```
<?xml version="1.0" encoding="UTF-8"?>
<!DOCTYPE plist PUBLIC "-//Apple Computer//DTD PLIST 1.0//EN"
"http://www.apple.com/DTDs/PropertyList-1.0.dtd">
<plist version="1.0">
<dict>
```

Because the widget is going to access the Internet, you have to declare your intentions here by setting AllowNetworkAccess to True. Because of this, the first time the user runs the widget, Dashboard will display a warning asking the user to confirm that it's okay to run the widget (Figure 17-5).

FIGURE 17-5: This dialog appears the first time you run Top Tunes.

```
<key>AllowNetworkAccess</key>
<true/>
```

The CFBundleDisplayName, CFBundleIdentifier, CFBundleName, CFBundleShortVersionString, and CFBundleVersion properties all provide identifying information for the bundle, just as they do for application bundles.

```
<key>CFBundleDisplayName</key>
<string>Top Tunes</string>
<key>CFBundleIdentifier</key>
<string>com.javworld.toptunes</string>
<key>CFBundleName</key>
<string>Top Tunes</string>
<key>CFBundleShortVersionString</key>
<string>1.0</string>
<key>CFBundleVersion</key>
<string>1.0</string>
```

When the user starts the widget, Dashboard displays the widget's default image until the widget is loaded. The `DefaultImage` property gives the name of the file that contains the default image.

```
<key>DefaultImage</key>
<string>Default</string>
```

The `MainHTML` property gives the name of the file that describes the widget's user interface and basic features.

```
<key>MainHTML</key>
<string>TopTunes.html</string>
```

The `Height` and `Width` properties specify the dimensions for the widget. If these properties are not present, the widget uses the height and width of the default image.

```
<key>Height</key>
<integer>220</integer>
<key>Width</key>
<integer>370</integer>
</dict>
</plist>
```

Extra Credit

When you use the Calculator widget, you can't drag the widget around by holding the mouse down on the buttons—you have to grab the Calculator by its edges or by its display. Dashboard implements this capability through the *control regions* feature, which uses CSS styles to specify parts of your widget that can't be dragged. You can use control regions to prevent Top Tunes from being dragged around by its arrow buttons.

 Cross-Reference For more information on this subject, see the section "The CSS File" in Chapter 16.

Summary

As RSS becomes more popular, we're seeing an explosion of data that's available through RSS feeds. Top Tunes shows what you can do with widgets that read RSS feeds. Widgets are as close as a function key or mouse button, and RSS provides fast access to information from far away. The combination is very powerful.

Video Desktop

Cool hacks are not always about the newest and shiniest features. Sometimes, a great hack comes from unearthing wonderful and wacky code hidden in an obscure location. Apple's sample code repository is a great source for this sort of digital archeology. In this chapter, you see a wonderful hack that takes advantage of a little-known bit of sample code for processing video camera input into QuickTime video. The hack, Video Desktop, takes the camera input and turns it into a continuously changing Mac OS X desktop (see Figure 18-1). The technology it uses isn't new or particularly fancy, but the effect it produces is extremely cool.

Video Desktop

Video Desktop works by creating an `NSWindow` and filling it with video grabbed from a camera, such as an Apple iSight, that's connected to the computer. The crucial act of grabbing frames and getting them to the screen is done by code derived from a sample application named SGDataProc, available at developer.apple.com/samplecode/Cocoa_-_SGDataProc/Cocoa_-_SGDataProc.html.

The SGDataProc sample instantiates `NSQuickDrawView`, a class that draws graphics using QuickDraw, the Mac's original graphics technology. The sample wires up a view with the input from a video camera, performing the necessary processing to get the image into a window.

FIGURE 18-1: Video Desktop in action.

The main part of the application creates a window that uses NSQuickDrawView to do its drawing. The most interesting part of this process is a call to the setLevel method of NSWindow which makes the window holding the video input appear in front of the desktop picture but behind any windows just above the desktop. The window also uses NSBorderlessWindowMask as its style, which ensures that no border will mar the incoming video as it plays on the desktop.

Buzz Andersen is a smart young programmer from the mean streets of Denver. Buzz is best known for his cool software contributions to the world: Cocoalicious, an open-source client for the popular del.icio.us social bookmark system, and PodWorks, a terrific utility that grants you greater control over copying songs to and from your iPod. Both products are available at Buzz's Web site, www.scifihifi.com.

Video Desktop Source Code

This section lists the key source files for Video Desktop, including the AppController files present in most Cocoa applications, along with the header and implementation for MyQuickDrawView, the code that pulls video in from the camera and puts it into a window.

AppController.h

The AppController.h file defines the interface for the application controller class, which includes three members:

- videoWindow, the window object you can use to display video on the desktop.
- gdView, an object of type MyQuickDrawView that takes video from the camera and associates it with the window.
- glView, an OpenGL view that's currently unused but is included as a possible technique to use for displaying video in a future version of this hack.

Note For more information on OpenGL and other graphics technologies used in Mac OS X, see http://developer.apple.com/referencelibrary/GettingStarted/GS_Graphics Imaging/index.html.

```
#import <Foundation/Foundation.h>
#import "MyQuickDrawView.h"
#import <QuickTime/QuickTime.h>
#import <Carbon/Carbon.h>

@interface AppController : NSObject {
    NSWindow *videoWindow;
    NSOpenGLView *glView;
    MyQuickDrawView *qdView;
}

@end
```

AppController.m

The AppController.m file holds the implementation for the `AppController` class. It defines three methods: `init`, `awakeFromNib`, and `applicationWillTerminate`.

```
#import "AppController.h"

@implementation AppController
```

The `init` method performs one task: It sets up the `AppController` object to receive a notification when the application is about to be terminated. This gives the application a chance to clean up the frame grabber function before it goes away.

```
- (id) init {
    [[NSNotificationCenter defaultCenter] addObserver:self
        selector:@selector(applicationWillTerminate:)
        name:@"NSApplicationWillTerminateNotification"
        object:NSApp];

    return self;
}
```

The `awakeFromNib` method is the place where `AppController` does its work. First, it allocates a rectangle to define the bounds of the video image and a view to be placed in the window.

```
- (void) awakeFromNib {
    NSRect screenRect = [[[NSScreen screens]
      objectAtIndex: 0] frame];

    qdView = [[MyQuickDrawView alloc] init];
```

Next, it creates the window object and initializes its fields, including the no-border mask and the all-important call to `setLevel` that makes the window appear on the desktop.

```
    videoWindow = [[NSWindow alloc]
        initWithContentRect: screenRect
        styleMask: NSBorderlessWindowMask
        backing: NSBackingStoreBuffered
        defer: NO];
    [videoWindow setBackgroundColor: [NSColor blackColor]];
    [videoWindow setLevel:
        CGWindowLevelForKey(kCGDesktopWindowLevelKey)];
    [videoWindow setIgnoresMouseEvents: YES];
    [videoWindow setContentView: qdView];
    saveQDViewObjectForCallback(qdView);
```

Now it's time to start the show by calling `doSeqGrab`, which begins grabbing frames from the video camera. The video appears in a window that's 800 by 600.

```
OSErr err = [qdView doSeqGrab: NSMakeRect(0, 0, 800, 600)];
```

Finally, the code does some error checking. If the `doSeqGrab` call returns an error, the error is reported to the user by calling `NSRunAlertPanel` with the error code returned from `doSeqGrab`.

```
if (err != noErr) {
    NSString *errorStr = [[NSString alloc]
      initWithFormat:@"%d" , err];
    int choice;

    /* now display error dialog and quit */
    choice = NSRunAlertPanel(@"Error", errorStr,
      @"OK", nil, nil);
    [errorStr release];
}

[videoWindow makeKeyAndOrderFront: self];
}

- (void) applicationWillTerminate:
    (NSNotification *) notification {
    [qdView endGrab];
}

@end
```

MyQuickDrawView.h

`MyQuickDrawView` is the deceptively named object that hooks up to a camera and captures its output. This file defines the interface for `MyQuickDrawView`.

```
#import <Cocoa/Cocoa.h>
#import <QuickTime/QuickTime.h>

@interface MyQuickDrawView : NSQuickDrawView
{
    NSTimer *gMyTimer;    // our timer for idling the sequence
                          // grabber
    SeqGrabComponent gSeqGrab; // the sequence grabber
                               // component
    SGChannel gSGChanVideo; // the sequence grabber channel
                            //component
```

```
        GWorldPtr gPGWorld; // gworld used for decompression
        Rect gBoundsRect; // rect we are drawing into
        ImageSequence gDecomSeq; // unique identifier for our
                                 //decompression sequence
        ImageSequence gDrawSeq; // unique identifier for our draw
                                //sequence
        long gImageSize; // size of the image in our buffer to draw
}

-(ComponentResult)setupDecomp;
-(ComponentResult)decompToWindow;
-(void)doDecomp:(NSRect)rect;
-(void)drawRect:(NSRect)rect;
-(void) sgIdleTimer:(id)sender;
-(OSErr) doSeqGrab:(NSRect)grabRect;
-(GWorldPtr)gworld;
-(ImageSequence)decomSeq;
-(ImageSequence)drawSeq;
-(SGChannel)sgChanVideo;
-(Rect)boundsRect;
-(void)endGrab;

@end
```

The mySGDataProc function is the heart of the video capture process. This is the function that actually captures the video and processes it, as shown in detail in the next section.

```
pascal OSErr mySGDataProc(SGChannel c,
                          Ptr p,
                          long len,
                          long *offset,
                          long chRefCon,
                          TimeValue time,
                          short writeType,
                          long refCon);
void saveQDViewObjectForCallback(void *theObject);
```

MyQuickDrawView.m

The MyQuickDrawView.m file contains the implementation for the MyQuickDrawView class. Much of this code is deep QuickTime-fu, created by Apple as sample code. If you modify it, you might find it no longer works the way you thought it would. However, you can't really damage anything (in the physical world) by experimenting, so you should feel free to mess around and see what interesting things you can create.

```
#import <QuickTime/QuickTime.h>
#import <Carbon/Carbon.h>

#import "MyQuickDrawView.h"

static MyQuickDrawView *myQDViewObject; // our MyQuickDrawView
                                        // object
static TimeScale gTimeScale; // time scale for our grabbed
                             // video
static TimeValue gLastTime;  // time value when a frame was
                             // last given to us

@implementation MyQuickDrawView

#define BailErr(x) {err = x; if(err != noErr) goto bail;}
#define BailIfNull(x) {gSeqGrab = x; if(gSeqGrab == nil) goto
bail;}
```

setupDecomp

The setupDecomp method prepares decompression for the raw video coming in from the camera. The function decompresses to an off-screen gWorld, which is a graphics buffer with state information. This buffer is defined by QuickTime. The frame eventually moves from the gWorld to the window on the screen.

```
//////////
//
// setupDecomp
//
// Code to setup our decompression sequences. We make
// two, one to decompress to a gworld, and the other
// to decompress to the window
//
//////////

-(ComponentResult)setupDecomp
{
   ComponentResult      err = noErr;
   Rect                 sourceRect = { 0, 0 }, bounds;
   MatrixRecord         scaleMatrix;
   ImageDescriptionHandle    imageDesc = (
     ImageDescriptionHandle)NewHandle(0);
   PixMapHandle         hPixMap;

   /* Set up getting grabbed data into the GWorld */
```

```
// retrieve a channel's current sample description, the
// channel returns a sample description that is
// appropriate to the type of data being captured
err = SGGetChannelSampleDescription(gSGChanVideo,
   (Handle)imageDesc);
BailErr(err);

// make a scaling matrix for the sequence
sourceRect.right = (**imageDesc).width;
sourceRect.bottom = (**imageDesc).height;
RectMatrix(&scaleMatrix, &sourceRect, &gBoundsRect);
```

Next, you begin the process of decompressing frames. This method is called once for the frame sequence. The video codecs provide information that's used to construct a decompression chain, and this process is too time-consuming to be repeated for every frame.

Cross-Reference

To learn more about this process, see the Apple document at `http://developer.apple.com/quicktime/icefloe/dispatch008.html`.

```
err = DecompressSequenceBegin(&gDecomSeq,
        // pointer to field to receive unique ID for
        // sequence
        imageDesc,      // handle to image description
                        // structure
        gPGWorld,       // port for the DESTINATION image
        NULL,           // graphics device handle, if port
                        // is set, set to NULL
        NULL,           // source rectangle defining the
                        // portion of the image to
                        // decompress
        &scaleMatrix,   // transformation matrix
        srcCopy,        // transfer mode specifier
        NULL,           // clipping region in dest.
                        // coordinate system to use as a
                        // mask
        0,              // flags
        codecNormalQuality, // accuracy in decompression
        bestSpeedCodec); // compressor identifier or
                        // special identifiers
                        // ie. BestSpeedCodec
BailErr(err);

DisposeHandle((Handle)imageDesc);
imageDesc = NULL;
```

```
    /* Set up getting grabbed data into the Window */
    hPixMap = GetGWorldPixMap(gPGWorld);
    GetPixBounds(hPixMap,&bounds);
    gDrawSeq = 0;

    // returns an image description for the GWorld's PixMap
    // on entry the imageDesc is NULL, on return it is
    // correctly filled out
    // you are responsible for disposing it
    err = MakeImageDescriptionForPixMap(hPixMap, &imageDesc);
    BailErr(err);

    gImageSize = (GetPixRowBytes(hPixMap) *
        (*imageDesc)->height);
            // ((**hPixMap).rowBytes & 0x3fff)
        * (*desc)->height;

    // begin the process of decompressing a sequence of frames
    // - see above notes on this call. Destination is specified
    // as the QuickDraw port for our NSView
    err = DecompressSequenceBegin(&gDrawSeq,
            imageDesc,
            [self qdPort],
                // Use the QuickDraw port for our NSView as
                // destination!
            NULL,
            &bounds,
            NULL,
            ditherCopy,
            NULL,
            0,
            codecNormalQuality,
            anyCodec);
    BailErr(err);

bail:

    if (imageDesc)
        DisposeHandle((Handle)imageDesc);

    return (err);
}
```

decompToWindow

The decompToWindow method is called during the drawing process to decompress video from the gWorld off-screen buffer to the window.

```
//////////
//
// decompToWindow
//
// Decompress an image to our window (the QuickDraw port for
// our NSView)
//
//////////

-(ComponentResult)decompToWindow
{
    ComponentResult err = noErr;
    CodecFlags       ignore;

    err = DecompressSequenceFrameS(gDrawSeq,
   // sequence ID returned by DecompressSequenceBegin

        GetPixBaseAddr(GetGWorldPixMap(gPGWorld)),
   // pointer to compressed image data
        gImageSize,    // size of the buffer
        0,             // in flags
        &ignore,       // out flags
        NULL);         // async completion proc
    return err;
}
```

doDecomp

The doDecomp method is basically a wrapper that's called during the drawing process. It decompresses the raw video by calling decompToWindow.

```
//////////
//
// doDecomp
//
// Setup and run our decompression sequence, plus display
// frames-per-second data to our window
//
//////////

-(void)doDecomp:(NSRect)rect
{
    if(gPGWorld)
    {
        if (gDecomSeq == 0)
        {
            [self setupDecomp];
```

```
        }
        else
        {
            [self decompToWindow];
        }
    }
}
```

drawRect

Subclasses of NSView override the drawRect method to do their drawing. In this case, the override simply calls doDecomp, which decompresses and draws video into the window, and that's all there is.

```
//////////
//
// drawRect
//
// Overridden by subclasses of NSView to draw the receiver's
// image within aRect. It's here we decompress our frames
// to the window for display
//
//////////

-(void)drawRect:(NSRect)rect
{
    [self doDecomp:rect];
}
```

sgIdleTimer

The SGIdle function is the system routine that provides the time when frames are grabbed from the camera. When an application has a sequence grabber to get frames from a camera, the application should call SGIdle often enough to get frames that display the desired video quality. This function sets up a timer to call SGIdle 10 times per second.

Note For more information on SGIdle and how often it should be called, see Apple's technical note at developer.apple.com/qa/qa2001/qa1349.html.

```
//////////
//
// sgIdleTimer
//
// A timer whose purpose is to call the SGIdle function
// to provide processing time for our sequence grabber
// component.
//
//////////
```

```
-(void) sgIdleTimer:(id)sender
{
    OSErr err;

    err = SGIdle(gSeqGrab);
    /* put up an error dialog to display any errors */
    if (err != noErr)
    {
        NSString *errorStr = [[NSString alloc]
            initWithFormat:@"%d" , err];
        int choice;

        // some error specific to SGIdle occurred - any errors
        // returned from the data proc will also show up here
        // and we don't want to write over them

/* now display error dialog and quit */
        choice = NSRunAlertPanel(@"Error", errorStr, @"OK",
            nil, nil);
        [errorStr release];

        // ...to fix this we simply call
        // SGStop and SGStartRecord again
        // calling stop allows the SG to release and re-prepare
        // for grabbing hopefully fixing any problems, this is
        // obviously a very relaxed
        // approach

        SGStop(gSeqGrab);
        SGStartRecord(gSeqGrab);
    }

}
```

doSeqGrab

The doSeqGrab method gets the sequence grabber ready to start pulling in video frames from the camera. A call to OpenDefaultComponent does initialization by hooking up with the default device that supports sequence grabbing. It exits with an error if no such device is found or some other undesirable event occurs. Calls to other sequence grabber functions complete the setup, including SGInitialize, SGSetDataRef, SGNewChannel, and SGSetChannelBounds.

To begin processing frames, the function calls SGSetDataProc to set up the function that performs the actual frame processing, and then it calls SGPrepare and SGStartRecord. Finally, the function creates an NSTimer to call SGIdle every 1/10th of a second.

```
//////////
//
// doSeqGrab
//
```

```
// Initialize the Sequence Grabber, create a new
// sequence grabber channel, create an offscreen
// GWorld for use with our decompression sequence,
// then begin recording. We also set up a timer to
// idle the sequence grabber
//
//////////

-(OSErr) doSeqGrab:(NSRect)grabRect
{
    OSErr   err = noErr;

    gTimeScale    = 0;
    gLastTime     = 0;

    /* initialize the movie toolbox */
    err = EnterMovies();
    BailErr(err);

    // open the sequence grabber component and initialize it
    gSeqGrab = OpenDefaultComponent(SeqGrabComponentType, 0);
    BailIfNull(gSeqGrab);

    err = SGInitialize(gSeqGrab);
    BailErr(err);
```

Next, you specify the destination data reference for a recording operation. You're not keeping the frames to make a movie, so you use the seqGrabDontMakeMovie flag to make sure that frames are not saved in a movie file.

```
    err = SGSetDataRef(gSeqGrab, 0, 0, seqGrabDontMakeMovie);
    BailErr(err);

    // create a new sequence grabber video channel
    err = SGNewChannel(gSeqGrab, VideoMediaType,
            &gSGChanVideo);
    BailErr(err);

    gBoundsRect.top      = grabRect.origin.y;
    gBoundsRect.left     = grabRect.origin.x;
    gBoundsRect.bottom   = grabRect.size.height;
    gBoundsRect.right    = grabRect.size.width;
    err = SGSetChannelBounds(gSeqGrab, &gBoundsRect);

    // create the GWorld
    err = QTNewGWorld(&gPGWorld,       // returned GWorld
            k32ARGBPixelFormat,        // pixel format
            &gBoundsRect,              // bounding rectangle
            0,                         // color table
            NULL,                      // graphic device handle
                0);                    // flags
```

```
        BailErr(err);

        // lock the pixmap and make sure it's locked because
        // we can't decompress into an unlocked PixMap
        if(!LockPixels(GetPortPixMap(gPGWorld)))
        {
            BailErr(-1);
        }

        err = SGSetGWorld(gSeqGrab, gPGWorld, GetMainDevice());
        BailErr(err);

        // set the bounds for the channel
        err = SGSetChannelBounds(gSGChanVideo, &gBoundsRect);
        BailErr(err);
```

Next, you set the video channel to *not* play the frames as they're captured—you'll use a different technique to display them. You specify a function to be called whenever the frame grabber writes data.

```
        err = SGSetChannelUsage(gSGChanVideo, seqGrabRecord);
        BailErr(err);

        err = SGSetDataProc(gSeqGrab,NewSGDataUPP(&mySGDataProc)
                            ,0);
        BailErr(err);

        /* lights...camera... */
        err = SGPrepare(gSeqGrab,false,true);
        BailErr(err);

        // start recording!!
        err = SGStartRecord(gSeqGrab);
        BailErr(err);

        /* setup a timer to idle the sequence grabber */
        gMyTimer = [[NSTimer scheduledTimerWithTimeInterval:0.1
                    // interval, 0.1 seconds
            target:self
            selector:@selector(sgIdleTimer:) // call this method
            userInfo:nil
            repeats:YES] retain];    // repeat until we cancel it
    bail:

        return err;
    }
```

Accessor Methods

The next five functions are simply accessor methods that retrieve the values of variables.

```
//////////
//
// gworld
//
// Accessor method for the gPGWorld class variable
//
//////////

-(GWorldPtr)gworld
{
    return gPGWorld;
}

//////////
//
// decomSeq
//
// Accessor method for the gDecomSeq class variable
//
//////////

-(ImageSequence)decomSeq
{
    return gDecomSeq;
}

//////////
//
// drawSeq
//
// Accessor method for the gDrawSeq class variable
//
//////////

-(ImageSequence)drawSeq
{
    return gDrawSeq;
}

//////////
//
// sgChanVideo
//
// Accessor method for the gSGChanVideo class variable
//
//////////
```

```
-(SGChannel)sgChanVideo
{
    return gSGChanVideo;
}


//////////
//
// boundsRect
//
// Accessor method for the boundsRect class variable
//
//////////

-(Rect)boundsRect
{
    return gBoundsRect;
}
```

endGrab

The application calls endGrab from its applicationWillTerminate override, just before it quits. The endGrab function cleans up by performing several tasks:

- Releases the NSTimer that calls SGIdle.
- Calls SGStop to turn off *Recording*, which is the process QuickTime is using to get video from the camera.
- Calls CDSequenceEnd to stop the decompression sequences.
- Shuts down the sequence grabber component by calling CloseComponent.
- Releases the gWorld object and its memory.

```
//////////
//
// endGrab
//
// Perform clean-up when we are finished recording
//
//////////

-(void)endGrab
{
    ComponentResult result;
    OSErr           err;

    // kill our sequence grabber idle timer first
    [gMyTimer invalidate];
    [gMyTimer release];
```

```
    // stop recording
    SGStop(gSeqGrab);

    // end our decompression sequences
    err = CDSequenceEnd(gDecomSeq);
    err = CDSequenceEnd(gDrawSeq);

    // finally, close our sequence grabber component
    result = CloseComponent(gSeqGrab);

    // get rid of our gworld
    DisposeGWorld(gPGWorld);
}

@end
```

mySGDataProc

The mySGDataProc function is called at SGIdle time, which in this application happens 10 times per second. QuickTime's sequence grabber calls mySGDataProc to process raw video data that's available from the camera. This function is responsible for converting the raw video to a format suitable for an off-screen gWorld, which is then transferred to the Video Desktop window. A call to DecompressSequenceFrameS grabs a frame from the camera and places it into the gWorld. Next, the function calculates the number of frames per second using saved timing values, and then it draws that information to the gWorld buffer using QuickDraw calls. Finally, the whole masterpiece is drawn in the window by calling the view's display method.

The comments in this function provide an overview of its variables and process.

```
/* ---------------------------------------------------- */
/* sequence grabber data procedure, where the work is done */
/* ---------------------------------------------------- */
/* mySGDataProc - the sequence grabber calls the data function
/* whenever any of the grabber's channels write digitized data
/* to the destination movie file.

/* NOTE: We really mean any, if you have an audio and video
/* channel then the DataProc will be called for either channel
/* whenever data has been captured. Be sure to check which
/* channel is being passed in. In this example we never create
/* an audio channel so we know we're always dealing with video.

This data function decompresses captured video data into an
offscreen GWorld, then transfers the frame to an onscreen
window.

    c - the channel component that is writing the digitized
        data.
```

```
p - a pointer to the digitized data.
len - the number of bytes of digitized data.
offset - a pointer to a field that may specify where you are
         to write the digitized data, and that is to receive
         a value indicating where you wrote the data.
chRefCon - per channel reference constant specified using
           SGSetChannelRefCon.
time    - the starting time of the data, in the channel's
          time scale.
writeType - the type of write operation being performed.
       seqGrabWriteAppend - Append new data.
       seqGrabWriteReserve - Do not write data. Instead,
          reserve space for the amount of data specified in
          the len parameter.
       seqGrabWriteFill - Write data into the location
          specified by offset. Used to fill the space
          previously reserved with seqGrabWriteReserve. The
          Sequence Grabber may call the DataProc several
          times to fill a single reserved location.
   refCon - the reference constant you specified when you
       assigned your data function to the sequence grabber.
*/

pascal OSErr mySGDataProc(SGChannel c,
                          Ptr p,
                          long len,
                          long *offset,
                          long chRefCon,
                          TimeValue time,
                          short writeType,
                          long refCon)
{
#pragma unused(offset,chRefCon,time,writeType)

    CodecFlags       ignore;
    ComponentResult  err = noErr;
    CGrafPtr         theSavedPort;
    GDHandle         theSavedDevice;
    char             status[64];
    Str255           theString;
    Rect             bounds;
    float            fps;

    /* grab the time scale for use with our fps calculations -
       but this needs to be done only once */
    if (gTimeScale == 0)
    {
        err = SGGetChannelTimeScale([myQDViewObject
           sgChanVideo], &gTimeScale);
        BailErr(err);
    }
```

```
    if([myQDViewObject gworld])
    {
```

At this point, the code decompresses a frame of video into the gWorld off-screen buffer.

```
        err = DecompressSequenceFrameS([myQDViewObject
            decomSeq],
// sequence ID returned by DecompressSequenceBegin
          p,       // pointer to compressed image data
          len,     // size of the buffer
          0,       // in flags
          &ignore, // out flags
          NULL);   // async completion proc
        BailErr(err);

        // ******  IMAGE IS NOW IN THE GWORLD ****** //

    }

    /* compute and display frames-per-second */
    GetGWorld(&theSavedPort, &theSavedDevice);
    SetGWorld([myQDViewObject gworld], NULL);
    TextSize(12);
    TextMode(srcCopy);
    bounds = [myQDViewObject boundsRect];
    MoveTo(bounds.left, bounds.bottom-3);
    fps = (float)
        ((float)gTimeScale /
        (float)(time - gLastTime));
    sprintf(status, "fps:%5.1f", fps);
    CopyCStringToPascal(status, theString);
    DrawString(theString);
    SetGWorld(theSavedPort, theSavedDevice);

    /* remember current time, so next time this routine is
       called we can compute the frames-per-second */
    gLastTime = time;

    /* calling the display method will invoke this NSView's
       lockFocus, drawRect and unlockFocus methods as
       necessary.
       Our drawRect method (above) is used to decompress one of
       a sequence of frames. This method draws the image
       back to the window from the GWorld and could be used as
       a "preview" */
    [myQDViewObject display];

bail:

    return err;
}
```

saveQDViewObjectForCallback

The SGDataProc function, listed previously, must be able to call methods of this class. To make the methods available, saveQDViewObjectForCallback stashes a reference to the object in the global variable myQDViewObject.

```
//////////
//
// saveQDViewObjectForCallback
//
// This routine stores a reference to our MyQuickDrawView
// object. We'll need this so we can call into methods in this
// class from outside the implementation of the class methods
// (specifically, from our SGDataProc
// C routine above).
//
//////////

void saveQDViewObjectForCallback(void *theObject)
{
    myQDViewObject = (MyQuickDrawView *)theObject;
}
```

 Note The full Video Desktop project includes a few other files, including main.m and Info.plist, that aren't included here. The full project is available from this book's companion Web site at www. wiley.com/compbooks/extremetech.

Extra Credit

If you want to play with getting video into your Mac and onto the desktop, here are a few ideas of how you might tweak and expand the Video Desktop project:

- Visiting the old school is fun, as we did in this hack with QuickDraw, but maybe you want to bring the code into the modern era. Try to find a way to use OpenGL instead of QuickDraw to do your processing. To accomplish this, you probably have to replace or reengineer everything in the MyQuickDrawView code.

- See what you can do to improve the performance of getting video onto the screen. Try tweaking the timer interval or work on optimizing the code.

- This version is hard-coded for a window that's 800 by 600. Add a way to pick the size dynamically.

Summary

Just when you think you know everything there is to know about Mac OS X, you realize that there's an immense collection of stuff that might have been created back when you were in grade school. In the case of this chapter's hack, we reach deep into Apple's treasure chest of sample code, all the way down to where the QuickTime and QuickDraw code lives, and we find a real gem that works well for grabbing video from a camera. If you're out of ideas for your next fun project, check out the sample code pages at developer.apple.com/samplecode/index. html. You're practically guaranteed to find something cool.

TextFilter

In this chapter, you learn how to take advantage of the Services menu in Mac OS X applications. If you're not an aficionado of the Services menu, you can find it as a submenu of the application menu in every running OS X app. In this chapter, you play around with the Services menu by creating an application that does its work as a service. The chapter also describes how to install the service, and I'll present a few hacky tricks as we go along. This service is a simple hack called TextFilter, created by Mark Dalrymple, that removes HTML tags from a mess of text.

About Services

The Services menu is an odd but valuable feature that appears as a submenu in the application menu (Figure 19-1). The Services menu provides a way to make some of your application's features available directly to users of other applications without requiring them to run your app directly. Items in the Services menu are officially called *standard services* by Apple, but are more commonly known as *system services*.

To use a service, you generally select something in the current application, and then pull down the application menu, navigate to the Services submenu, and pick the service you want. For example, when you install the Camino Web browser, Camino adds the Open URL In Camino item to the Services menu. So, when you're running another application, such as Microsoft Word or Preview, and you want to open a URL from some of its text, you can select the text and choose Open URL In Camino from the Services menu. Mac OS X finds the necessary code in the other application—Camino, in this case—passes the data to it from the current application, and the service does its thing. When you install an application, the system finds any services that application provides so that they can be added to the Services menu.

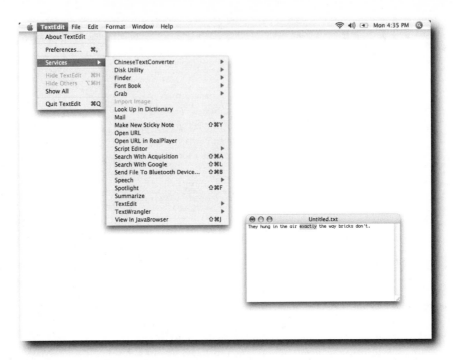

FIGURE 19-1: A typical Services menu.

Not all services are provided by applications. Mac OS X also supports standalone services that have no associated applications. The system searches for these services in various Services directories, such as ~/Library/Services (in the user's Home directory) and /Library/Services.

Problems When Using Services

Services provide some very cool features, but many Mac users don't even know that services exist, and Apple doesn't do a lot to promote their existence. Why aren't services more popular? First, they're hard for users to find. Putting features into a hierarchical submenu is not the best way to advertise their availability. In addition to their obscure location, many users have trouble with the mouse dexterity necessary for picking items out of a submenu.

When you do find services, it's not always easy to figure out how to use them. I asked a friend if he used services, and he replied "Those things that are always disabled?" All Cocoa applications support services, so if you're using a non-Cocoa app, like Microsoft Word, you're likely to find that services indeed are all disabled. Even if you're using a Cocoa application, services are grayed out if they don't have anything to operate on, and there's no hint about what you need to do to enable them. For example, if you're running Safari, but you have no text selected when you pull down the Services menu, you can't do anything.

A final problem with the Services menu is that it only grows, never shrinks, and you have little control over what appears in it. If you install an application that has a service, it's added to the Services menu—you don't get to decide. So, chances are your Services menu is filled with items you'll never use. That's not nice.

Tip You can remove unwanted services from the Services menu, although the process is a little messy. Find the application that provides the service, and then open that application's Info.plist file in Property List Editor. Find and delete the NSServices entry to remove the service from the menu and make it inaccessible. Some services aren't provided by applications—they have `.service` files in the ~/Library/Services folder. To get rid of one of those, just trash the `.service` file. In both of these cases, you might have to log out and log in again for the change to take effect.

The TextFilter Hack

The TextFilter service handles the task of taking text laden with HTML tags and removing all the tags, leaving only the nice text behind. This is useful for humanizing a chunk of text from a Web page. Mark Dalrymple, who wrote the code, uses it to clean up text before he feeds it to the Mac's speech synthesizer. Text sounds a lot better with the tags removed.

Here's a brief description of what you have to do to provide a service, with full details to come later in this chapter:

- Include a method that Mac OS X can call when the user wants to run your service. In this example, it's the `stripTags:userData:error` method.

- In Interface Builder, set your `AppController` object to be the application's delegate. This enables you to register your service so that users can see it.

- In your application's information property list (Info.plist), add a branch describing the service.

Building and running the application registers the service for other applications to see. Users can take advantage of the service by selecting text and then choosing Strip HTML Tags from the Services menu.

This hack uses the standard techniques for building an application, plus a couple of unusual ones: including a bit of code written in Perl. You tell Xcode to use that Perl code in your application with a technique called a *copy phase*. You also have to do some hacking around in the application's property list to make the service work.

To start creating TextFilter, go to Xcode and make a new Cocoa application project. Name it *TextFilter*.

Interface Builder

The Interface Builder steps for TextFilter are very simple. You subclass NSObject to create an AppController class and then instantiate the AppController—steps that are common to many Cocoa projects. Next, make sure the application's delegate outlet is set to the AppController object. This allows you to register the application's service. In the Interface Builder window, control-drag from File's Owner to AppController. Double-click the delegate outlet to make the connection, as shown in Figure 19-2.

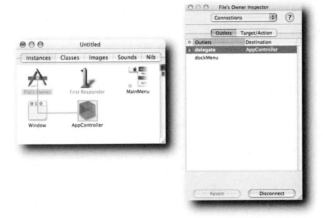

FIGURE 19-2: Connecting the delegate outlet to AppController.

Because TextFilter has no user interface—remember, it's just a front for an item that will appear in the Services menu— there's no more work to do here in Interface Builder.

Note Even though the application provides a service, which is an item in every application's Services menu, you don't explicitly create the menu item. Mac OS X constructs it automatically based on an entry you make in the application's property list.

Source Code

The source for this hack is contained in a standard header file (AppController.h) and implementation (AppController.m), with a little extra—the Perl script—in stripper.pl.

AppController.h

The application is pretty simple and accomplishes its work without having to declare very much in the header file. All you need is the AppController class. It doesn't even define any of its own methods.

```
// AppController.h starts here.

// Always import Cocoa framework headers.
#import <Cocoa/Cocoa.h>

// We instantiate an AppController in Interface Builder.
// Not much to AppController this time!
@interface AppController : NSObject
{
}

@end // AppController
```

AppController.m

Because the AppController object has no methods, AppController.m simply contains the code that implements TextFilter's features. I'll go through the logic in each method, including the Perl script at the heart of the hack that performs the actual work.

AppController.m begins in the usual way.

```
// AppController.m starts here.

#import "AppController.h"

@implementation AppController
```

stripTags:userData:error:

Remember, you're building an application that nobody ever needs to run. Instead, users will tap its features via the Services menu in some other application. What exactly happens when that Service menu item is invoked? As described earlier in this chapter, Mac OS X will look through all the registered services and then call this application, based on an entry in the Info.plist file. In addition to advertising the service, that entry tells the system which method to call in order to perform the service.

In this case, we want Mac OS X to call stripTags:userData:error: when somebody wants to use our service.

```
// stripTags:userData:error: starts here
```

When the system calls this method, it passes the current selection as a pasteboard object. Your job is to get the selection, remove any HTML tags, and then put the text, now devoid of unsightly tags, back on the pasteboard.

```
- (void) stripTags: (NSPasteboard *) pboard
   userData: (NSString *) userData
   error: (NSString **) error
{
```

Next, you need to find out which data types are on the pasteboard.

```
NSArray *types;
types = [pboard types];
```

The next step is to look for text on the pasteboard. If there is no text, you can't perform this service, so set an error and give up, sadly.

```
if (![types containsObject: NSStringPboardType]) {
    *error = @"Error: No plain text on the clipboard";
    goto done;
    }
```

If you made it this far, you know text exists on the pasteboard. Use `stringForType:` to extract the text so you can mess with it.

```
NSString *pboardString;
pboardString = [pboard stringForType: NSStringPboardType];
```

The next bit of code is an error check: You need to make sure that you actually got some text out of the pasteboard. If not, you can't do what you've been asked, so again, report the error and return to the caller.

```
if (pboardString == nil) {
    *error =
@"Error: Could not read plain text from the clipboard";
    goto done;
    }
```

At this point, you have the text (with nasty tags). To strip the tags, pass the text (in `pboardString`) to the magic tag-stripping method, `stringStrippedOfTags:`. See the following for the scoop on `stringStrippedOfTags:`.

```
NSString *newString;
newString = [self stringStrippedOfTags: pboardString];
```

`stringStrippedOfTags` returns the denuded string in the `newString` parameter. Now you just have to put it on the pasteboard and return it to the caller.

Next, you have to prepare a new types array with only one type: `NSStringPboardType`.

```
types = [NSArray arrayWithObject: NSStringPboardType];
```

Now you have to put the stripped string and the single type on the pasteboard.

```
[pboard declareTypes: types  owner: nil];
[pboard setString: newString
        forType: NSStringPboardType];
```

```
done:
   return;

} // stripTags
```

stringStrippedOfTags:

The `stripTags:userData:error:` method calls `stringStrippedOfTags:` when it's time to remove the HTML tags from the target string. If you examine the code in this method, looking for the part that scans the string and takes out the tags, you'll search in vain: It's not there. Instead, `stringStrippedOfTags:` is a big ruse. The real work is done by a tiny Perl script, which is called by `stringStrippedOfTags`. This is kind of a hack within the hack: demonstrating how to call a script from inside an application.

```
// stringStrippedOfTags: starts here
```

`stripTags:userData:error:`, described earlier, calls this method after extracting text from the pasteboard. `stringStrippedOfTags:` takes an `NSString` object, which holds the text to be stripped, and returns another `NSString`, containing the stripped text.

Most of the work in this routine is to set up a call to a Perl script that does the actual tag stripping.

```
- (NSString *) stringStrippedOfTags: (NSString *) string
{
```

The Perl script is included in the application's bundle. Before you call it, you have to find it, so the next step is to get a reference to the bundle and find the script using its filename.

```
NSBundle *bundle = [NSBundle mainBundle];
NSString *stripperPath;
stripperPath =
   [bundle pathForAuxiliaryExecutable: @"stripper.pl"];
```

Now you have to get ready to call the script. You need to instantiate an `NSTask` for the execution and two pipes to handle reading and writing data with the script.

```
NSTask *task = [[NSTask alloc] init];
[task setLaunchPath: stripperPath];

NSPipe *readPipe = [NSPipe pipe];
NSFileHandle *readHandle = [readPipe fileHandleForReading];
```

```
NSPipe *writePipe = [NSPipe pipe];
NSFileHandle *writeHandle =
    [writePipe fileHandleForWriting];
```

Now you have all the data structures for calling the Perl script. You finish setting up by telling the NSTask object to use the pipes you created for input and output, and then starting the script with a call to the NSTask's launch method.

```
[task setStandardInput: writePipe];
[task setStandardOutput: readPipe];

[task launch];
```

The script is now running, but it's waiting for input. Feed it, it's hungry! The text you want to operate on is in the string variable. Pipe it to the script by calling writeData on standard input.

```
[writeHandle writeData:
    [string dataUsingEncoding: NSASCIIStringEncoding]];
[writeHandle closeFile];
```

Next, create an NSData buffer to hold the data returned by the script and an NSMutableData object to get it ready for the function return value.

```
NSMutableData *data = [[NSMutableData alloc] init];
NSData *readData;
```

Read the script's output from the buffer and append it to the NSMutableData object.

```
while ((readData = [readHandle availableData])
   && [readData length])
   {
       [data appendData: readData];
   }
```

At this point, the Perl script has done its work. You have the stripped string in the NSMutableData object. Now you have to get it into an NSString and return it as the function result. You initialize the string by calling initWithData, using the data from the script, and encoding it as an ASCII string.

```
NSString *strippedString;
strippedString = [[NSString alloc]
                initWithData: data
                encoding: NSASCIIStringEncoding];
```

Now it's time to clean up. Make sure to autorelease strippedString because it's going to be returned as the function result.

```
[task release];
[data release];
[strippedString autorelease];
```

```
        return (strippedString);

} // stringStrippedOfTags
```

applicationDidFinishLaunching:

When an application provides a service, it has to register with the system as a service provider. To do this, you call the application object's `setServicesProvider:` method. The easiest way to do this is to set the application's delegate in Interface Builder to the `AppController` object, as described earlier in the Interface Builder section, and then handle the `applicationDidFinishLaunching:` delegate message by registering the service.

```
// applicationDidFinishLaunching: starts here
```

Because you set `AppController` as the delegate for NSApplication, you get the `applicationDidFinishLaunching:` message.

```
- (void) applicationDidFinishLaunching:
                          (NSNotification *) notification
{
```

You can only do one thing here: Tell Mac OS X that the application itself will be handling calls for the service that it provides. You register the service by calling the application's `setServicesProvider` method.

```
    [NSApp setServicesProvider: self];

} // applicationDidFinishLaunching
```

stripper.pl

The real work of removing tags from the string happens here, in a Perl script that's called by `stringStrippedOfTags`. To create the script, choose File → New File, pick Empty File in Project, and name it stripper.pl. If you're not familiar with Perl, you might find the syntax a little opaque. Here's the script and a brief explanation of what's going on:

```
#!/usr/bin/perl
```

This first line is a directive that tells the system which program is going to execute the code in this script. In this case, it's Perl. This MUST be the first line in the script, or it will fail to execute. When a line starts with a # followed by a space, the whole line is a comment.

Next is the functional part of the stripper script. The first line tells the script to keep scanning text from the standard input until you've seen it all.

```
while (<>)
{
```

In the following cryptic code, the *s* means "search for what's between the first and second slashes and replace it with what's between the second and third slashes." [^>] means "any character other than a closing angle bracket." * means "any number of repetitions of those characters." So, s/<[^>]*>// means "Look for sequences of characters that fall between angle brackets, and then replace all those characters with nothing." (That is, delete them.) The *s* at the end means, "Don't worry about whether the tag is entirely on one line," and the *g* means, "Do this repeatedly." Now you see why programmers use Perl instead of English.

```
    $_ =~ s/<[^>]*>//gs;
    print $_;
}
```

Be sure #!/usr/bin/perl is the first line in the file, or the service won't work. To get an idea about what happens when a service fails, you can open Console and check for an error message. For example, if you try to run this service without #!/usr/bin/perl as the first line, you get an error like this in Console:

```
2004-10-18 13:44:08.692 TextFilter[1658] *** NSTask: Task create
for path
/Users/scott/TextFilter/build/TextFilter.app/Contents/MacOS/
stripper.pl failed: 8, "Exec format error".
```

Editing the Information Property List

To include a service in an application, you have to specify it in the application's information property list (Info.plist). The easiest way to edit an Info.plist is with Apple's handy Property List Editor. In Xcode, find Info.plist in the list of files. Then choose Open With Finder from the File menu. This starts up Property List Editor and opens the property list.

In Property List Editor, click Root and then click New Child. Rename the new item NSServices and change its type to Array. Using the New Child and New Sibling buttons, continue adding to the NSServices item until it matches the hierarchy, as shown in Figure 19-3.

This property list entry specifies five important elements of your service:

- The name of your service's menu item (Strip HTML Tags).
- The name of the method the system will call to implement the service (stripTags).
- The name of your application (TextFilter).
- An array of data types your application will take as input (NSStringPboardType).
- An array of data types your application will return as output (NSStringPboardType).

FIGURE 19-3: Property list for service entry.

Adding the Perl Script

This hack includes a file, stripper.pl, that you want to put into the application bundle without any processing by Xcode or other tools. At runtime, the Perl interpreter that comes with OS X handles the script; but at build time, we just want Xcode to put the text file into the bundle and leave it alone.

To handle cases like this, Xcode lets you add a copy files build phase to your project. This phase simply copies a file you specify into your application bundle. To add stripper.pl to your project, follow these steps:

1. In Xcode, choose Project → New Build Phase → New Copy Files Build Phase.

2. In the Copy Files Phase Info window, click the Destination pop-up and choose Executables.

3. Close the Copy Files Info window.

4. In the Groups & Files panel, in the Targets section, click the disclosure triangle next to TextFilter. The last item revealed should be named Copy Files (see Figure 19-4).

FIGURE 19-4: Copy Files phase in TextFilter project.

5. Drag stripper.pl from the file list to the Copy Files group you revealed in Step 4.

6. Finally, you need to make stripper.pl an executable file. Start Terminal and type the following command:

```
chmod +x TextFilter/stripper.pl
```

After you add stripper.pl to the copy phase, Xcode makes sure the latest version of stripper.pl is copied into the application bundle whenever you build.

Extra Credit

You can expand your service to infinite proportions. Here are some modest ideas for more things to do:

- Assign a keyboard shortcut to your service by adding an NSKeyEquivalent dictionary to the NSServices branch in your Info.plist file.
- Create an application that provides more than one service.

Summary

Mac OS X services are kind of a secret cult feature: hard to find and a little bit difficult to use, but handy. If your application has a cool feature that makes sense when used outside the context of the application itself, you might want to play around with implementing it as a feature.

Spotlight for XML

The most highly touted new feature of Mac OS X Tiger is Spotlight, shown in Figure 20-1. Every user searches for information, and Spotlight makes searching faster and more powerful than it's ever been on a Mac.

Spotlight searches *metadata*: information that's not necessarily in a file, but describes attributes of the file and its data. For example, photos often contain metadata about the image type, dimensions, color space, and other details. Word processing documents might include the author's name, revision history, and printing information as metadata. Spotlight can search all these details.

Metadata is created by Spotlight *importers*, programs that process information in files and provide metadata for Spotlight to search. Tiger ships with a set of Spotlight importers for common types, including images, audio files, Mail messages, iChat transcripts, and many more. To make Spotlight powerful, Apple asks software developers to create importers for their own types of documents and data. In this chapter, I'll demonstrate how that works by creating a custom Spotlight importer for a reasonably common file type, XML documents.

About Spotlight

The main user interface for Spotlight is the ubiquitous, blue-encircled magnifying glass at the right end of the menu bar. When users click there, they see the simplest search interface possible: a box to type in (Figure 20-2).

As soon as users type in the box, Spotlight begins searching metadata for matches, refining the search as more text is typed. Eventually, the list of results dangles below the search box, starting with a *Search All* item, followed by *Top Hit* (Figure 20-2). Every item in the list is clickable. The user can click any item to open it directly in its application. Clicking Search All displays the results in more detail and with filtering options. You can, for example, choose to display only items created or modified today, or you can sort items by author.

FIGURE 20-1: Spotlight is new in Mac OS X Tiger.

FIGURE 20-2: Spotlight search results.

Spotlight Importers

Spotlight importers work by extracting information from files and creating metadata keys for appropriate data. Some types of metadata are obvious, such as file system information like creation and modification dates. Spotlight installs a metadata daemon (background process) that calls the appropriate importers when files are created or modified.

Usually, you create an importer that understands information that's specialized for your application. In this chapter, you are building an importer for a type that already exists: XML files. In Tiger, the importer RichText.mdimporter handles XML as well as many other kinds of text, but the project in this chapter is specialized for XML files. Although this project won't index any additional files for Spotlight, it's useful as an example of how to create an importer for an existing file type.

When you create an importer, you specify the file types you're interested in using uniform type identifiers (UTIs) in the importer's Info.plist in the `LSItemContentTypes` key. Like most other hunks of code in Mac OS X, Spotlight importers are code bundles.

As you process the file, you create metadata keys. Spotlight defines a long list of standard key types, such as `kMDItemAuthors` for a document's authors and `kMDItemFSCreationDate` for a file's creation date. When you write an importer, you should use existing keys wherever you can. You can define additional keys if you need to.

Writing an importer presents an interesting challenge: You have to be able to process data that's in your documents, but you can't use code that's in your application because that application might not even be running when your importer is called. Your importer must be quick and stealthy when it runs—users shouldn't be able to detect any noticeable delay while an importer is running.

Creating an Importer

To create a Spotlight importer, start by choosing File → New Project in Xcode. In the Standard Apple Plug-Ins section of the New Project Assistant window, choose Metadata Importer (Figure 20-3). In the New Project Assistant, name your project **XMLImporter**. Xcode generates a skeleton project for your importer.

FIGURE 20-3: Starting a Spotlight importer project in Xcode.

The fundamental part of your Spotlight importer is a C function named GetMetadataFor
File. In the project that Xcode generates, this function is defined in a file named GetMeta
dataForFile.c. The function prototype for GetMetadataForFile is the following:

```
Boolean GetMetadataForFile(void* thisInterface,
     CFMutableDictionaryRef attributes,
     CFStringRef contentTypeUTI,
     CFStringRef pathToFile)
```

When a file of your specified type is created or modified, Spotlight calls your importer's
GetMetadataForFile function. The attributes parameter is a dictionary that you
use to store any metadata you extract from the file. The type of the file is passed in the
contentTypeUTI parameter. Your importer gets access to the file's contents by using the
pathToFile parameter. In your GetMetadataForFile function, you read the file, examine
its contents, extract any metadata, and add it to the attributes dictionary. Then you sit back
and enjoy watching Spotlight search your files.

Info.plist and Other Files

In addition to the all-important GetMetaDataForFile.c file, importer code bundles include an information property list (Info.plist). The property list for a Spotlight importer includes the following keys:

- `CFBundleDevelopmentRegion` gives the name of the base language used by the importer.

- `CFBundleDocumentTypes` is a dictionary with two keys. The first is `CFBundle TypeRole`, which simply specifies that this plug-in is used by Spotlight as a metadata importer. The second key, `LSItemContentTypes`, is an array of file-content types processed by this importer. When you create your own Spotlight importer, you should change the second key to list the content types you want your plug-in to handle. For example, because this importer works on XML files, the `LSItemContentTypes` key contains the value `public.xml`.

- `CFBundleExecutable` is the name of the file that holds the executable code for the importer. Xcode sets this to the same name as the project, so you shouldn't have to change it unless you have a bizarre desire to rename your importer executable.

- `CFBundleIconFile` points to a custom icon for the importer bundle. If you don't specify a custom icon, you get the generic Spotlight importer icon.

- `CFBundleIdentifier` is the unique identifier for the importer, using the reverse domain name system, as in com.papercar.myimporter.

- `CFBundleInfoDictionaryVersion` gives the version of the importer bundle's information property list. This key is set to 6.0 by Xcode, and there's no need to change it.

- `CFBundleVersion` provides a version number for the importer bundle. When you create a new importer project, Xcode sets this key to 1.0.

- `CFPlugInDynamicRegistration` is a Boolean key used in plug-in bundles. If it's set to `True`, the plug-in host—in this case, Spotlight—calls a function you specify when loading and registering the plug-in. If this key is set to `False`, Spotlight uses registration information in the property list instead of calling a function at load time.

- `CFPlugInDynamicRegisterFunction` is the name of the function called by the plug-in host if you're using dynamic registration, as described in the preceding point. You can leave this key blank if you're not using dynamic plug-in registration.

- `CFPlugInFactories` is a funny name, isn't it? Every importer includes a universally unique identifier (UUID), a 128-bit value that gives this importer an identity that's distinct from all others. Xcode generates this value automatically when you create the project. It places the UUID into the property list for you, so you don't have to change it.

- `CFPlugInTypes` associates the UUID for the importer with another UUID, this one identifying the interfaces supported by the plug-in. This value is the same for all Spotlight importers. It's automatically generated by Xcode and you don't have to deal with it directly.

- `CFPlugInUnloadFunction` is the name of a function that's called when the plug-in is unloaded. Because Spotlight is a system feature that runs all the time, you shouldn't rely on this function being called.

In addition to the Info.plist, Xcode generates a few other pieces when it creates a Spotlight importer project:

- main.c file: Contains the main entry point for the importer. This code is pure boilerplate. It's interesting to check out, but you shouldn't modify it.

- schema.xml: Used in the unlikely event that your importer requires you to define any custom metadata keys.

- Info.plist strings and schema.strings: Provide places for you to put localized strings if you're going to localize your importer.

After you have created your custom Spotlight importer, you have to install it to turn it loose on the user's metadata. You can put importers in any of several directories: inside your application bundle in the Contents/Library/Spotlight directory, in /Library/Spotlight, or in ~/Library/Spotlight.

Command-Line Tools

Like so much of Mac OS X, Spotlight doesn't stop at the graphical-user-interface level. Apple provides a nice suite of command-line tools for fooling around with Spotlight. These are useful for debugging Spotlight importers, searching for things if you spend a lot of time in Terminal, or writing shell scripts that include Spotlight inquiries. I'll discuss the Spotlight shell commands in this section. All the shell commands start with the letters *md*, which stand for metadata.

mdimport

The `mdimport` command is the Swiss Army Knife of Spotlight shell commands. As its name indicates, you can use it import metadata, but it has many other features. Here are some of the cool things you can do with `mdimport`:

- The `-A` option prints a list of all the metadata types that are currently defined. It's a long list. Here's just a portion of the result you see when you type `mdimport -A`:

```
'kMDItemAudioSampleRate'   'Sample rate'   'Sample rate of the file's audio
data'
'kMDItemAuthorEmailAddresses'  '(null)'  '(null)'
'kMDItemAuthors'  'Authors'  'Authors of this item'
'kMDItemBitsPerSample'   'Bits per sample'  'Number of bits per sample'
```

```
'kMDItemCity'  'City'  'City of the item'
'kMDItemCodecs'   'Codecs'  'Codecs used to encode and decode the media'
'kMDItemColorSpace'   'Color space'  'Color space model of this image'
'kMDItemComment'  'Comment'   'Comments about this item'
'kMDItemComposer'  'Composer'   'Composer of the song in the audio file'
'kMDItemFSCreationDate'  'Created'  'Date the file was created'
'kMDItemFSExists'  'File exists'  '(null)'
'kMDItemFSInvisible'  'File invisible'   'Whether the file is visible'
'kMDItemFSIsExtensionHidden'  'File extension hidden' 'File extension is hidden'
'kMDItemFSIsReadable'  'File readable'   'File can be opened but not changed'
'kMDItemFSIsWriteable'  'File writable'  'Whether the file can be changed'
```

- You can see all the registered importers by using the -L option. The mdimport -L command on my Mac produced the following result:

```
2005-03-19 12:46:01.625 mdimport[499] Paths: id(501) (
    "/System/Library/Spotlight/Image.mdimporter",
    "/System/Library/Spotlight/Audio.mdimporter",
    "/System/Library/Spotlight/Font.mdimporter",
    "/System/Library/Spotlight/PS.mdimporter",
    "/Library/Spotlight/Microsoft Office.mdimporter",
    "/System/Library/Spotlight/RichText.mdimporter",
    "/System/Library/Spotlight/QuickTime.mdimporter",
    "/System/Library/Spotlight/Mail.mdimporter",
    "/Library/Spotlight/AppleWorks.mdimporter",
    "/Library/Spotlight/Keynote.mdimporter",
    "/Library/Spotlight/SourceCode.mdimporter",
    "/System/Library/Spotlight/QuartzComposer.mdimporter",
    "/System/Library/Spotlight/vCard.mdimporter",
    "/System/Library/Spotlight/Application.mdimporter",
    "/Library/Spotlight/Pages.mdimporter",
    "/System/Library/Spotlight/PDF.mdimporter",
    "/System/Library/Spotlight/Bookmarks.mdimporter",
    "/System/Library/Spotlight/Chat.mdimporter",
    "/System/Library/Spotlight/SystemPrefs.mdimporter",
    "/System/Library/Spotlight/iCal.mdimporter"
)
```

Note that Apple supplies a bunch of importers for basic document types—images, audio, vCards, QuickTime—and stores them in the /System/Library/Spotlight/ folder. A few more Apple importers for applications, such as Keynote and AppleWorks, are stored in /Library/Spotlight/.

- Use the -r option to ask Spotlight to import all the files associated with a particular importer. This is especially useful for testing your newly developed importer. For example, after you build your importer, you can use this command:

```
mdimport -r /Library/Spotlight/myGreatImporter.mdimporter
```

Spotlight usually gets its claws on files only when they're created, modified, moved, or copied. By using mdimport -r, you can force Spotlight to get involved without having to touch all the files to be imported.

- The -d option lets you control how much information is displayed in response to an mdimport command. You can specify values from 1 to 4 after the d. The higher the value, the more output detail you get. For example, you can find out which importer will be used for a particular file by calling mdimport -d1, as in the following example:

```
mdimport -d1 aqualung/GetMetadataForFile.c
```

This command produces the following:

```
2005-03-19 13:49:44.699 mdimport[638] Import
'/Users/scott/aqualung/GetMetadataForFile.c' type 'public.c-
source' using
'file://localhost/Library/Spotlight/SourceCode.mdimporter/'
```

This output tells us that Spotlight has classified the file as type public.c-source, and it will be processed by the importer named SourceCode. That sounds right.

mdls

Use the mdls command to list the metadata information in any particular file. For example, here's the result of pointing mdls at a file of source code, the GetMetadataForFile.c file discussed later in this chapter:

```
aqualung/GetMetadataForFile.c -------------
kMDItemAttributeChangeDate       = 2005-03-19 11:18:35 -0800
kMDItemContentCreationDate       = 2005-03-19 11:18:21 -0800
kMDItemContentModificationDate = 2005-03-19 11:18:21 -0800
kMDItemContentType               = "public.c-source"
kMDItemContentTypeTree           = (
    "public.c-source",
    "public.source-code",
    "public.plain-text",
    "public.text",
    "public.data",
    "public.item",
    "public.content"
)
kMDItemDisplayName               = "GetMetadataForFile.c"
kMDItemFSContentChangeDate       = 2005-03-19 11:18:21 -0800
kMDItemFSCreationDate            = 2005-03-19 11:18:21 -0800
kMDItemFSCreatorCode             = 0
kMDItemFSFinderFlags             = 0
kMDItemFSInvisible               = 0
kMDItemFSLabel                   = 0
kMDItemFSName                    = "GetMetadataForFile.c"
kMDItemFSNodeCount               = 0
kMDItemFSOwnerGroupID            = 501
kMDItemFSOwnerUserID             = 501
kMDItemFSSize                    = 2318
kMDItemFSTypeCode                = 0
kMDItemID                        = 408956
kMDItemKind                      = "C Source File"
```

This information is useful for learning and debugging, to see if a file's metadata contains what you expect it to. You can use `mdls` with the `-name` option to list only a specific metadata key for the file.

mdfind

The `mdfind` command lets you take advantage of Spotlight searches from the command line. You can use `mdfind` to search the full metadata store, just as when you click the Spotlight icon on the right side of the menu bar and type. For example, the following command searches for the word *jungle* anywhere in metadata, just as it would if you clicked the Spotlight icon and typed the same word:

```
mdfind jungle
```

To narrow your search, you can use an expression for the search term. For example, to find every MP3 file, you can use this command:

```
mdfind "kMDItemKind == '*MP3*'"
```

A couple of interesting options are available with `mdfind`. The `-onlyin` option lets you limit the search to a specified directory. The `-live` option keeps the query going, giving updated results if the metadata changes—until you press Control-C to stop it.

mdutil

The `mdutil` command provides some powerful and scary options you can use to control Spotlight. For example, the `-E` option erases the metadata store for a given disk volume. Be careful with that one. The `-i` option lets you turn Spotlight indexing on or off for any particular volume. The harmless `-s` option shows the Spotlight status for the given volume.

Creating XML Importer

In this section, you examine the code for an actual custom Spotlight importer. This one examines XML files and extracts textual information and then builds keys in the metadata dictionary that feature that information. Josh Carter, our old friend from Chapter 17, created the XML Spotlight importer presented here.

GetMetadataForFile.c

Almost all the work of creating a Spotlight importer is writing the `GetMetadataForFile` function, so you start by taking a look there. The basic technique Josh uses in his XML importer is to take advantage of libxml, an open source library for swimming around in XML files. Josh calls libxml to find textual data inside XML files before assigning metadata keys for that text.

The parseXMLFile function in libxml does the dirty work of pulling out text from the XML file, You call parseXMLFile with the filename that Spotlight provides when it calls a meta-data importer, and you also pass a CFMutableStringRef object to parseXMLFile to receive the extracted text.

After parseXMLFile produces some text, it's time to create a metadata key for that text. To accomplish that, you call this function:

```
CFDictionaryAddValue(attributes, kMDItemTextContent, allText);
```

This call creates a key of type kMDItemTextContent with the text in allText, adding it to the metadata store.

Note To find out much more about libxml and download a copy, see the project Web site at xmlsoft.org.

```
/* XML character data indexer for Spotlight.
 * by Josh Carter <josh@multipart-mixed.com>
 */

#include <CoreFoundation/CoreFoundation.h>
#include <CoreServices/CoreServices.h>
#include <libxml/parser.h>

/**
 * Uncomment to enable logging via printf, which is useful for
 * debugging using the mdimport command.
 */
#undef  PRINTF_LOGGING

/**
 * Apple docs say to not submit more than 100K of text at once.
 * We'll cap ours at 50K. Alternatively we could skip indexing
 * of files past a certain size limit.
 */
#define kMaxCharactersToHandle 50 * 1024

/**
 * Callback from libxml which gives us only character data.
 */
void HandleSAXCharacters(void* castToAllText,
                         const xmlChar *str,
                         int len)
{
    CFMutableStringRef allText =
      (CFMutableStringRef) castToAllText;

    /* We need a holding buffer because incoming data
     * is *not* null terminated.
     */

static char buf[1024];
```

```
        while (len > 0)
        {
            int appendSize = len > 1023 ? 1023 : len;
            len -= appendSize;

            /* Copy and terminate a chunk */
            memcpy(buf, str, appendSize);
            buf[appendSize] = 0;

            /* Append that to the master string */
            CFStringAppendCString(allText, buf,
                kCFStringEncodingUTF8);

#ifdef PRINTF_LOGGING
            printf("appending: %s\n", buf);
#endif
        }
}


/**
 * Sets up and starts libxml parser.
 */
Boolean ParseXMLFile(const char *filename,
    CFMutableStringRef allText)
{
    /* Set all handlers to null by default */
    xmlSAXHandler saxHandlers;
    memset(&saxHandlers, 0, sizeof(xmlSAXHandler));

    /* Register our character data handler */
    saxHandlers.characters = HandleSAXCharacters;

    /* Fire up the parser */
    if (xmlSAXUserParseFile(&saxHandlers,
      (void*) allText, filename) >= 0)
        return TRUE;
    else
        return FALSE;
}


Boolean GetMetadataForFile(void* thisInterface,
                           CFMutableDictionaryRef attributes,
                           CFStringRef contentTypeUTI,
                           CFStringRef pathToFile)
{
    /* Copy CFString path to C string for libxml */
    char cStringPath[512];
    CFStringGetCString(pathToFile, cStringPath,
      512, kCFStringEncodingUTF8);
```

```
    /* Create string used to hold text we'll index */
    CFMutableStringRef allText = CFStringCreateMutable
      (kCFAllocatorDefault, kMaxCharactersToHandle);

#ifdef PRINTF_LOGGING
    printf("\n\n=== starting XML parsing: %s ===\n",
            cStringPath);
#endif

    if (ParseXMLFile(cStringPath, allText))
    {
#ifdef PRINTF_LOGGING
        printf("parsing done: successful\n");
#endif

        /* Add our master string to Spotlight's dictionary
         * for this file.
         */

        CFDictionaryAddValue(attributes,
          kMDItemTextContent, allText);
        return TRUE;
    }
    else
    {
#ifdef PRINTF_LOGGING
        printf("parsing done: FAILED\n");
#endif

        /* Parsing error; don't index this file */
        return FALSE;
    }
}
```

Info.plist

Most of the keys in the information property list for our XML importer are generated automatically by Xcode's New Project Assistant and then left untouched. The only keys you must change are the following:

- In the `CFBundleDocumentTypes` key, you edit the `LSItemContentTypes` entry to contain `public.xml`, which identifies the type of document that this importer handles.
- The `CFBundleIdentifier` key is `com.multipart-mixed.xmlDataImporter`, a unique identifier for this importer, which follows the standard reverse-domain system used by all OS X code bundles.

```
<?xml version="1.0" encoding="UTF-8"?>
<!DOCTYPE plist PUBLIC "-//Apple Computer//DTD PLIST 1.0//EN"
"http://www.apple.com/DTDs/PropertyList-1.0.dtd">
```

```xml
<plist version="1.0">
<dict>
    <key>CFBundleDevelopmentRegion</key>
    <string>English</string>
    <key>CFBundleDocumentTypes</key>
    <array>
        <dict>
            <key>CFBundleTypeRole</key>
            <string>MDImporter</string>
            <key>LSItemContentTypes</key>
            <array>
                <string>public.xml</string>
            </array>
        </dict>
    </array>
    <key>CFBundleExecutable</key>
    <string>XMLMetadataImporter</string>
    <key>CFBundleIconFile</key>
    <string></string>
    <key>CFBundleIdentifier</key>
    <string>com.multipart-mixed.xmlDataImporter</string>
    <key>CFBundleInfoDictionaryVersion</key>
    <string>6.0</string>
    <key>CFBundleVersion</key>
    <string>1.0</string>
    <key>CFPlugInDynamicRegisterFunction</key>
    <string></string>
    <key>CFPlugInDynamicRegistration</key>
    <string>NO</string>
    <key>CFPlugInFactories</key>
    <dict>
        <key>50A8F8E0-FBBD-458D-8B84-C6F93B6B0B77</key>
        <string>MetadataImporterPluginFactory</string>
    </dict>
    <key>CFPlugInTypes</key>
    <dict>
        <key>8B08C4BF-415B-11D8-B3F9-0003936726FC</key>
        <array>
            <string>50A8F8E0-FBBD-458D-8B84-C6F93B6B0B77</string>
        </array>
    </dict>
    <key>CFPlugInUnloadFunction</key>
    <string></string>
</dict>
</plist>
```

main.c

The main.c file that appears when you create a new Spotlight importer project in Xcode is pure template code. It's interesting to look at, but you shouldn't change anything in the file. The main.c file implements functions for the standard plug-in interface defined by the Mac OS X plug-in architecture. Because the code is standard and shouldn't be changed, it's not reprinted here. If you want to see it, just take a look at the main.c file in any Spotlight Importer project.

 To learn about the Mac OS X plug-in architecture in more detail, see "Introduction to Plug-ins" at `http://developer.apple.com/documentation/CoreFoundation/Conceptual/CF PlugIns/index.html`.

Build and Install

Here are the steps for getting XML Importer running after you have all the code in place:

1. In Xcode, click Build to compile the project. If you get any compile errors, check to make sure your code matches what's in the book.

2. In the Finder, look in your Home directory for the Library/Spotlight folder. If this folder doesn't exist, choose File ➔ New Folder to create a folder; then rename it Spotlight.

3. Copy the file XMLImporter.mdimporter from your Xcode project folder to ~/Library/Spotlight.

4. In Terminal, type the command **mdimport -L** to list all known importers, and make sure ~/Library/Spotlight/XMLImporter.mdimporter is on the list (it's probably the last item).

5. Tell Spotlight to use your new importer to collect metadata: Type the command **mdimport -r ~/Library/Spotlight/XMLImporter.mdimporter**.

6. Test Spotlight to see if everything worked. Click the Spotlight button in the menu bar and search for text in an XML file. For example, search for XMLMetadataImporter, which is in the importer's own Info.plist file. You should see the file in the Spotlight search results.

Extra Credit

If you're interested in playing around more with Spotlight, here are a few projects you might be interested in trying:

- Apple has done a good job of creating importers for most of the common file types in the system, and I've shown you XML in this chapter; but there are likely other types that could use importers. Take a look around your Mac and see if you can create an importer for a forgotten file type or two.

- Spotlight works better when importers use the standard data types that are already defined. But it's always more fun to do it yourself. Try writing an importer that defines its own custom data type.

- Want to build Spotlight inquiries into your applications? Go right ahead! You can use `MDQuery` or `NSMetadataQuery` (in Cocoa) to talk directly to Spotlight.

- Become a plug-in expert. Study CFPlugIn and figure out how to do something really cool by modifying the main.c file that's part of your Spotlight importer—that's the one that says "DO NOT MODIFY THE CONTENT OF THIS FILE."

Summary

Spotlight is the most visible and most user-accessible new feature in Tiger. In fact, it's so prominent that it appears on the screen all the time, at the right end of the menu bar. Buried beneath this cool feature is a powerful set of tools for geeks who want to make searching better in Mac OS X. Spotlight makes a great platform for fun and useful hacking.

Commando

I n this chapter, you're going to look at something a little different from what you've seen before. Instead of merely moving technology forward, you're going to reach back for a wonderful old tool that's been lost in the mists of time, drag it forward, dust it off, and reinvent it for a new generation.

This chapter describes Commando, a cool and useful hack created by Shane Looker. Commando provides a nice Aqua interface to help you specify and execute Unix shell commands. When you use Commando, you don't have to remember the syntax and options of shell commands. Instead, Commando presents a nifty dialog for the command—you just click check boxes and radio buttons and type in text boxes to specify what you want the shell command to do.

The Original Commando

Commando was a brilliant idea that was originally implemented in the venerable Macintosh Programmer's Workshop (MPW), a development environment used by most Mac programmers from its inception in the mid-1980s until well into the 1990s, when Metrowerks tools began to take over. MPW was a powerful development environment that included regular expressions, scripting, and a broad set of command-line tools, sort of a mini-Unix for developers. Figure 21-1 shows the MPW Shell window.

MPW was a great step forward for Mac developers, but Apple wanted to make it even more Mac-like in form and function. After all, Apple was touting a graphical user interface that gave everyday folks windows, menus, and a mouse; so why should programmers have to suffer with a command line? To help make the command line friendlier to Mac-loving developers who hadn't seen (or didn't like) Unix, Commando was born (Figure 21-2).

FIGURE 21-1: MPW window.

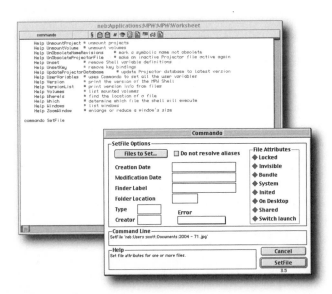

FIGURE 21-2: Commando in MPW made it easier to execute shell commands.

There are a couple of ways to start Commando from the MPW Shell. Commando itself is a shell tool, which you can activate by typing the word **commando** followed by the name of another tool. For example, you can use Commando to run the compare tool by typing this command:

```
commando compare
```

MPW displays the dialog shown in Figure 21-3.

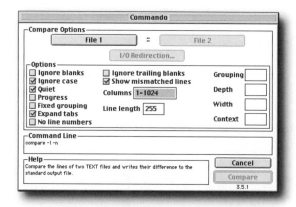

FIGURE 21-3: Commando dialog for the compare tool.

You can also trigger Commando by typing the name of a tool, followed by Option-semicolon and Enter, or just by typing the command and pressing Option-Enter. The Option-semicolon produces an ellipsis, which also happens to be the character used in Mac menus to indicate an item that produces a dialog box, so it's especially appropriate for Commando, which is all about putting up dialog boxes.

For thousands of Macintosh programmers in a bygone era, Commando provided a vital bridge between the worlds of graphical user interfaces and command lines. If you want to see for yourself what it was like, you can download MPW from Apple for free at http:// developer.apple.com/tools/mpw-tools/.

Note MPW requires Mac OS 7, 8, or 9 in order to run. On a modern Macintosh, you can run MPW in the Classic environment. There is apparently an OS X native version of MPW, and although it has been demonstrated in public and even seen outside of Apple's halls, Apple has never shipped it.

Commando Reborn

Mac OS doesn't need a fake Unix any more—it has the real thing. Now that every Mac has Unix, it seemed to Mac programmer Shane Looker that a new version of Commando would come in handy. This modern Commando runs in Terminal and offers assistance to folks who wanted an easier to way to summon shell commands and provide all the correct options. The result is a new Commando, brought into the 21st century for Mac OS X. You can see what a new Commando dialog looks like in Figure 21-4.

FIGURE 21-4: The Commando dialog.

Shane Looker has been programming Macs since 1984, before MPW was the coolest tool around. His current coding specialty is nifty tricks involving printer drivers, but he's tackled a zillion different kinds of projects. He created Commando out of reverence for the past, a desire for a better future, and the need to stop reading man pages.

Specifying Shell Commands

This modern version of Commando is implemented as a tool named cmdo. To use it, just type cmdo followed by the name of a shell command. In order for Commando to work with a particular shell command, there must be a template file for that command in the /Library/ Preferences/Commando folder. As an example, here is the template file for the top command.

When you install Commando, notice that it already comes with template files for some commands. To support additional commands, you can create your own template files. The first line in the template file gives the name of the command, followed by all its possible options, each one represented by a number and enclosed in brackets.

```
top [1][2][3][4][5]
```

The <pane> tag divides options into separate panes in the Commando dialog. Commando automatically adds an I/O Settings pane to every command.

```
<pane Options>
```

Each possible option is listed on its own line, with a vertical bar used to separate parts of the option. First is a number, corresponding to the option numbers in the first line of the template. Next is a letter that indicates the type of control that appears in the dialog box for this option:

- s (for switch) produces a check box.

- R followed by a group number (for example, R1) is for a radio button. All items with the same group number are placed together in a radio button group.

- T stands for a text entry field.

After the control type, the text of the option appears, followed by helpful text that shows up in a tooltip when the user hovers over the control. The </pane> tag closes the definition for that pane. You can specify as many panes as you like for a command.

```
1|R1|-cn|-cn Non-event mode (default)|Calculate CPU usage
   since the previous sample
1|R1|-ca|-ca Accumulative Mode|Count events accumulatively,
   starting at launch of top. Calculate CPU usage and time.
1|R1|-cd|-cd Delta mode|Count events relative to the previous
   sample. Calculate CPU usage since the previous sample.
1|R1|-ce|-ce Absolute mode|Count events using absolute
   counters.
2|S|-F|-F Ignore Frameworks (shared libraries)|Dont calculate
   statistics for shared libraries. Reduces top
   processor time.
3|S|-f|-f Include Frameworks (default)|
4|S|-h|-h Print command line help|
5|T|-s<t>|-s <t>delay in seconds|
</pane>
```

Commando Source Code

This section provides listings for some of the key Commando source files. In the interests of space, not all source files are listed here. To see all the sources, you can download the entire project from the book's companion Web site at http://www.wiley.com/compbooks/extremetech.

The heart of Commando is CommandoWindowController, which kicks off Commando and produces the dialog.

CommandoWindowController.h

This is the header file for the vital `CommandoWindowController` section.

```
/* CommandoWindowController */
```

```
#import <Cocoa/Cocoa.h>
```

These are constants for the various parts of the dialog: buttons, text fields, and so on.

```
enum
{
 kInputPopupTerminal = 1000,
 kInputPopupChooseFile,
 kInputPopupTextField,

 kOutputPopupTerminal = 1100,
 kOutputPopupDevNull,
 kOutputPopupChooseFile,
 kOutputPopupTextField,
 kOutputPopupPipe,

 kStderrPopupToOutput = 1200,
 kStderrPopupTerminal,
 kStderrPopupDevNull,
 kStderrPopupChooseFile,
 kStderrPopupTextField
};
```

```
@class ToolParser;
@class AssociatedTable;
```

Next, the following define the outlets for the `CommandWindowController` class that will be hooked up with other objects.

```
@interface CommandoWindowController : NSWindowController
{
 IBOutlet NSTextField *mCommandName;
 IBOutlet NSTextView  *mOutputLine;
 IBOutlet NSTabView   *myTabView;
 IBOutlet NSImageView  *myImageTest;
 IBOutlet NSTextView  *mAdditionalCommandLine;
 IBOutlet NSTextView  *mInputTextView;
 IBOutlet NSTextView  *mOutputTextView;
 IBOutlet NSTextView  *mErrorTextView;

 int  mStdinTypeTag;
    // These tags identify how to handle stdio on the output
    // line
 int  mStdoutTypeTag;
 int  mStderrTypeTag;
```

```
ToolParser *mToolParser;
AssociatedTable *mPanelTable;
NSString *mPrototypeLine;
NSString *mShellPathStr;
}
```

The following code defines the actions that will be connected to buttons in the Commando dialog, and declare other miscellaneous methods.

```
- (IBAction)doCancel:(id)sender;
- (IBAction)doDisplay:(id)sender;
- (IBAction)doExecute:(id)sender;
- (IBAction) ioPopupActionHandler: (id) sender;

- (void) returnTerminalToFront;

- (void) buildInterfaceTabs;
- (void) fillControlTable: (AssociatedTable**) theCmdoControls
  andUniqueSet: (NSMutableSet**) uniqueSet fromTabControlList:
  (NSMutableArray*) tabControlList;

- (NSMutableString*) buildExecutionString;
- (void) displayCommandLine;

- (BOOL) findShell;

- (NSString*) stdinHandlingString;
- (NSString*) stdoutHandlingString;
- (NSString*) stderrHandlingString;

@end
```

CommandoWindowController.mm

CommandoWindowController.mm contains the code that does most of the work in Commando, including these methods:

- awakeFromNib gets everything ready when Commando starts up.
- buildInterfaceTabs creates the views for the dialog.
- buildExecutionString puts together the command-line string that matches the chosen shell command and options.
- doExecute forks off a new shell and runs the command in that shell.

```
#import "CommandoWindowController.h"
#import "CmdoControl.h"
#import "AssociatedTable.h"
#import "ToolParser.h"
#import <string>
```

```
#import <fstream>

extern int gArgc;
extern char **gArgv;
extern char **environ;

NSMutableDictionary *gSubstitutionDictionary;
NSMutableDictionary *gRadioDict;
NSMutableDictionary *gAllOptionControls;

static void signalCatcher(int signal);
static NSTask *gSubTask = nil;

@implementation CommandoWindowController
```

The awakeFromNib method gets Commando started. First, check to make sure there's a command name and an available shell to execute it. If not, provide helpful information and then bail out.

```
- (void) awakeFromNib
{
 BOOL isOK;

 if ((gArgc < 2) || ([self findShell] == NO))
{
  printf ("Command usage:\n");
  printf ("commando [toolName]\n... [toolName]\n",
    gArgv[1]);
  [self doCancel: self];
 }

 mStdinTypeTag = kInputPopupTerminal;
 mStdoutTypeTag = kOutputPopupTerminal;
 mStderrTypeTag = kStderrPopupToOutput;
```

Prepare for the dialog by removing the tabs. You can build them back later. Then, create a set of global dictionaries for handling command substitution, radio button sets, and options.

```
 [myTabView removeTabViewItem:
   [myTabView tabViewItemAtIndex: 1]];
 [myTabView setDelegate: self];

 gSubstitutionDictionary =
[[NSMutableDictionary alloc] initWithCapacity: 40];
 gRadioDict =
[[NSMutableDictionary alloc] initWithCapacity: 40];
 gAllOptionControls =
[[NSMutableDictionary alloc] initWithCapacity: 40];
```

Call the tool parser that will find and load the data file containing Commando information. If the file isn't there, report an error and quit.

```
mToolParser = [[ToolParser alloc] init];
if (mToolParser == nil) // No data file to parse
{
 printf("Unable to find commando data for %s\n",
    gArgv[1]);
 [self doCancel: self];
}
isOK = [mToolParser loadCommandDefinitionArgc:
   gArgc Argv: gArgv];
mPanelTable = [mToolParser panelDictionary];

[[self window] setTitle: [NSString stringWithCString:
   gArgv[1]]];
```

At this point, everything seems to be going well, so put the Commando dialog in the front.

```
ProcessSerialNumber psn;
MacGetCurrentProcess(&psn);
SetFrontProcess(&psn);

[self buildInterfaceTabs];
[self displayCommandLine];

NSNotificationCenter *theNC = [NSNotificationCenter
   defaultCenter];
[theNC addObserver: self
   selector: @selector(textChangedNotificationHandler:)
   name:@"NSTextDidChangeNotification" object: nil];

signal(SIGHUP, signalCatcher);
signal(SIGINT, signalCatcher);
signal(SIGQUIT, signalCatcher);
signal(SIGABRT, signalCatcher);
}
```

The doCancel method is called if the user clicks the Cancel button, or if Commando decides it must quit due to an error.

```
- (IBAction)doCancel:(id)sender
{
 [self returnTerminalToFront];
 [[NSApplication sharedApplication] terminate: self];
}
```

Commando calls the doDisplay method to create the string that contains the shell command to be executed.

```
- (IBAction)doDisplay:(id)sender
```

```
{
 NSMutableString *commandStr = [self buildExecutionString];

 [self returnTerminalToFront];
 printf("%s\n", [commandStr cString]);
 [self doCancel: sender];

 [[NSApplication sharedApplication] terminate: self];
}
```

The doExecute method takes the shell command string defined by the dialog and sends it to the shell for execution.

```
- (IBAction)doExecute:(id)sender
{
 NSTask *subTask;

 NSMutableString *commandStr = [self buildExecutionString];
 NSMutableArray *argArray =
   [NSMutableArray arrayWithObject: commandStr];
```

Add –c as the first argument to the shell. This indicates to the shell that the next argument is the command to be executed. The command string is also written to the command line so it will appear in Terminal.

```
[argArray insertObject: [NSString stringWithString: @"-c"]
   atIndex:0];

 printf("%s\n", [commandStr cString]);
 subTask = [NSTask launchedTaskWithLaunchPath:
             mShellPathStr
             arguments: argArray];
 gSubTask = subTask;

 [self returnTerminalToFront];
 [subTask waitUntilExit];

 [self returnTerminalToFront];

 [[NSApplication sharedApplication] terminate: self];
}
```

When Commando is done building the command string, make Terminal the frontmost application again.

```
- (void) returnTerminalToFront
{
 char  bigArray[1024];

 ProcessInfoRec procInfo;
 procInfo.processName = nil;
 procInfo.processAppSpec = nil;
```

```
procInfo.processLocation = bigArray;
procInfo.processInfoLength = sizeof(procInfo);

ProcessSerialNumber psn;
MacGetCurrentProcess(&psn);
GetProcessInformation(&psn, &procInfo);

SetFrontProcess(&procInfo.processLauncher);
}
```

Commando calls `buildInterfaceTabs` to create the various I/O and View panels and the controls in them that are associated with tabs in the Commando window.

```
- (void) buildInterfaceTabs
{
  int count = [mPanelTable count];
  int i;

  for (i = 0; i < count; i++)
  {
    NSString *key;
    key = [mPanelTable keyAtIndex: i];

    NSMutableArray *tabControlList =
      [mPanelTable objectForKey: key];

    NSTabViewItem *aTabView = [NSTabViewItem new];
    [aTabView setLabel: key];
    [myTabView insertTabViewItem: aTabView atIndex: i];

    NSRect tabViewRect = [myTabView contentRect];

    AssociatedTable *myCmdoControls =
      [[AssociatedTable alloc] init];

    NSMutableSet *goodControls;
    [self fillControlTable: &myCmdoControls
        andUniqueSet: &goodControls
        fromTabControlList: tabControlList];
```

At this point, you have a unique list of controls for the window. Now start to lay them out in the window.

```
    int max = [myCmdoControls count];
    NSView *subView = [aTabView view];

    float subViewBottom = 0;
    float subViewTop = NSHeight(tabViewRect);
```

```
float lastControlBottom = subViewTop;
float currentLeftEdge = 20.0;

for (int controlIndex = 0; controlIndex < max;
    controlIndex++)
{
 float fHeight;
 NSControl *aControl =
    [myCmdoControls objectAtIndex: controlIndex];

 if ([goodControls containsObject: aControl])
 {
  [goodControls removeObject: aControl];
  CmdoControl *cCon =
    [myCmdoControls keyAtIndex: controlIndex];
  NSView *tempView;
```

Put a box around the control.

```
 if ([[cCon control] isKindOfClass:
                    [NSMatrix class]])
 {
  NSBox *theBox = [[NSBox alloc] init];
  [theBox setBoxType: NSBoxSecondary];
  [theBox setTitlePosition: NSNoTitle];// ;
  [theBox setContentView: [cCon control]];
  [theBox sizeToFit];
  tempView = theBox;
  fHeight = NSHeight([theBox frame]);
 }
 else {
   tempView = [cCon control];
   fHeight = [cCon height];
 }

 [subView addSubview: tempView];
```

You now know the frame, the size of the tab view, and the location of the last control placed in the view. Use this information to figure out where this control goes. The layout leaves 3 pixels between controls. It must start over at the top of a new column if there's no more room in the current one.

```
 int height = (int) fHeight + 3;
 if ((lastControlBottom - height) < subViewBottom)
 {
  lastControlBottom = subViewTop;
  currentLeftEdge += NSWidth(tabViewRect) / 2.0;
 }
```

```
        lastControlBottom -= height;
        [tempView setFrameOrigin:
                NSMakePoint(currentLeftEdge,
                    lastControlBottom) ];
    }
  }
 }

 [myTabView selectFirstTabViewItem: self];
}
```

The `fillControlTable` method creates a table containing all the controls for the dialog.

```
- (void) fillControlTable:
                    (AssociatedTable**) theCmdoControls
            andUniqueSet: (NSMutableSet**) uniqueSet
        fromTabControlList: (NSMutableArray*) tabControlList
{
 int max = [tabControlList count];
 AssociatedTable *myCmdoControls =
   [[AssociatedTable alloc] init];
```

Create all the controls first.

```
 for (int controlIndex = 0; controlIndex < max;
     controlIndex++)
 {
  NSMutableArray *controlInfo =
   [tabControlList objectAtIndex: controlIndex];
  CmdoControl *cCon =
    [CmdoControl initWithData: controlInfo
          forController: self];

  if (cCon != nil)
   [myCmdoControls setObject: [cCon control]
        forKey: cCon ];
 }
 NSMutableSet *goodControls =
  [NSMutableSet setWithArray:
          [myCmdoControls allObjects]];
 *uniqueSet = goodControls;
 *theCmdoControls = myCmdoControls;
}
```

Commando calls `buildExecutionString` to create a character string with the desired command and all options selected by the user.

```
- (NSMutableString*) buildExecutionString
```

```
{
 NSString *protoString = [mToolParser prototypeLine];
 NSMutableString *cmdString;
 cmdString =
   [NSMutableString stringWithString: protoString ];
 NSMutableArray *subsList =
   [NSMutableArray arrayWithCapacity: 50];
int    startP, stopP;

 unsigned int lengthOfString = [protoString length];
 unsigned int i;

 for (i = 0; i < lengthOfString; i++)
 {
  unichar aChar = [protoString characterAtIndex: i];
  if (aChar == '[')
    startP = i;
  if (aChar == ']')
  {
   stopP = i;
   NSString *matchToken =
     [protoString
        substringWithRange:
           NSMakeRange(startP, (stopP - startP + 1))];
   [subsList addObject: matchToken];
  }
 }
```

Now that we have command strings, look for substitutions in the dictionary. If one doesn't exist, replace it with a null string.

```
 for (i = 0; i < [subsList count]; i++)
 {
  NSString *matchStr = [subsList objectAtIndex: i];
  NSString *newStr = [gSubstitutionDictionary
                 objectForKey: matchStr];
  if (newStr == nil)
     newStr = @"";

  [cmdString replaceOccurrencesOfString: matchStr
       withString: newStr
       options: NSLiteralSearch
       range: NSMakeRange(0,[cmdString length])];
 }
```

Look through the string for hyphens that have no options with them. If any are found, delete them.

```
[cmdString replaceOccurrencesOfString: @" - "
    withString: @" "
    options: NSLiteralSearch
    range: NSMakeRange(0, [cmdString length])];

if ([cmdString characterAtIndex: [cmdString length] - 1]
  == '-')
{
 [cmdString deleteCharactersInRange:
      NSMakeRange([cmdString length]-1, 1)];
}
```

Finish by adding the options for I/O handling.

```
[cmdString appendFormat: @" %@ %@ %@ %@",
  [mAdditionalCommandLine string],
  [self stdinHandlingString],
  [self stdoutHandlingString],
  [self stderrHandlingString] ];

return cmdString;
}
```

If the user clicks the Display button in the dialog, Commando uses the `displayCommandLine` method to show the command in the shell instead of executing it.

```
- (void) displayCommandLine
{
 NSMutableString *dispString = [self buildExecutionString];
 NSTextStorage *textStore = [mOutputLine textStorage];
 [textStore replaceCharactersInRange:
      NSMakeRange(0, [textStore length])
      withString: dispString];
}
```

Look for a shell to use for executing the command. If there's no shell, you can't do anything with the command.

```
- (BOOL) findShell
{
 char **ePtr = environ;

 std::string aStr;
 bool done = false;
 BOOL found = NO;

 do
 {
  aStr = *ePtr;
  if (aStr.size() == 0)
```

```
   done = true;
  else
  {
   if (aStr.find("SHELL=", 0) == 0)
   {
    mShellPathStr = [NSString stringWithCString:
       aStr.substr(6).c_str()];
    [mShellPathStr retain];
//    printf("shell = %s\n", aStr.substr(6).c_str());
    found = TRUE;
    done = true;
   }
   ePtr++;
  }
 }while (!done && (*ePtr != nil));

 return (found);
}
```

The `ioPopupActionHandler` method manages the pop-up menus that let the user choose
what to do with input, output, and errors.

```
- (void) ioPopupActionHandler: (id) sender
{
 NSPopUpButton *thePopup = sender;
 NSString  *selectedFileStr;

 [[self window] makeFirstResponder: self];
int theTag = [[thePopup selectedItem] tag];
if (theTag >= kStderrPopupToOutput)
  mStderrTypeTag = theTag;
else if (theTag >= kOutputPopupTerminal)
  mStdoutTypeTag = theTag;
else
  mStdinTypeTag = theTag;
```

The next chunk of code includes case labels for handing the input, output, and error redirection.

```
 switch (theTag)
 {
 case kInputPopupTerminal:
   [mInputTextView setEditable: NO];
   break;

 case kInputPopupChooseFile:
   [mInputTextView setEditable: NO];
   NSOpenPanel *thePanel = [NSOpenPanel openPanel];
   [thePanel retain];
   [thePanel setCanChooseDirectories: YES];
   [thePanel setCanChooseFiles: YES];
```

```
    [thePanel setAllowsMultipleSelection: NO];
    if ([thePanel runModalForDirectory: nil file: nil
            types: nil] == NSOKButton)
    {
     selectedFileStr = [[thePanel filenames]
                objectAtIndex: 0];
     [mInputTextView setString: selectedFileStr];
    }
    [thePanel release];
    break;

 case kInputPopupTextField:
    [mInputTextView setEditable: YES];
    [mInputTextView selectAll: self];
    [[self window] makeFirstResponder: mInputTextView];
    break;

case kOutputPopupTerminal:
    [mOutputTextView setEditable: NO];
    break;

case kOutputPopupDevNull:
    [mOutputTextView setEditable: NO];
    [mOutputTextView setString: @"/dev/null"];
    break;

case kOutputPopupChooseFile:
    [mOutputTextView setEditable: NO];

    NSSavePanel *savePanel = [NSSavePanel savePanel];
    [savePanel retain];
    if ([savePanel runModal] == NSFileHandlingPanelOKButton)
    {
     selectedFileStr = [savePanel filename];
     [mOutputTextView setString: selectedFileStr];
    }
    [savePanel release];
    break;

 case kOutputPopupTextField:
    [mOutputTextView setEditable: YES];
    [mOutputTextView selectAll: self];
    [[self window] makeFirstResponder: mOutputTextView];
    break;
```

```
case kOutputPopupPipe:
  [mOutputTextView setEditable: NO];
  break;

case kStderrPopupToOutput:
case kStderrPopupTerminal:
  break;

case kStderrPopupDevNull:
  [mErrorTextView setString: @"/dev/null"];
  break;

case kStderrPopupChooseFile:
  NSSavePanel *errPanel = [NSSavePanel savePanel];
  [errPanel retain];
  if ([errPanel runModal] == NSFileHandlingPanelOKButton)
  {
   selectedFileStr = [errPanel filename];
   [mErrorTextView setString: selectedFileStr];
  }
  [errPanel release];
  break;

 case kStderrPopupTextField:
  [mErrorTextView setEditable: YES];
  [mErrorTextView selectAll: self];
  [[self window] makeFirstResponder: mErrorTextView];
  break;
}

[self displayCommandLine];

}
```

The next three methods, stdinHandlingString, stdoutHandlingString, and stderrHandlingString, create the appropriate redirection string according to the user's choice from the pop-up menus in the Commando window.

```
- (NSString*) stdinHandlingString
{
  NSMutableString    *theString = nil;

  switch (mStdinTypeTag)
  {
  case kInputPopupTerminal:
    theString = [NSMutableString string];
    break;
```

```
    case kInputPopupChooseFile:
      theString = [NSMutableString
              stringWithFormat: @"<%@",
            [mInputTextView string] ];
      [theString replaceOccurrencesOfString: @" "
            withString: @"\\ "
            options: NSLiteralSearch
            range: NSMakeRange(0, [theString length])];
      break;

    case kInputPopupTextField:
      theString = [NSMutableString stringWithFormat: @"<%@",
                    [mInputTextView string]];
      break;
    }

    return theString;
}

- (NSString*) stdoutHandlingString
{
    NSMutableString    *theString = nil;

    switch (mStdoutTypeTag)
    {
    case kOutputPopupTerminal:
      theString = [NSMutableString string];
      break;

    case kOutputPopupDevNull:
      theString = [NSMutableString
              stringWithString: @">/dev/null"];
      break;

    case kOutputPopupChooseFile:
      theString = [NSMutableString stringWithFormat: @">%@",
                    [mOutputTextView string] ];
      [theString replaceOccurrencesOfString: @" "
            withString: @"\\ "
            options: NSLiteralSearch
            range: NSMakeRange(0, [theString length])];
      break;

    case kOutputPopupTextField:
      theString = [NSMutableString stringWithFormat: @">%@",
                    [mOutputTextView string] ];
      break;
```

```
  case kOutputPopupPipe:
    theString = [NSMutableString stringWithString: @"| "];
    break;
  }

  return theString;
}

- (NSString*) stderrHandlingString
{
  NSMutableString    *theString = nil;
  switch (mStderrTypeTag)
  {
  case kStderrPopupToOutput:
    if (mStdoutTypeTag == kOutputPopupTerminal)
      theString = [NSMutableString stringWithString: @""];
    else
      theString = [NSMutableString
              stringWithString: @"2>&1"];
    break;

  case kStderrPopupTerminal:
    theString = [NSMutableString string];
    break;

  case kStderrPopupDevNull:
    theString = [NSMutableString stringWithString:
                    @"2>/dev/null"];
    break;

  case kStderrPopupChooseFile:
    theString = [NSMutableString stringWithFormat: @"2>%@",
                  [mErrorTextView string] ];
    [theString replaceOccurrencesOfString: @" "
          withString: @"\\ "
          options: NSLiteralSearch
          range: NSMakeRange(0, [theString length])]];
    break;

  case kStderrPopupTextField:
    theString = [NSMutableString stringWithFormat: @"2>%@",
                  [mErrorTextView string] ];
    break;
  }

  return theString;
}
```

The `textChangedNotificationHandler` method simply shows the command line. Commando calls this method after its interface comes to the front.

```
- (void) textChangedNotificationHandler:
    (NSNotification *) theNotification
{
 [self displayCommandLine];
}

- (void)tabView:(NSTabView *)tabView
    didSelectTabViewItem:(NSTabViewItem *)tabViewItem
{
 [[self window] makeFirstResponder: self];
}
```

The `signalCatcher` method handles termination signals received by Commando. If any of these signals are received, `signalCatcher` calls `terminate` to kill the task.

```
void signalCatcher(int signal)
{

switch (signal)
 {
 case SIGHUP:
 case SIGINT:
 case SIGQUIT:
 case SIGABRT:
 case SIGTERM:
  [gSubTask terminate];
  exit(1);
  break;
 }
}

@end
```

ToolParser.h

This header file provides the definitions for the *tool parser*, the part of Commando that interprets shell command template files. The tool parser finds a file with the name of the given command and the .cmdo extension. It creates dialog panels and controls for each panel.

```
#import <Cocoa/Cocoa.h>
#import <fstream>

@class AssociatedTable;

@interface ToolParser : NSObject
{
  NSString *mPrototypeLine;
  AssociatedTable  *mPanelTable;
```

```
}

-  (NSString*) prototypeLine;

-  (AssociatedTable*) panelTable;

-  (BOOL) loadCommandDefinitionArgc: (int) argc
                            argv: (const char**) argv;
-  (void) readCommandPrototype: (std::ifstream*) inStream;
-  (void) readPanels: (std::ifstream*) inStream;

-  (void) parseOptionLine: (std::string*) line
              intoArray: (NSMutableArray*) controlArray;

@end
```

ToolParser.mm

ToolParser.mm contains the code that opens a command's template file, builds the panes for the Commando dialog, and creates the controls that go in the dialog panes. Key methods include the following:

- readPanels loads panes for the Commando dialog.

- loadCommandDefinitionArgc controls the process of reading the shell command definition.

- parseOptionLine processes an option definition, including the option name, control type, and tool tip.

```
#import "ToolParser.h"

@implementation ToolParser

- (id) init
{
 if (self = [super init])
   mPanelTable = [[AssociatedTable alloc] init];

 return [super init];
}

- (void) dealloc
{
    [mPanelTable release];
    [mPrototypeLine release];

    [super dealloc];
}
```

```
- (NSString*) prototypeLine
{
 return mPrototypeLine;
}


- (AssociatedTable*) panelDictionary
{
 return mPanelTable;
}

- (BOOL) loadCommandDefinitionArgc: (int) argc
                   argv: (char**) argv
{
 std::ifstream *inStream = new std::ifstream();
 std::string lookupString("/Library/Preferences/Commando/");
 std::string tryString = lookupString;

 tryString += argv[1];
 tryString += ".cmdo";
```

Look for the command definition file and try opening it.

```
 inStream->open(tryString.c_str());

 if (inStream->is_open() == true)
 {
  [self readCommandPrototype: inStream];
  [self readPanels: inStream];

  inStream->close();
  return YES;
 }
  else
    return NO;
}
```

The readCommandPrototype and readPanels methods get information from the .cmdo file and use it to help construct the Commando dialog.

```
- (void) readCommandPrototype: (std::ifstream*) inStream
{
 char protoLine[512];

 inStream->getline(protoLine, sizeof(protoLine) - 1);
 mPrototypeLine = [NSString stringWithCString: protoLine];

 [mPrototypeLine retain];
}

- (void) readPanels: (std::ifstream*) inStream
```

```
{
 BOOL doneWithPanes = NO;
 BOOL doneWithThisPane = NO;

 std::string paneTag = "<pane ";
 std::string endPaneTag = "</pane>";
 do
 {

 char paneLine[1024];
 inStream->getline(paneLine, sizeof(paneLine) - 1);
 std::string paneLineStr = paneLine;

 int findPost = paneLineStr.find(paneTag);
 if (findPost != -1)
 {
  findPost += paneTag.size();
  int endPost = paneLineStr.find(">");

  std::string paneNameStr =
     paneLineStr.substr(findPost, endPost - findPost);

  NSString *labelString =
     [NSString stringWithCString: paneNameStr.c_str()];
```

Assemble the `panelTable` object. For items in this table, the tab name is the key and the value is an array of control data arrays.

```
  NSMutableArray *tabControlList =
   [NSMutableArray arrayWithCapacity: 10];
  do
  {
  inStream->getline(paneLine, sizeof(paneLine) - 1);
  paneLineStr = paneLine;
  if (paneLineStr.find(endPaneTag) != -1)
  {
   doneWithThisPane = YES;
   [mPanelTable setObject: tabControlList
     forKey: labelString];
  }
  else
  {
   NSMutableArray *controlArray =
     [NSMutableArray arrayWithCapacity: 5];

   [self parseOptionLine: &paneLineStr
      intoArray: controlArray];
   [tabControlList addObject: controlArray];
  }
```

```
 } while (!doneWithThisPane);
}
else
 doneWithPanes = TRUE;

} while (!doneWithPanes);
}
```

The parseOptionLine method takes a string of elements separated by a vertical bar and breaks them up into individual fields that are added to the control array.

```
- (void) parseOptionLine: (std::string*) line intoArray:
  (NSMutableArray*) controlArray //intoTab: (NSTabViewItem*)
  theTab
{
 int lastPost = 0;
 int fencePost;

 [controlArray addObject: [NSObject new]];

 do {
 std::string matchItem;

 fencePost = line->find("|", lastPost);
 BOOL foundEscape;
 do
 {
  foundEscape = NO;
  if ((fencePost > 0)
      && ((*line)[fencePost-1] == '\\'))
  {
  line->erase(fencePost-1, 1);
  fencePost = line->find("|", fencePost);
  foundEscape = YES;
  }
 } while (foundEscape);

 if (fencePost == -1)
  matchItem = line->substr(lastPost);
 else
  matchItem = line->substr(lastPost,
                  fencePost - lastPost);

 lastPost = fencePost + 1;

 [controlArray addObject:
     [NSString stringWithCString: matchItem.c_str()]];

 } while (fencePost != -1);
}

@end
```

Summary

Commando proves that technology does not always move forward in a tidy linear fashion. Sometimes great ideas and implementations get left behind in the rush of progress. But great old ideas can become great new ones, as Commando proves. In a Unix world, Commando is possibly even more useful now than it was back in the MPW days.

mach_override and mach_inject

chapter

22

in this chapter
- ☑ Learn about dynamic overriding
- ☑ Find out how mach_override and mach_inject work
- ☑ See an example of dynamic overriding

In this final chapter, you'll learn about our hackiest hack yet: mach_override and mach_inject, a pair of packages for writing code that customizes the way applications behave, using a technique called *dynamic overriding*. If you're looking for a way to add a feature to the Finder, change the way iCal does something, or generally bend your Macintosh to your will, you'll be very interested in mach_override and mach_inject, coded by Jonathan "Wolf" Rentzch.

The packages in this chapter are cleverly designed so that you can create your own override code without having to understand anything about what's going on when mach_override and mach_inject do their thing. However, if you're curious about how these functions harness the lowest levels of Mac OS X, you can explore the source listings and commentary. The concepts involved in creating mach_override and mach_inject are very low level, and if you're mainly used to application programming, studying them will probably involve learning some new concepts. However, I think it's more than worthwhile, and it's a rare chance to go behind the scenes of a true virtuoso feat of programming.

Dynamic Overriding

When a person in authority says not to do something, it's human nature (for some humans, anyway) to want to do that very thing. So it is with operating systems and independent developers. The OS vendor has an honest interest in maintaining a stable, usable system, so it creates and enforces rules of behavior that are encoded primarily as application programming interfaces (APIs). Developers want their programs to be better, more clever, and cooler than everybody else's; and sometimes they break the rules to achieve those ends, or more commonly, they push into gray territory that's not specifically covered by the rules.

In the ancient days before Mac OS X, the important Mac system routines all passed through a single table of addresses using a microprocessor feature called *trap dispatching*. By changing the address of a system trap, developers could intercept and customize routines, adding and changing features. But Mac OS X abandoned this mechanism for new schemes, leaving developers to wonder how they would get access to what's inside the system.

In 2001, a group of veteran Mac developers got together to ponder this question. In due time, a prolific developer named Jonathan "Wolf" Rentzch came up with a solution, which he called *dynamic overriding*. He implemented his scheme in two packages: mach_override, for inserting your own code in place of a system function, and mach_inject for launching your code into another application's address space and getting it to run there. And it was good: many other developers are now using Wolf's code to make cool applications and utilities. By studying this chapter, you'll be able to create cool hacks with mach_override and mach_inject.

The software described in this chapter takes advantage of Mach, the low-level part of OS X that manages memory and processes. Because Mac OS X is built on Mach, you can take advantage of Mach features and interfaces in your software. To learn more about Mach, see the Mach home page at www-2.cs.cmu.edu/afs/cs.cmu.edu/project/mach/public/www/mach.html. You might also be interested in learning more about the architecture of the Mac's PowerPC microprocessor. For that information, see the information at http://www.lightsoft.co.uk/Fantasm/Beginners/begin1.html and http://www-106.ibm.com/developerworks/library/l-ppc.

Jonathan "Wolf" Rentzch knows an amazing amount of stuff about programming. As the sole proprietor of Red Shed Software, he programs using Cocoa, Carbon, WebObjects, Mach, Unix, and a zillion other technologies. Wolf likes to explore the obscure but vital corners of systems, such as how to make Mac OS X better through dynamic overriding. You can find out more by visiting http://rentzsch.com.

How Dynamic Overriding Works

The functions described in this chapter let you dynamically override functions. What is dynamic overriding? It's *overriding* because you're changing the way functions work by replacing them with your own code. It's *dynamic* because it happens at runtime and goes away when the code you're overriding (usually an application) is gone, leaving no bitter aftertaste.

The runtime for Mac OS X (and for most operating systems) calls functions by constructing a table of addresses, then jumping to the appropriate function when it's called. In OS X, every process gets its own table of function addresses. This fact, along with Mach's *lazy binding* feature that helps give OS X programming its terrific versatility, makes it impossible to override a system function by changing a value in one central place.

The mach_override package works by replacing the first instruction of the function itself with a branch to other code—sort of like installing a detour sign at the beginning of the function. Instead of executing the function as it was written, this technique, which is called *single-instruction overwriting*, runs your overridden version of the code. This technique is illustrated in Figure 22-1.

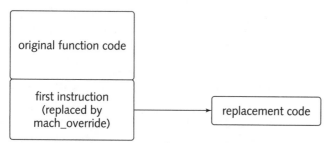

FIGURE 22-1: Single-instruction overwriting detours to your code.

In a world of preemptive multitasking like the OS X runtime, you have to be careful about changing code that's already loaded and running. Because you're only changing a single instruction in the code—the first instruction—you can take advantage of the PowerPC's capability to replace a 32-bit value in one processor cycle, a feature called *atomic replacement*.

Branch Islands

In the scheme described so far, you only get to replace one assembly language instruction, and you can't do much in that tight space. The most productive use of that precious single instruction is a branch instruction to another location where you can deploy a little bit more code. The strategy mach_override uses is to load that little-bit-more code, then make the original routine branch to that location. The place where you put your code is called a *branch island* (see Figure 22-2).

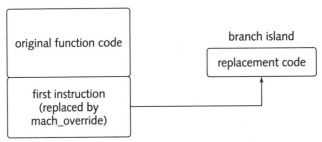

FIGURE 22-2: New instruction points to a branch island.

The PowerPC instruction set defines many kinds of branch instructions, but most of them can't be used here. Some branch instructions require loading a register first, and that would take more than a single instruction space, so they're out. Other branch instructions change the link register when they're executed. These wouldn't be very nice to the routine you're overriding because the link register contains the calling routine's return address. There's a branch relative instruction that jumps to an address within 32MB of the calling instruction, but you don't have an easy to way to guarantee that your branch island will actually be within 32MB of the caller, so you can't use that one.

This process of elimination leaves one possible branch instruction: *branch absolute*. The branch absolute instruction can jump to the lowest and highest 32MB of the process address space. The first 32MB is usually pretty busy, but the last 32MB generally has plenty of room for code. So the plan is to create a branch island in the last 32MB of address space, and put the branch island there.

You could conceivably put the entire override in that space in the last 32MB, but locating the whole function there would take some work, and you might eventually run into memory limitations. Instead, mach_override makes the branch island into a level of indirection that points to your actual code. This is called an *escape branch island*, which incidentally would also make a terrific name for an action movie. Figure 22-3 provides a picture of how this works:

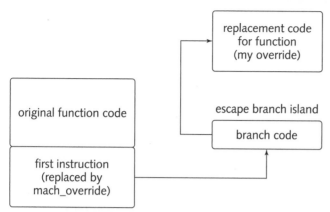

FIGURE 22-3: mach_override makes the original function point to the branch island, which then points to the replacement code.

Often, when you override a function with mach_override, you'll want to return to the original function's code at some point. To make this possible, mach_override creates a *reentry branch island* that contains the original first instruction and a branch back to the function's second instruction. If you want to return to the original function after your custom code is done, you can execute the code in this reentry branch island.

After mach_override has done all that, you've successfully imposed your will on the overridden function. In most cases, you'll also want to use mach_inject, which, conveniently, is the subject of the next section.

Code Injection

Overriding a function with mach_override is a fine way to change what happens when a function runs in the current process. To make really cool stuff happen, however, you need to be able to install the override in *another* process and get it running there. That's where you turn to mach_inject, the other half of your code customizing kit.

Like overriding, injecting code into another process is a delicate procedure, but most of the tricky parts are handled for you in mach_inject. To oversimplify what happens, it's basically a four-part process: Create a thread for the injected code, allocate memory in the remote process, put the code there, and start it running. The Mach magic you need is canonized for you in mach_inject.

When you create your injection project, you use the interface provided by mach_inject_bundle. It's possible to call the lower-level mach_inject directly, but there's no practical reason to do so. To learn how to use mach_inject_bundle, see the Dynamic Overriding Example section later in this chapter.

By combining mach_override with mach_inject, you can gain the remarkable power of introducing new features into existing applications. Of course, you still need plenty of sleuthing and ingenuity to decide exactly which features you want to add and which functions to override to make those happen.

Source Code

This section lists the code for mach_override.c and mach_inject_bundle.c. You might be surprised to see that although the Mach-laden code is often dense and highly technical, it's not very long compared to the amazing capabilities it provides, proving that good things come in small packages. You probably won't modify the code in mach_override and mach_inject_bundle. They're listed here to provide you with a better understanding of how these features work and perhaps to inspire you to find out more about the low levels of Mac OS X.

This section also lists a short example, DisposeWindow+Beep, along with the code that injects it, DisposeWindow+Beep_Injector. You can use these as the prototypes for your own cool injection projects.

mach_override.c

This file implements the logic for mach_override. As described earlier in this chapter, it allocates the branch island and reentry branch island, creates the branch instruction, then puts the original first instruction into the reentry branch island.

The mach_override function takes the following parameters:

- `originalFunctionSymbolName`: The name of the function to override. C function names should be prefixed with an underscore.

- `originalFunctionNameLibraryNameHint`: The name of the library that contains the symbol to be overridden. This parameter is optional.

- `overrideFunctionAddress`: The address of the replacement code that's taking the place of the original.

- `originalFunctionReentryIsland`: The address of a pointer to the reentry island.

The function returns a result that's either zero for no error, or err_cannot_override if the override failed because the first instruction can't be replaced.

```
/***********************************************************
    mach_override.c
    Copyright (c) 2003-2005 Jonathan 'Wolf' Rentzsch:
        <http://rentzsch.com>
    Some rights reserved:
        <http://creativecommons.org/licenses/by/2.0/>
***********************************************************/

#include "mach_override.h"

#include <mach-o/dyld.h>
#include <mach/mach_host.h>
#include <mach/mach_init.h>
#include <mach/vm_map.h>
#include <sys/mman.h>

#include <CoreServices/CoreServices.h>

/***********************************
 *
 *    Constants
 *
 ***********************************/
#pragma mark    -
#pragma mark    (Constants)

#if !defined(__ppc__) && !defined(__POWERPC__)
    #error "this code is currently PowerPC-only"
#endif

long kIslandTemplate[] = {
    0x9001FFFC,    //    stw      r0,-4(SP)
    0x3C00DEAD,    //    lis      r0,0xDEAD
    0x6000BEEF,    //    ori      r0,r0,0xBEEF
    0x7C0903A6,    //    mtctr    r0
    0x8001FFFC,    //    lwz      r0,-4(SP)
    0x60000000,    //    nop      ; optionally replaced
    0x4E800420     //    bctr
};
#define kAddressHi        3
#define kAddressLo        5
#define kInstructionHi     10
#define kInstructionLo     11

#define    kAllocateHigh     1
#define    kAllocateNormal    0
```

```
/************************
 *
 *    Data Types
 *
 ************************/
#pragma mark    -
#pragma mark    (Data Types)

typedef   struct   {
   char   instructions[sizeof(kIslandTemplate)];
   int      allocatedHigh;
}  BranchIsland;

/************************
 *
 *    Funky Protos
 *
 ************************/
#pragma mark    -
#pragma mark    (Funky Protos)

   mach_error_t
allocateBranchIsland(
      BranchIsland    **island,
      int             allocateHigh );

   mach_error_t
freeBranchIsland(
      BranchIsland    *island );

   mach_error_t
setBranchIslandTarget(
      BranchIsland    *island,
      const void      *branchTo,
      long            instruction );

/************************************************************
 *
 *    Interface
 *
 ************************************************************/
#pragma mark    -
#pragma mark    (Interface)
```

The mach_override function itself is defined here, with the parameters described previously.

```
      mach_error_t
mach_override(
      char *originalFunctionSymbolName,
      const char *originalFunctionLibraryNameHint,
      const void *overrideFunctionAddress,
      void **originalFunctionReentryIsland )
{
    assert( originalFunctionSymbolName );
    assert( strlen( originalFunctionSymbolName ) );
    assert( overrideFunctionAddress );

    mach_error_t   err = err_none;
```

First, mach_override finds the address of the function you want to override. To do this, mach_override calls _dyld_lookup_and_bind or dyld_lookup_and_bind_with_hint, depending on whether the caller supplied the name of the library that holds the original function.

Warning

Be sure the function exists before asking mach override to override it, or OS X may kill the process. To be certain the function exists, you can call NSIsSymbolNameDefined or NSIsSymbolName DefinedWithHint before using mach_override.

```
    long    *originalFunctionPtr;
    if( originalFunctionLibraryNameHint )
      _dyld_lookup_and_bind_with_hint(
          originalFunctionSymbolName,
          originalFunctionLibraryNameHint,
          (void*)&originalFunctionPtr,
          NULL );
    else
      _dyld_lookup_and_bind( originalFunctionSymbolName,
          (void*) &originalFunctionPtr,
          NULL );
```

Next, mach_override examines the first instruction in the target function—the one that's going to be replaced. Although most instructions tolerate being shipped out to a branch island, the mfctr instruction can't be moved, so mach_override bails out if that's the case.

```
    #define   kMFCTRMask         0xfc1fffff
    #define   kMFCTRInstruction  0x7c0903a6

    long   originalInstruction = *originalFunctionPtr;
    if( !err && ((originalInstruction & kMFCTRMask) ==
        kMFCTRInstruction) )
      err = err_cannot_override;
```

mach_override is going to put code on the last memory page of the process, a space that's normally not writable. But making it writable is easy, merely requiring a call to vm_protect.

```
if( !err ) {
    err = vm_protect( mach_task_self(),
         (vm_address_t) originalFunctionPtr,
         sizeof(long), false, (VM_PROT_ALL | VM_PROT_COPY) );
    if( err )
        err = vm_protect( mach_task_self(),
             (vm_address_t) originalFunctionPtr,
             sizeof(long), false,
             (VM_PROT_DEFAULT | VM_PROT_COPY) );
}
```

After making the appropriate memory space writable, mach_override allocates the branch island by calling allocateBranchIsland, which in turn does the actual allocation by calling vm_allocate.

```
BranchIsland    *escapeIsland = NULL;
if( !err )
    err = allocateBranchIsland( &escapeIsland,
        kAllocateHigh );
if( !err )
    err = setBranchIslandTarget( escapeIsland,
        overrideFunctionAddress, 0 );
```

Next, build the branch absolute instruction to the escape island.

```
long    branchAbsoluteInstruction;
if( !err ) {
    long escapeIslandAddress = ((long) escapeIsland)
        & 0x3FFFFFF;
    branchAbsoluteInstruction = 0x48000002
        | escapeIslandAddress;
}
```

If the caller asked for a reentry island, allocate and return it next.

```
BranchIsland    *reentryIsland = NULL;
if( !err && originalFunctionReentryIsland ) {
    err = allocateBranchIsland( &reentryIsland,
        kAllocateNormal );
    if( !err )
        *originalFunctionReentryIsland = reentryIsland;
}
```

Finally, mach_override hooks everything up by atomically installing the function's first instruction into the reentry branch island. This makes the reentry island executable and puts the branch instruction detour at the start of the original function.

```
if( !err ) {
    int escapeIslandEngaged = false;
    do {
        if( reentryIsland )
            err = setBranchIslandTarget( reentryIsland,
                    (void*) (originalFunctionPtr+1),
                        originalInstruction );
        if( !err ) {
            escapeIslandEngaged = CompareAndSwap(
                originalInstruction, branchAbsoluteInstruction,
                (UInt32*)originalFunctionPtr );
            if( !escapeIslandEngaged ) {
                originalInstruction = *originalFunctionPtr;
                if( (originalInstruction & kMFCTRMask)
                  == kMFCTRInstruction )
                    err = err_cannot_override;
            }
        }
    } while( !err && !escapeIslandEngaged );
}

//   Clean up on error.
if( err ) {
    if( reentryIsland )
        freeBranchIsland( reentryIsland );
    if( escapeIsland )
        freeBranchIsland( escapeIsland );
}

return err;
}
```

mach_inject_bundle.c

This section lists mach_inject_bundle.c The code in this file assembles the replacement code and ships it off to the remote address space, hooks it up, and kicks it off. The mach_inject_bundle takes your function and adds the primitive code block that gets injected into the remote process. There's also a lower-level interface, mach_inject, that you rarely need to use, if ever.

```
/*************************************************************
    mach_inject.bundle.c
Copyright (c) 2005 Jonathan 'Wolf' Rentzch:
    <http://rentzsch.com>
    Some rights reserved:
        <http://creativecommons.org/licenses/by/2.0/>
 *************************************************************/

#include "mach_inject_bundle.h"
#include "mach_inject.h"
#include "mach_inject_bundle_stub.h"
#include <CoreServices/CoreServices.h>

    mach_error_t
mach_inject_bundle_pid(
        const char    *bundlePackageFileSystemRepresentation,
        pid_t         pid )
{
    assert( bundlePackageFileSystemRepresentation );
    assert( pid > 0 );

    mach_error_t    err = err_none;
```

First, mach_inject_bundle locates its own bundle in memory, returning an error if something goes awry.

```
    CFBundleRef frameworkBundle = NULL;
    if( !err ) {
        frameworkBundle = CFBundleGetBundleWithIdentifier(
            CFSTR("com.rentzsch.mach_inject_bundle"));
        if( frameworkBundle == NULL )
            err =
              err_mach_inject_bundle_couldnt_load_framework_bundle;
    }
```

Next, it looks around to find the code to be injected. Again, the routine checks for errors and indicates if the bundle can't be found.

```
    CFURLRef injectionURL = NULL;
    if( !err ) {
        injectionURL = CFBundleCopyResourceURL(frameworkBundle,
            CFSTR("mach_inject_bundle_stub.bundle"),NULL,NULL);
        if( !injectionURL )
            err =
              err_mach_inject_bundle_couldnt_find_injection_bundle;
    }
```

An instance of the injection bundle is created next.

```
CFBundleRef injectionBundle = NULL;
if( !err ) {
    injectionBundle =
        CFBundleCreate( kCFAllocatorDefault, injectionURL);
    if( !injectionBundle )
        err =
      err_mach_inject_bundle_couldnt_load_injection_bundle;
}
```

After the injection bundle has been built, mach_inject_bundle creates a thread to execute the code. The parameter block is created and set up, and everything is ready to go.

```
void *injectionCode = NULL;
if( !err ) {
    injectionCode =
        CFBundleGetFunctionPointerForName( injectionBundle,
        CFSTR( INJECT_ENTRY_SYMBOL ));
    if( injectionCode == NULL )
        err =
   err_mach_inject_bundle_couldnt_find_inject_entry_symbol;
}

mach_inject_bundle_stub_param *param = NULL;
size_t paramSize;
if( !err ) {
    size_t bundlePathSize =
          strlen(bundlePackageFileSystemRepresentation)
        + 1;
    paramSize = sizeof( ptrdiff_t ) + bundlePathSize;
    param = malloc( paramSize );
    bcopy( bundlePackageFileSystemRepresentation,
          param->bundlePackageFileSystemRepresentation,
          bundlePathSize );
}
```

After the injection bundle is all ready, calling the low-level routine mach_inject sends the code to the remote process and gets it started.

```
if( !err ) {
    err = mach_inject( injectionCode, param,
        paramSize, pid, 0 );
}
```

Finally, there are a few items left to clean up by calling `CFRelease`.

```
    if( param )
        free( param );
    if( injectionBundle )
        CFRelease( injectionBundle );
    if( injectionURL )
        CFRelease( injectionURL );
    if( frameworkBundle )
        CFRelease( frameworkBundle );

    return err;
}
```

Other Sources

This section contains the source listings for the most relevant files and functions in the mach_override and mach_inject projects. There are other sources, but in the interests of space, they're not listed here. You can get the full sources by downloading the projects from the book's Web site at www.wiley.com/compbooks/extremetech or from http://rentzsch.com/mach_override and http://rentzsch.com/mach_inject.

Dynamic Overriding Example

This section contains a tiny sample that uses mach_override and mach_inject_bundle to override the `DisposeWindow` function in the Finder, causing it to produce a beep every time `DisposeWindow` is called. After the override does its beeping, it calls the original `DisposeWindow` to make sure that the original routine gets a chance to do its normal window disposal business.

DisposeWindow+Beep

This code uses mach_override to create a custom version of `DisposeWindow`. The new version simply writes a little text to the log and then beeps to announce its presence.

```
#include <Carbon/Carbon.h>
#include "mach_override.h"

//   Override type & global.
typedef   void (*DisposeWindowProc)( WindowRef window );
DisposeWindowProc    gDisposeWindow;

//   Funky Protos.
void   DisposeWindowOverride( WindowRef window );

#pragma CALL_ON_LOAD load
void load() {
```

```
   printf( "DisposeWindow+Beep loaded\n" );
   mach_override( "_DisposeWindow", NULL,
      DisposeWindowOverride, (void**) &gDisposeWindow );
}
```

Here's the replacement method itself. The `fflush` call seems to be necessary to make the `printf` work.

```
void DisposeWindowOverride( WindowRef window ) {
   printf( "beep!\n" );
   fflush(0);
   SysBeep( 20 );
   gDisposeWindow( window );
}
```

DisposeWindow+Beep_Injector

This is the matching bookend to the replacement function in the previous section. In this one, the code uses mach_inject_bundle to install the overridden function in the Finder, thus producing a beep whenever a Finder window goes away. This example includes a handy utility routine, FindProcessBySignature, which locates a process serial number given its type and creator codes. For the Finder, these codes are FNDR and MACS, respectively.

```
#import "InjectorAppDelegate.h"
#import <mach_inject_bundle/mach_inject_bundle.h>

@implementation Injector
```

The FindProcessBySignature function takes a type and creator and returns a process serial number. You can use this function in your own override projects if you want to be able to locate the target process by type and creator.

```
   static
   OSErr
FindProcessBySignature(
   OSType               type,
   OSType               creator,
   ProcessSerialNumber  *psn )
{
   ProcessSerialNumber tempPSN = { 0, kNoProcess };
   ProcessInfoRec procInfo;
   OSErr err = noErr;

   procInfo.processInfoLength = sizeof( ProcessInfoRec );
   procInfo.processName = nil;
   procInfo.processAppSpec = nil;
```

The following code walks through the list of processes, using `GetNextProcess`, until it finds one that matches the given type and creator.

```
while( !err ) {
    err = GetNextProcess( &tempPSN );
    if( !err )
        err = GetProcessInformation( &tempPSN, &procInfo );
    if( !err
        && procInfo.processType == type
        && procInfo.processSignature == creator ) {
        *psn = tempPSN;
        return noErr;
    }
}

return err;
}
```

The `applicationDidFinishLaunching` implementation is the place to put the actual work of the replacment code. First, create a bundle path string. Then, identify the process that's going to receive the injected code. Finally, call `mach_inject_bundle_pid` to actually perform the injection.

```
-(void)applicationDidFinishLaunching:
    (NSNotification*) notification_
{
    NSString *bundlePath = [[NSBundle mainBundle]
        pathForResource:@"DisposeWindow+Beep" ofType:@"bundle"];

    ProcessSerialNumber psn;
    FindProcessBySignature( 'FNDR', 'MACS', &psn );

    pid_t pid;
    GetProcessPID( &psn, &pid );

    mach_error_t err = mach_inject_bundle_pid(
        [bundlePath fileSystemRepresentation], pid );
    NSLog( @"err = %d", err );
    [NSApp terminate:nil];
}

@end
```

Extra Credit

Of all the "Extra Credit" sections in this book, this is the toughest one to write, because mach_override and mach_inject hold the most possibilities for adding untold features to Mac OS X applications. For your first projects, you might want to start with DisposeWindow+Beep and add to it. When you're ready to do more, there are a bunch of shareware and commercial apps in the world already that use mach_override and mach_inject, including Stuffit Deluxe, Desktop Manager, and Virtual Desktop. Maybe you can get inspiration from one of those. Or, just think about which cool features you would like to see added to your favorite applications, and then go for it.

Because mach_override and mach_inject are open source projects, you can choose to contribute to them and make them even better.

Summary

With great power comes great responsibility, and mach_override and mach_inject give you great power. Dynamic overriding is a fine way to make your Mac more capable. Just be sure you use yourself as a guinea pig for testing any particularly hairy changes before you turn your overriding masterpiece loose in the world.

For more information on mach_override and mach_inject, see Wolf Rentzch's thoughts on the topic at `http://rentzsch.com/mach_override` and `http://rentzsch.com/mach_inject`. Both packages are available as open source under a Creative Commons license.

Goodbye

With this final chapter, we've reached the end of our hacky journey through Mac OS X Tiger. I hope that you've enjoyed the tricks we've covered, and that you'll keep learning and playing with OS X—there's enough cool stuff in there to keep you busy 24 hours a day. Good luck, and have fun!

Index

Continued

Continued